BARÇA

THE MAKING OF THE GREATEST TEAM IN THE WORLD

GRAHAM HUNTER

BackPage Press

About the author

Born in Aberdeen and a lifelong supporter of that club, Graham Hunter made his first pilgrimage to football in Spain for the 1982 World Cup. Barcelona has been his home for the last 10 years.

His career in writing and broadcasting about football began in the late 1980s and progressed through work for the *Sunday Times Scotland*, *Scottish Daily Mail*, *The Daily Mail*, Sky, *The Sunday Herald*, *The Scottish Mail on Sunday*, Newstalk 106, BBC Radio 5 Live, Talksport, ESPN US and the *Melbourne Age*.

Graham is uefa.com's Barcelona correspondent, their Spain correspondent for the last five years and was FIFA TV producer for Spain at World Cup 2010.

CONTENTS

INTRODUCTION

T HE FIRST THING TO SAY is that while researching and writing this book has been far harder work than I had ever expected, there are a handful of things which sustained me.

Firstly, I genuinely believe that the current FC Barcelona era, its football and its personalities, has given us something which, if not unique, I don't expect to see rivalled, let alone equaled in my lifetime.

From Ronaldinho and Eto'o at their best, through to the magical combinations weaved by Iniesta, Xavi and Messi, I have been privileged to work at football stadia around Europe where Barça have been absolutely jaw-droppingly good.

Perhaps we could have titled this "… The Greatest Team Ever" but what would be the point? Some important football people already believe that. My opinion matters less than theirs, but my job is to chronicle the manner in which this squad, under a brilliant man, Pep Guardiola, proved that they have been the greatest team in the world between 2008 and publication in 2012.

The greatest ever is, almost always, a matter of debate and opinion and entrenched position. I suspect that we are witnessing something close to all-time excellence but it's for others, you included, to judge whether the evidence of your eyes and what this book explains convinces you that this team is unique.

What is beyond reasonable argument, even for those teams who have fallen victim to Guardiola's sides, is that Barça regularly produce football which is uplifting to the spirit. That alone has kept me believing that the book has been worth doing.

I hope, and I think I believe, that some of the Spanish football which Sky has been showing for over 15 years will gradually influence how talented young players in the UK and Ireland conceive of their sport while they develop. I want them and their coaches to say, 'No, I'm not following hackneyed ideas about height, power, route one,' etc. The first touch, the technique, the obsession with maintaining possession, the flowing passing movements, half-touch football – I want all of this to influence young boys and girls who first play and then coach football, so that it becomes the norm for people to want to play like that (notwithstanding our inherent need to compete aggressively) and the dummies and thugs become outcasts.

Secondly, I am constantly thrilled by how passionately people around the world, not just those who were born in Catalonia and are therefore drawn to FC Barcelona, feel about this team, this era.

Football has shown many faces since I started watching it with my Dad at Pittodrie in the late 1960s, but its capacity to inspire and to thrill has rarely, if ever, entranced the entire world like this Barça era has managed.

Graham Hunter, Barcelona. January 2012

I – THE ROAD TO WEMBLEY

"Nobody's given us a hiding like that, but Barça deserve it. In my time as manager, it's the best team we have played"
— Sir Alex Ferguson

Wembley, London. May 28, 2011

SIR ALEX FERGUSON shakes Pep Guardiola by the hand; his body language speaks of an acceptance that his Manchester United team have just been bettered and of an admiration at a contest won brilliantly by Barcelona.

Éric Abidal, having fought back from tumour surgery to play some three months ahead of medical prognosis, is handed the armband by the Barcelona captain, Carles Puyol, and told to collect the cup.

An odd little army of co-conspirators are recruited by Gerard Piqué to cut down the Wembley goal net.

The entire Barça squad and staff hold hands and dance round the centre circle with the Champions League trophy, draped in a Catalan flag, placed squarely on the centre spot like some pagan festival worshipping 'The Cup with the Big Ears'.

Iconic moments to match the goals scored by Pedro, Wayne Rooney, Leo Messi and David Villa.

Then, from some of the greatest names in the sport, a flood of such unrestrained admiration that the response to this masterpiece by Guardiola's incredible Barcelona team begins to compete in terms of impact with those extraordinary images the final produced.

"Nobody's given us a hiding like that, but Barça deserve it. In my time as manager, it's the best team we have played," said Ferguson, who has won over 40 trophies.

"They play the right way and they enjoy their football. They do mesmerise you with their passing and we never really did control Messi. But many people have said that."

Terry Venables, who has inspired a performance or two out of his teams at Wembley and who coached Barcelona to a Spanish title plus the final of the European Cup, told me: "United got a tanning. They got a lesson – it must have been a nightmare for Fergie. He just had to come out and say, 'They were great,' because Barça didn't just beat them, they showed United what's possible. I think everybody should be standing up and applauding."

Graeme Souness was part of the dynastic Liverpool team of the late 1970s and early 80s that won three European Cups. "I think that for young boys today who are interested in football they are not only watching the best player ever [Messi] but arguably the best team ever," he said. "They should watch every video, sit down and watch them every time they are on television, because this is a unique group of players."

Before the match, Ossie Ardiles, a World Cup winner with Argentina in 1978, had been one of the few to admit he saw "no chance" of Manchester United beating Barcelona. Afterwards, he said: "For some time I thought that Diego Maradona could never be surpassed, and nor could Pelé, but no longer. I would now say that Lionel Messi will go down in history as the No 1 player of all time, the best that there ever was. This Barça is the greatest team of all time."

Bixente Lizarazu, winner of the World Cup, European Championships and Champions League with France and Bayern Munich, said of Messi: "When you see him dressed normally he looks like a kid on his way to school. But when you see him in shorts on the pitch he makes all the other players look like students in front of a master."

Gary Neville, recently retired after a trophy-laden career at Manchester United: "Seven of those Barcelona players tonight came through the ranks of their club and that helps to make them an unstoppable force," he said. "You have to hand it to them, they're brilliant and Messi was absolutely magnificent — one of the best players that we've ever seen.

"For the past two decades football has been about greater physical fitness and athleticism and now Barcelona are taking it back to the days of the great Brazil teams. Total football."

Roy Keane, whose United captaincy epitomises Ferguson's glorious reign as manager, said Barcelona are "the best team I've ever seen. They're on a different level and that might make it a touch easier [for United to take]. United didn't disgrace themselves tonight. They just came up against the best team ever."

Ottmar Hitzfeld managed both Borussia Dortmund and Bayern Munich to victory in the Champions League. "This Barcelona is the most intelligent team of all time," he said. "They have a golden generation which will continue to impact on the Champions League in the coming years. I've no idea when we will once again have a team with such technical perfection."

Marcello Lippi, a Champions League and World Cup winning coach, said: "There has never previously been a team which played like this in the history of football. This Barcelona has all the characteristics to be considered the strongest of all time. We are watching a unique phenomenon."

To add some historical context, Just Fontaine, the 78-year-old fourth-top scorer in World Cup history (13 for France in the 1958 finals alone) is our next witness: "No team has ever been better in possession of the ball than this Barcelona. Brazil were immense in 1958 and 1970, the Ajax of Cruyff, the Madrid of the five European Cups, too. But, technically, Barcelona reach perfection.

"As far as Leo Messi is concerned, I thought Pelé was the best, shining for his club and winning three World Cups. Di Stéfano was sublime, too. But Messi is superior to both of them."

Mestalla Stadium, Valencia. April 20, 2011

Thirty-eight days previously this team of shimmering excellence sat, tired, defeated, angry and sore, on the playing surface of Valencia's Mestalla stadium, watching Real Madrid celebrate victory in the Copa del Rey final.

Guardiola's players assumed the blank expressions which are the mark of the losers at a big occasion. Dull eyes, thousand-yard stares – pain.

It was the second Clásico in three days. Domination and a 1-0 lead had been tossed away in a 1-1 draw at the Bernabéu in the league then this epic, nerve-wracking cup final was lost to a glorious Cristiano Ronaldo header in extra time.

It looked like a 'perfect storm' might be engulfing Barcelona. The first cup final to be lost in the Guardiola era was a difficult experience, and these were tired soldiers, the majority of whom had been playing, and winning for the previous three seasons – and during the summers, too. Euro 2008, followed by the Confederations Cup, followed by the 2010 World Cup was a gruelling way to spend your 'down time'. Domestically, Real Madrid had been mean-eyed pursuers for the last three seasons. It was tiring beyond belief for Barcelona.

Might this defeat puncture morale, self-belief or unlock a dam-full of exhaustion?

The teams faced a third Clásico in seven days' time. It would certainly be the most important of the season. The first leg of the Champions League semi-final had always looked like a brutal test, but Madrid appeared to have a competitive and psychological advantage. They had set Barcelona a physical challenge and Guardiola's team had come up just short.

The argument from the white corner was best summed up when I spoke to Emmanuel Adebayor in the mixed zone – where players talk with gathered media – this time down in the Mestalla basement. The Madrid striker explained: "Mourinho told us that Barça are not Robocop. They are one of the best sides in the world, but they are just human, just players like us which means if we try to play our football and if you press them high, for sure they will make some mistakes, they will lose the ball. So we just went at them like tigers or lions.

"The team that wanted to win it more was Real Madrid and so we won it."

The Barcelona and Madrid players who also represented Spain had been enforcing an unwritten rule that no matter how feisty their matches got, they wouldn't forget their national team bond. There would be standards, respect would be shown. A deal something along the lines of: 'Compete to the absolute limit, but not beyond.'

Fairly or unfairly, some Barça players felt that lines

were crossed and friendships corroded in the Copa del Rey final.

Referee Undiano Mallenco awarded 26 fouls against Madrid and 24 against Barcelona, booking five of the winners and three of the losers – hardly a blatant disparity between the teams. However, he was very permissive.

Álvaro Arbeloa stamped on Villa in the first half and the Barça players were irate that Sergio Ramos and Arbeloa immediately combined to bend down and brusquely haul Villa to his feet. There were various incidents when Madrid, without behaving criminally, went over the top, and the referee was content to allow it.

The game was titanic. A flow of chances missed, saved or off the woodwork. Iker Casillas and José Pinto both made jaw-dropping saves.

The night was topped off by the footage which zipped around the world of Ramos dropping the trophy as Madrid's bus toured the capital en route to their traditional place of celebration, Los Cibeles, and the trophy emerging battered from under the wheels. It was a metaphor for how Barça felt.

Reports surfaced that a combination of unfair actions by security staff and poor planning by the Spanish FA left Guardiola's players stranded out on the pitch, fuming, while Madrid went up to collect the cup and take the acclaim of their delirious fans.

Not true. Guardiola's consigliere, Manel Estiarte, will be one of our principal guides through the incredible events that closed out season 2010-11. A multi-Olympian, gold medal winner and for long periods of his career the best water polo player in the world, Estiarte was Guardiola's first appointment when he became first team coach. Advisor, friend, sounding board, protector – Estiarte sees all, but tells very little. However, he did provide me with rare insight into Barça's journey from the Mestalla to Wembley.

"At the Mestalla, it was our choice to stay out on the pitch," says Estiarte. "In 2009 we had watched Manchester United suffer in Rome and Athletic Bilbao sitting crying in the Mestalla after that Copa del Rey [final in 2009, which Barcelona won 4-1]. We admired their dignity and their pride, so we decided we had to stay on the pitch too if we lost. Nobody made us do it."

Tito Vilanova, Guardiola's assistant, told me: "I never like losing, but I learned very early that you can't win every time. If you know you've done everything you could and that you've had chances, then you accept losing is just part of the game. You take it on the chin and try to improve. You show respect to the other team, just as we did at the Mestalla."

Gerard Piqué sought out every single Real Madrid player, shook their hands and congratulated them. "Losing the final was hard because you know how many people you have made sad, and you feel for your team-mates who have given everything, but sometimes it's your turn to lose," he recalled. "I think this team has won the right to lose occasionally, just so long as we show the kind of attitude and Barcelona playing style as we did here."

After the defeat, I felt that perhaps Messi had dropped too deep in trying to find 'clean' possession without Pepe hounding him and hacking at him. Messi's customary position has been branded the 'false nine' because he starts as the central striker but is given licence to roam far beyond the position normally occupied either by a centre forward or a No 10. First trialled under Rijkaard at Sevilla in 2008, his form in this role became explosive during the 6-2 win at Madrid and using him there permanently, a master-stroke of Guardiola's, has contributed immensely to his prolific goalscoring since the Catalan took over in 2008. However, this time Barça's most important foot-baller had occasionally drifted back to just in front of his own penalty box before being served a short pass from Sergio Busquets or Piqué.

Had Messi helped Real Madrid? It also echoed the way Mourinho's Inter had successfully policed him in each of the Champions League semi-finals the previous year.

I put that question to the Barça manager and Guar-diola told me: "I've asked Leo to be much more than a goalscorer. His role is to participate fully in the game. He can go to the areas of the pitch he thinks are best for him to do that. The idea is that he's involved in all aspects of the game much more than someone who is just a finisher, because he's our decisive player."

At the time I was unsure if that addressed what I'd seen in those two consecutive Clásicos, but the matter of seven days would prove Guardiola's point and ban-ish my scepticism.

After victory, Mourinho looked and sounded exhausted. "Barcelona seemed psychologically tired in the second half because they're used to being much more successful," he said. "Some people say that to play great football you have to keep lots of possession, but I think that counter-attacking and dominating the spaces also makes for a great match. We don't consider ourselves better than Barça just because we won. Nor are they inferior because they've lost. Every game is different."

However, one gentle remark made after this match became extremely important. It probably shaped the destiny of a season.

Just over 20 minutes before the end of normal time, it looked like Pedro had scored a glorious goal which stemmed from one of the greatest dribbling movements I have ever seen Messi, or anyone else, produce. However, a marginal offside call against the winger annulled the goal. Despite it being an exceptionally narrow decision and despite Barcelona's website match report admitting that 'referee Undiano got it right in disallowing the goal', Guardiola's mild post-match reaction was to fire up José Mourinho's Machiavellian imagination.

Guardiola started his press conference with: "Congratulations to Real Madrid, they played an excellent game."

He refused to criticise the referee, but pointed out that the night had turned on small details. "A two-centimetre decision from a linesman with a good view ruled out a goal from Pedro." Those were Guardiola's exact words. Nothing more. Keep them in mind for a page or two.

Camp Nou. April 23, 2011. Barcelona v Osasuna

There was a minefield immediately in front of them, even before the next bout with their conquerors in the Bernabéu.

Guardiola's squad had won the two previous La Liga

titles, each time after a riveting fight with Real Madrid. Nobody was prepared to sacrifice another championship to increase their chances of reaching the Champions League final. Only once in the club's entire history had Barça won more than two consecutive leagues – and that was Johan Cruyff's 'Dream Team'.

"There was a period where everyone was exhausted physically and psychologically," recalls Vilanova, "but there was no time for feeling sorry for ourselves. When you are a truly great player, you know how important it is to pick yourself up after a defeat and that's exactly what our players did."

Going into Jornada 33, against Osasuna, Barça were eight points clear and there were 18 left to play for. Their position at the top of the table was comfortable, but not assured. Guardiola begged the fans to turn up and get behind the team.

His press conference quote of the day was, "Any of my players who are sad or down in the dumps about losing the cup final – well, let them run harder!"

He went on: "My guys have to react because this is their work and that is their responsibility. Sadness can be left behind you on the football pitch if you work hard and battle a bit more. Anyone I see who is a bit affected by losing will be on the bench or in the stand."

"*Campeones, campeones,*" the Camp Nou fans chanted that Saturday, as Osasuna, during a rather cumbersome performance, were defeated 2-0. David Villa's first goal in 12 matches and a late second from Messi (his 50th of the season) saw them meet Guardiola's demands.

Madrid went back to Valencia that same night, scored six times to defeat Unai Emery's team and looked still more menacing for the looming Champions League semi-final.

Barça were eight points clear with only 15 left in play.

Months afterwards, Guardiola admitted to us that the Osasuna game was "horrendous" but, at the time, we had to figure out what health the squad was in. Tiredness, both mental and physical, had to be factored in. There might easily have been a crumbling of morale – simply through exhaustion.

Madrid. Tuesday, April 26, 2011. Champions League press conference

Real Madrid went first, holding their press conference at 2.45pm in their training centre, Valdebebas, out near Barajas airport. Barcelona were to train at the Santiago Bernabéu (helpful given the huge debate raging about the playing surface) following which, at 8pm, Javier Mascherano (now widely called the 'Little Boss') and Guardiola would give their press conference.

It was the third of four Clásicos in 16 days – football fans and media the world over were agog.

By the time Guardiola sat down to talk he was ready to hit us with a 2 minute 27 second thunderbolt of controlled aggression and indignation which was at least as well planned as any tactic his team enforced during the following night's game.

Earlier that afternoon, the Real Madrid manager had made a mistake.

Mourinho's sardonic press conference diatribe against Guardiola was, in turns, snide, extravagant, colourful and dripping with sarcasm. It was all about

Guardiola's tame "two-centimetre decision" comment regarding Pedro's disallowed goal in the Copa del Rey final.

"Until now, managers could be divided into two groups," Mourinho opened, in mock amazement. "The small one comprises those who don't talk about referees at all and the other, huge one, in which I figure, is made up of those who only criticise refs if they make important errors. We can't control our frustration when they get it wrong, but congratulate them when they get it right.

"But, now, there is a third group with only one member – Pep! It's a new era – never seen in world football – someone who criticises a referee for getting it right!

"The explanation is that in Guardiola's first season coaching Barça he experienced the scandalous refereeing at Chelsea in the Champions League semi-final and, since then, he's never happy when a referee gets it right."

No reference to how Guardiola complimented Madrid on a merited win, no admission that Guardiola had not criticised the officials or even suggested that he thought the goal was onside. The mere mention of an offside goal and a linesman, by Pep Guardiola, was enough to send the Portuguese spinning off into his own dark universe.

Mourinho believes 'the game starts in the press room the day before kick-off' and he has had some success with his calculated statements. So, having left the world's media drooling at his performance, he was no doubt reaching round to pat himself on the back as he left the press conference. *Trabalho bem feito*, he'd have grinned to himself. Job well done.

However, it turned out he'd misjudged Guardiola. That evening, in the Santiago Bernabéu stadium press room, was a thousand times more riveting.

Guardiola, and the majority of his squad, had watched Mourinho's mid-afternoon press conference live on television.

Andoni Zubizarreta, Barça's director of football and nominally the coach's line manager, was also his team-mate during the Cruyff era. "More than ever, this is when we have to stick to talking about the football," 'Zubi' cautioned Guardiola after Mourinho's pantomime villain performance.

The former Barcelona and Spain goalkeeper knew a line had been crossed. Following the previous two bruising Clásicos, this was the time when his manager might cut loose. Guardiola made the right noises to placate his former team-mate, but he had decided that enough was enough.

Mascherano spoke first in the press conference and was typically eloquent, trying to focus on the football, getting away from the debate about the playing surface in Madrid. Guardiola gave him an appreciative nod and a pat on the back: 'Nice work fella.' The Barça manager didn't need anybody doing his work for him. He was ready to pull the trigger on his own.

Then, everything began to build towards ramming speed. Barça's senior press officer, Chemi Teres, selected the aptly named David Bernabéu for the first question. Barça is a Catalan club, yet instead of the dozens of print, radio and television Catalans who had travelled through, the first question was given to a Spanish speaker from a Madrid television station. David had an early deadline and had asked for that to be considered, but this suited Guardiola, also. The performance he had prepared was aimed at a Spanish-speaking audience: maximum voltage, maximum exposure.

The journalist asked: "I don't know whether anyone has notified you what Señor Mourinho said in his press conference this afternoon, but I've noted some parts of it down for you.

"It surprised him that you criticised the referee for getting something right, in relation to the offside decision against Pedro in the cup final last week. He even asked how you lived with the scandal of the semi-final at Chelsea two years ago and whether, because of it, you are accustomed to referees favouring Barça?

"So, 24 hours ahead of the big game, is there something you'd like to answer Mourinho with?"

The following lasted precisely two minutes and 27 seconds.

"Well, first of all, good evening everyone. Given that Señor Mourinho has chosen to use 'tú' [the less respectful form of 'you'] and call me 'Pep' all through his conference, I'll be referring to him as José tonight.

"I don't know which is his camera here [Guardiola looks down the barrel of the television cameras at the back of the room, rather than at the journalists], probably all of them.

"Tomorrow at quarter to nine we are going to play a game of football out on that pitch. Off the pitch he has already won, he's been winning all year, all season and he'll continue to do so in the future. I'm happy to award him his personal Champions League trophy off the pitch. He can take that home with him and enjoy it with his other stuff.

"As for us, we just play. Maybe we win, maybe we

lose. Normally he wins, as his CV shows. We will settle for our 'smaller' victories which seem to inspire admiration all round the world, and which make us very proud. I could produce a list of comparable complaints for you all, but then we'd never get finished.

"He talked about Stamford Bridge and I guess we could drag up 250,000 complaints of ours, but we don't have secretaries and ex-referees or managing directors on our staff to note those kind of grievances down for us, so we are only left with going out there at 8.45pm tomorrow and trying to win by playing the best football we know how.

"In this particular press room he's the f*****g boss, the big f*****g chief.

"He knows the ways of the world better than anyone else. I don't want to compete with him in this arena for one instant. I'd only remind him that we were together, he and I, for four years [at FC Barcelona in the late 1990s]. He knows me and I know him. That's enough for me. If he prefers to 'go' with statements and claims of newspaper journalist friends of Florentino [Pérez] about the Copa del Rey and prefers to put more weight on what they write than on the friendship, well, no, not quite friendship, but working relationship he and I had then, that's his right.

"He can continue reading Albert [Einstein, who Mourinho claimed to quote in speeches to his players]. Let him do all that with total freedom, or let him read the thoughts of the journalists who suckle on the teat of Florentino Pérez and then draw the conclusions he wishes to.

"I am not going to justify my words for one second. I said that we were defeated by a minute detail – because of the smart vision of a linesman who got it right. That night, I simply congratulated Real Madrid for winning the cup, deservedly, on the pitch, against a good team on the pitch – the team which I am proud to coach.

"So José, I don't know which is your camera [scans the back of the room] but … here we go."

This had been a long time coming.

I worked alongside the Spain team at the 2010 World Cup and by the time they brought the trophy home, the Barcelona contingent were already sick of fielding questions about Mourinho's arrival in Spain.

All Mourinho had to do was cough and raise an eyebrow for the Catalan media, never mind the rest of Spain, to pester Barça's players about the 'Special One'. My first interview of the new season was with Gerard Piqué and I simply asked whether he was already tired of hearing the man's name.

Piqué replied: "It's really difficult to go to every interview, every press conference and they ask you about 'him'. I understand he's new here and he's the coach of Real Madrid, but that's it!

"I think we have to talk about us – about Barcelona! About how we can play this year and to forget about Real Madrid and Mourinho. We won a lot of respect and titles showing the world how we play – we will try to play the same way this year."

Throughout the year, the Barcelona players felt more and more disrespected by Mourinho, even after their comprehensive 5-0 win in November.

He stated that other clubs 'handed' Barcelona the league by not trying to win at the Camp Nou but, instead, playing to minimise their defeat. Mourinho consistently stated that Barcelona were heavily favoured by refereeing decisions and then, the day before the semi-final, added that Guardiola couldn't live with referees not giving them an advantage.

Though the Barça players largely followed the club's orders in not sniping at Madrid, not entering into the traps Mourinho was laying for them, these are warriors, not shrinking violets. They had long wanted to bite back and, finally, when Guardiola felt personally disrespected, he chose that night to unleash some of the anger and frustration which had been gnawing at him, his squad and his staff.

The players loved it. Guardiola had lanced the boil. It set their minds on simply playing football the next night, not entering into more polemic about kicking, diving and angry confrontations.

Estiarte lifts the lid for us. "The team were travelling back from training to the hotel when mobile phones started bleeping – mostly SMS messages like: 'The boss has really started something this time'. As soon as we got back to the hotel ourselves, the players gave him a massive ovation. It was one of the most special nights of the last three years."

However the 'night before Christmas' feeling didn't end there. After dinner, the team salon had the lights dimmed. The majority of the players immediately expected another of Pep's inspirational motivational videos, although they were usually part of the game-day preparation.

Instead, they had a treat – Víctor Valdés had prepared a DVD of himself imitating a wide range of characters both within the Barça squad and more widely in Spanish football.

His team-mates loved it, Messi, Mascherano and

Milito in particular split themselves laughing and took their 'imitations' in great spirit.

However, it wasn't all about rabble rousing – there was a defined game plan.

Estiarte continues. "I'm not saying Pep is actually a genius, but in football terms he is extremely talented. I go to all the tactical meetings and at the beginning I didn't know that much about football. There he is, with a huge screen showing 25 minutes of footage. He says, 'Gentlemen, we're going to win because you are all here'. By the end they feel as if they have already played the match because his instructions are so clear cut. Pep shows them their opponents' weaknesses and says, 'This is what's going to happen here and here'.

"He doesn't say, 'You have to score a goal in such and such a way'. It's more like, 'If we can open up this space we can get through easily.' "

Publicly, Guardiola still betrayed the fact that he saw no connection between losing the cup final and Barça having diminished chances when returning to the hostile Bernabéu.

"We are going into the semi-final knowing that things are tight," he said. "Everything is against us and very few people are backing us. Public opinion seems to think they'll win, but we are looking forward to it immensely, all of us are fired up and enthusiastic."

Meanwhile Barça's captain, Carles Puyol, was winning the race to be fit. It felt significant. Until that point, Piqué and Puyol had played 18 matches together that campaign, with 15 wins, three draws and no defeats. In fact, their last defeat starting together had been the previous season's semi-final of the Champions League against Mourinho's Inter.

However, the 32-year-old was going to have to draw on all his vast experience and competitive hunger. He would end the season playing only four times in 30 matches, managing 90 minutes just twice. Each time it was in the heat of battle against Madrid. It was amazing commitment and bravery. He wasn't fully fit and had it been anything other than a Clásico, he'd likely not have played.

Vilanova: "It's true. Probably no-one else could achieve what Carles does. He deserves enormous recognition because he went through a very difficult time and then played the semi-final against Madrid having hardly trained at all. We weren't sure if he would make it or whether the injury would cause him problems. What Carles did last year is one of the greatest things I've ever seen in football. For that reason, we all felt so bad that he couldn't start the final."

Word emerged that the match official would be Wolfgang Stark. Initially, those at FC Barcelona who analyse such things were underwhelmed.

The German had sent off the Barcelona players Thiago Motta and Javier Saviola against Celtic in the 2003-04 UEFA Cup. And in the home leg of the 2009 Champions League semi-final against Chelsea, Guardiola's players had found him to be a referee who allowed 'northern European' levels of physical contact.

Barça had won one of their five matches with Stark.

So the match cast would include Puyol and Stark, plus a healthy 3590 Barça fans – probably 10 times more than for a Liga Clásico – but Andrés Iniesta would not take the stage. Injury robbed him of the moment, just as it had, crucially, in the previous season's semi-final, when Mourinho and Inter knocked Barça out.

Omens, omens. Wembley seemed like a long way away.

In the end, it was a stunning night.

Santiago Bernabéu. Wednesday, April 27, 2011. Champions League semi-final

Mourinho deployed Pepe in the middle of a defensive midfield with Lassana Diarra and Xabi Alonso. His job was to do another 'Terminator' on Messi.

Madrid left the grass long – three centimetres, rather than the one centimetre which Barcelona prefer. Barcelona's players take that subject seriously. Skinhead playing surface, ball flying at the speed of a hockey puck – advantage to the quick, technical ball players. Grass like the fringes on a 1970s country and western suede jacket, slower moving ball, happy days for the hasslers, the hackers and the horrible, defensive football which so many employ to try and shackle Messi, Iniesta and Xavi.

The latter commented: "It's a great pity that there are no rules about the grass. In 2011 we have rules about earrings, the media, our shirts, but none regarding the grass which can make the match so much more entertaining, or end up causing injuries."

Madrid, the nine-time European champions, only managed 26% possession of the ball in their own stadium in the Champions League semi-final. Partly that was down to the visitors, partly to Mourinho's gameplan.

El País is Spain's leading quality daily – it wears no club colours. Their lead writer, José Sámano, put it like this: "With Pepe, Madrid refused to play. Without Pepe, they couldn't play.

"Mourinho's bugle call to his team has been to play these matches on the dark side. He did it in the league the other week and again last night. Neither time brought him a result and that would have been the only excuse for playing this way."

'Without Pepe' refers to the straight red referee Stark showed the Portuguese, whose straight leg, knee-high challenge on Dani Alves would only not have been an ordering-off had it been part of the 'anything goes' 1970 FA Cup final between Leeds and Chelsea – recommended viewing online.

Mourinho was also red-carded for sarcastically mocking and applauding the refereeing team for the decision.

Without Pepe to shackle him, Messi ran wild. His first goal came when Ibrahim Afellay made Marcelo look like a statue before crossing for Messi, who had eluded Xabi Alonso.

The Argentinian's second was one of the all-time great Champions League goals. Receiving possession from Busquets, near halfway, Messi left four Madrid players in his wake, dragging them along with him as if they were fish in a trawler net, and culminated the dribble by clipping the ball past Casillas.

Gordon Strachan, the former Scotland, Aberdeen and Manchester United midfielder, who managed Celtic against Messi and Barcelona, was at the Bernabéu that night and called it "one of the greatest goals you'll see from, in my opinion, the best footballer who has ever played the game".

Tito Vilanova made a shrewd comment when

I spoke to him. I had thought the red card for Pepe utterly determining. He had a different perspective. "When Messi dribbles past six players, it's not important whether the rivals have 10 or 11 men on the pitch – what's important is that he's dribbled past six opponents."

Plenty more went on, but those were the key moments. Few, amid the sound and fury, made much of the fact that Guardiola used eight products of the FC Barcelona youth system that night, the youngest of whom was the 19-year-old substitute, Sergi Roberto, who became the 19th *canterano* (academy-trained youngster) to be given a debut by this coach since taking over in June 2008. Fewer than three full years, 19 new kids introduced to a team already packed full of home-bred talent. Utterly remarkable.

Sadly, I have to record that there was horrendous racist chanting at Barcelona's black players. Friends who were in the crowd at the Camp Nou the following week report that the same shameful thing happened there. It is a blight on all football, but Spain isn't fighting it properly.

Post-match, Mourinho matched the rubbish he'd produced on the pitch.

"*Por qué?*" he asked, over and over. Why? Although he didn't quite froth at the mouth, it all felt a bit rabid.

"If I were to speak my mind to UEFA and to the referee, then my career ends today."

He then named referees who he appeared to be accusing of favouring Barcelona in previous fixtures. "Øvrebø, De Bleeckere, Busacca, Frisk, Stark ... *por qué?*"

Mourinho had compiled a list of decisions he felt had gone Barça's way – mostly against his teams.

Tom Henning Øvrebø turned down several Chelsea penalty claims in the 2009 Champions League semi-final; Frank De Bleeckere was the referee who sent off Inter's Thiago Motta the following year at the same stage; Massimo Busacca red-carded Robin van Persie of Arsenal in the last-16 in 2011; Anders Frisk goes all the way back to 2005 and a red card for Didier Drogba of Chelsea against Barça.

Then he returned his focus to Stark and the match Barça had just won.

"We'll play the second leg without Pepe, who did nothing, without Ramos [whose yellow card resulted in a suspension] who did nothing. Without the coach.

"I only leave one question. Perhaps one day I'll get an answer. It is *por qué*?

"I don't know whether it's the UNICEF publicity. I don't understand what Øvrebø did two years ago, what happened today or the miracle that took place last year for Inter.

"They killed us once again. Today it's been demonstrated that we have no chance at all. We had a game plan which the referee wouldn't let us use. I don't know why. This football world sometimes makes me feel sullied. Today we saw that it's not difficult – it's mission impossible. And if by some chance we go ahead at the Camp Nou and make the tie a bit more open, well, they'll kill us again.

"I would be ashamed to win games like Josep Guardiola – apparently it was disrespectful of me calling him Pep yesterday. The guy's a fantastic coach, but he won his first Champions League after the scandal of Stamford Bridge – I'd be ashamed to win it that way – and if he wins this year, it'll be after the scandal of the

Bernabéu. He's a great coach and a great person and that's why I hope that one day he manages to win a Champions League which isn't tainted."

Just for the record, Guardiola's reaction was: "A team with nine European Cups in its trophy cabinet will never give up. I've seen Madrid play a thousand times in my life, from when I was just a kid, and we all know what they're capable of. Against any other team with a 0-2 result on the first leg, we'd be sitting pretty. Against this team that isn't the case.

"We were already playing well when they had 11 men. Obviously it was easier when they were down to 10, but we had the situation under control before then."

Piqué added: "The first 60 minutes they didn't attack at all and they were playing at home. When your football borders on out-and-out violence, it's always going to end badly for you."

The criticism came not just from Barcelona. Guti, arch-*Madridista* but at that time playing in Turkey, sided not with the incandescent Mourinho, but Guardiola. "Pep is a superstar; All my words about him are of respect and admiration, as much for his coaching as for how he played the game."

Then there was Cristiano Ronaldo. In the first 15 minutes at the Bernabéu, he had tried to press Barcelona and found that none of his colleagues had followed him. Waving his hands to the sky, he encouraged them to close down the Barça defenders high up the pitch – but they had their orders.

After the match, Ronaldo was asked about Mourinho's game plan.

"For an attacking player like you, do you like the style of play this team uses?"

"No, I don't like it, but I have to adapt because that's the way things are."

His goal had won them the Copa del Rey the previous week, his supply had been cut by Mourinho, not Wolfgang Stark, but for his comments he was dropped that weekend against Zaragoza (albeit his coach said it was because Ronaldo had had to play 10 against 11 for too long in the semi-final – 29 minutes). Madrid lost 3-2 in that match, allowing Barcelona to rest Puyol, Iniesta, Valdés, Villa and Pedro for their own 2-1 defeat at Real Sociedad.

It all meant that, ahead of the Champions League second leg and with each team lodging complaints with UEFA over the conduct of the other, the Catalans were eight points clear in La Liga, with four matches remaining.

Camp Nou. Tuesday, May 3, 2011. Champions League semi-final, second leg

For the semi-final return match, the heavens cried, either out of sympathy for poor old Mourinho, out of compassion for the return of Éric Abidal from his potentially fatal liver tumour, or from joy at the manner of Barcelona's qualification for the Wembley final. At any rate, the downpour nearly made the surface unplayable.

Madrid were adventurous, ambitious and vicious in almost equal manner. That Diarra, Ramos and particularly Marcelo were not sent off is not easy to explain.

Pedro put Barcelona 3-0 up on aggregate with a wonderful goal. Marcelo partially atoned for his culpability in all three Barça goals with the equaliser and Gonzalo Higuaín was denied a perfectly legitimate goal for a foul, by Ronaldo on Mascherano, which never was. That might have made the night a little interesting for both teams had it stood.

The 95,000 crowd – Madrid didn't fill their allocation – sang in the rain and it was a Mourinho special. To the tune of '*Oé oé oé oé*,' they roared "*Por qué, por qué, por qué, por qué*," although the Special One was in a suite at the Hotel Rey Juan Carlos, the first place I ever met him, back in 1997. He was suspended from the match and not allowed by UEFA rules to sit on the bench or instruct his team on the night.

Abidal only played a minute or two, but the crowd went absolutely wild. After an operation to take a tumour out of his liver he had somehow dragged himself back to match fitness months ahead of medical prognosis. His emergence from the bench was an incredibly moving moment.

Whether the surgeons were delighted to see the French defender's team-mates grabbing him and throwing him up and down in the air in celebration of his return, I couldn't say. But I couldn't watch either. "Please don't drop him," I prayed, silently, in the amazing din.

Guardiola, his squad and all the staff linked arms around shoulders and danced around the centre circle in a version of the traditional Catalan *sardana* – just as they had done in Rome after winning the competition in May 2009. Then the same staff formed a little guard of honour at the tunnel, the blue-collar workers slapping and cuffing the superstar heroes as they passed through.

Guardiola, post-match: "This has been one of the most wonderful nights of my life. I would like to congratulate Madrid for coming here to play us toe-to-toe. I'd like to congratulate everyone who has come to watch the match and my players because after we drew level, instead of just defending, they still wanted to play football. I am immensely grateful to them."

Valencia. Wednesday, May 11, 2011. Levante v Barcelona

The final was on May 28 and Guardiola, who immediately headed off to Old Trafford with Manel Estiarte to watch United eliminating Schalke, wanted business ruthlessly taken care of well in advance. Victory in the Catalan derby – 2-0 at home to Espanyol thanks to Iniesta and Piqué – meant that a point in Valencia, against Levante, would wrap up a third consecutive title.

However, life gives and takes. The return of Abidal was uplifting, the death of Seve Ballesteros a miserable blow. The day before the Espanyol game, at the pitifully young age of 54, a brain tumour ended his remarkable life.

Whilst he was a golfing genius and a lovable man, he was also a legendary Barça fan. He was invited by the club to the royal box at Wembley in 1992 to see Cruyff's team become European champions for the first time and no Barça player who was at the club for any length of time could fail to get to know and adore this charismatic man.

The last time any of this group saw Ballesteros was back in August 2010 in Seve's home town of Santander.

Guardiola and company had rolled into town, defeated Racing 3-0 and were delighted when the golfer, already deteriorating after what had been a decent remission from cancer, made his way down from the stand to the dressing room. He was welcomed by the players leaping to their feet and spontaneously applauding him for well over a minute. Seve cried and I guess they all knew it was their last time together.

I adored him and I wish he'd lasted just a little longer; long enough to see Barça take Wembley again.

Seydou Keita's goal on a night when Barcelona simply took the sting out of a valiant Levante earned the 1-1 draw at the same stadium where, six years before, another African, Samuel Eto'o, had given Frank Rijkaard's Barça the same result, which also confirmed the title.

That evening in 2005 Pep Guardiola had been at home in Barcelona, recently returned from Qatar, sitting on his couch watching 'his' team become champions for the first time in six years. He was still several months from beginning his coaching education. Quite a journey, from then until now.

The 2011 title win triggered mayhem. Nearly half a million people hit the streets of Barcelona or filled the Camp Nou – free entry – where the open-topped bus deposited the champions for a big fiesta that Friday night.

Down on the pitch, with families surrounding them, the manager, the squad and all the staff bathed in a sea of adoration.

The full house chanted "*¿Por qué, por qué, por qué?*" until their throats were raw and then David Villa took the microphone to give his version of 'My Way'.

One by one, they promised to return after May 28 with another Champions League trophy to parade. One by one, they spoke about what it all meant to them.

Guardiola: "Thanks for your support and my eternal gratitude to these players. Thanks lads, I admire you."

Puyol: "They have attacked us from all sides and they'll continue to do so, but we'll continue doing our thing, which is playing football well."

Xavi: "I'd only tell you all that it's not worth thinking about those around us – just concentrate on Barça: the greatest team in the world."

Abidal: "Thanks to all my team-mates and all the staff – you gave me strength."

Then, perhaps the biggest of the night.

Pinto: "If anyone wants to know why [*por qué*] we are here doing this then I'll tell them. It's … *por qué somos los mejores* [because we are the best]."

Messi chose a different tone. Back in 2009, he'd been shy and almost scared of the microphone when the league celebration took place – again in front of a packed Camp Nou. After the Champions League win in Rome a few days later, Messi had been encouraged into swallowing a beer or two on the open-topped bus journey round the city with the trophy. By the time he spoke on the pitch he was, at least, tipsy.

"Hellooooooooo, I love you all. We are going to win everything all over again," he announced boozily to the enormous amusement of the squad behind him.

This time he was short and to the point. "I'm saying nothing for the moment. I'll speak on May 29, because we'll be back here then." In his mind, the Champions League final was a formality.

1 — The Road to Wembley

Now Pep Guardiola once again took a step away from the norm.

Just as when they won the title in May 2009, the Barça coach ordered his troops to drink, dance, sing and disconnect. The Spanish champions, two weeks away from Wembley, were sent out on a huge party.

In 2009, it had been La Coruña's finest nightspots after the last league match – Restaurant Coral and Twenty Century Rock. In 2011, it was the massive new W Hotel down by Barceloneta beach where the party started. Up on the 26th floor it was dinner, dancing and karaoke (featuring backing vocals from Shakira) in the Eclipse disco, followed by the hardier elements of the group heading out to the Luz de Gas disco in town.

The Víctor Valdés impersonation show, which had been such a hit before the semi-final in Madrid, was back by popular demand. Team-mates were taken off, as well as Jorge Valdano, general manager of Real Madrid, Fernando Alonso, Mourinho and the singer Joaquín Sabina.

Guardiola and some of his stars opted for rooms at the five-star hotel shaped like a giant sail, from where, if you look left along the beach, you can see the Hotel Arts, where Manchester United celebrated their dramatic 1999 Champions League win, when Pep was still a key Barcelona player and Sergio Busquets was 10 years old.

Manel Estiarte was the organiser of the night – which Eto'o attended by invitation from Guardiola – and other high jinks over the following days.

"We had won the title and Wembley was two weeks away. Pep said, 'I want a break of three *días de locos* [crazy days]'. We had continuous parties and dinners and the players went out, enjoyed themselves and got drunk.

"Pep was very specific. He will often say 'three-day break' when the players can take a rest and enjoy free time with their families or girlfriends, but this was three days of celebrating together. He wanted to recognise the achievement and to ensure his squad didn't end up physically and mentally exhausted. Pep has these intuitions."

Those few days amounted to the first phase of the preparation for the Champions League final.

There were no casualties, but I watched the squad consume gallons and gallons of water out on the training pitch the following Saturday morning – hangovers were the order of the day and one or two were still, definitely, not completely sober.

The Camp Nou celebrated, again, after the 0-0 draw with Deportivo that night, after which Pep told his lads: "Now you have three more days off – I don't want to see you. Try and go out with friends or family who have nothing to do with this club and switch off. Wednesday morning it's back to work, full on, and the road to Wembley starts."

The road to Wembley

The fans already had that fever. There were 96,267 applications for 24,360 available Champions League final tickets but, suddenly, there was potentially a greater problem.

Barcelona had their hotel booked, 42 of the 154 suites

at the Wyndham Grand Hotel at Chelsea harbour. They had the post-match party venue sorted, the Natural History Museum in South Kensington.

The post-match party was important, and the venue was crucial, because many senior staff at Barcelona feel that the real golden moment is when the full FC Barcelona family is together – staff, players, directors plus assorted parents, girlfriends, wives, children and special guests – celebrating a year's hard work.

To some, such as Vilanova, that wonderful sense of union is almost more valuable than winning the trophy.

UEFA cleared Sergio Busquets to play, pushing aside Real Madrid's accusations that he had racially abused Marcelo. Everyone bar Afellay was fit; the title was wrapped up; there were no more dates with Mourinho on the horizon. Barça were locked and loaded.

Then Mother Nature intervened. The previous year it had been devastating to have to play a derby against Espanyol then take a coach trip to Milan because of volcanic ash from Eyjafjallajökull closing European air-space.

With brutal timing there were suddenly eruptions again: this time Grímsvötn.

It was unclear as to when flights might be hampered and, if there was a loud groan at the Camp Nou offices, it was drowned out by the sound of immediate action. There were to be no more avoidable errors. Barcelona would leave for London and get there two days early. The Wyndham couldn't accommodate them, so Barcelona stayed temporarily at the Grove and trained at London Colney, courtesy of Arsenal, despite having knocked them out in controversial circumstances just over a month earlier. Guardiola's gang was in town. "We went to London a good few days before, made ourselves feel at home there, and went into the match in really good shape," said Guardiola. "Things like that tend to get overlooked but they make the difference in big games."

Then, another problem. Puyol, a certain starter, experienced pain in the knee which would soon require surgery and only a last-minute fitness test would determine whether he, or Abidal, would start.

Two weeks before the final I'd sat down for a long interview with Mascherano, who had taken a seven-figure pay cut to join Barcelona because he, like Alves, Ibrahimovic, Fàbregas and Abidal, was absolutely determined to be part of that wonderful playing philosophy. This club calls to them. Money is nice, professional happiness is much rarer.

Many in England thought Mascherano wouldn't fit in. His combative qualities at Liverpool had masked something which Barça team-mates discovered almost instantly. Not only can he play, he's very football intelligent.

Our chat had a slightly comical side. When I mentioned Wembley to Mascherano he was soon on to 1966, Sir Alf Ramsey, Antonio Rattín and a World Cup quarter-final which is still infamous in both England and Argentina.

"I wasn't alive, but everyone knows we were robbed," Mascherano reckoned, as we roamed just slightly off the subject in hand.

I'd been convinced of the Argentinian captain's chances at Barça as soon as I'd heard Xavi praising his passing ability and instinctive understanding of the

Barcelona playing philosophy. I believe Xavi will coach Barcelona in the relatively near future and if he thinks a player 'gets it' then that player definitely 'gets it'.

Mascherano it would be. Puyol on the bench. Abidal left-back.

There were so many echoes surrounding the game that it was a match in a bubble.

United won their first European crown at Wembley, as did Barcelona. The two sides had played out a stirring but eventually one-sided European Cup final two years previously – and there to watch the rematch would be so many faces from the two great events.

I had the huge privilege to spend a few great hours the night before the game in a BBC radio studio with a fantastic football man, Pat Crerand, who was in midfield for Sir Matt Busby's side in 1968. Fiercely loyal to United, he knew his team was up against a rival to whom, if they hit form, it would be no shame to lose.

Ronald Koeman, Hristo Stoichkov, Johan Cruyff, Charly Rexach – they could all be seen around the UEFA hotel, the best local restaurants, then Wembley itself.

On Friday, I met and interviewed Gio van Bronckhorst, a smashing footballer who had added bite and brains to the 2006 Champions League-winning side of Ronaldinho, Eto'o and Henrik Larsson. He's far from a controversial man but, clearly, he could only really envisage one winner – speaking analytically, rather than with his heart.

Then, there was the Ferguson factor. Both Sir Alex and his brother Martin had been spectators at what is often called the greatest European final of all – Real Madrid 7 Eintracht Frankfurt 3 at Hampden in 1960.

Sir Alex turned down more than one opportunity to manage Barça and, had Pep Guardiola left in 2010, when Joan Laporta's reign ended, Sandro Rosell had long pondered whether he could tempt Ferguson for one last hurrah at the Camp Nou, coaching Xavi, Piqué, Iniesta and Messi.

On the Saturday morning of the match I arranged to meet Martin Ferguson, United's head of European scouting, for a drink and a quiet chat in the build-up to the match. He is a friend of over 10 years and, while hopeful for his brother and the United squad, he knew that this was an improved rival from that which had beaten United in 2009.

Finally, Sir Alex managed my hometown team, Aberdeen, to glory in Europe. On a personal level, victory for him and Darren Fletcher, another friend, would have been cause for celebration.

Before the game, Messi was asked about a statistical anomaly: he had never scored on English soil. He replied: "It's nothing more than a coincidence and while I'll be trying to score at Wembley, the only thing I care about is that Barça win the cup."

About his phenomenal goal record, which would make him Champions League top scorer for a second successive season, Barça's No 10 answered: "Every year I'm getting more experience and that helps me make the right decisions. I know precisely what I can and can't do in a given situation. During the game ideas pop up in my head about what to do, what to attempt and what happens is that you get increasingly bold about putting those into practice."

Guardiola warned: "You can't be favourites against a club like United. The guys need to concentrate, work hard and not be confused by the fact that this is their second final in three years. I want them to have the appropriate level of fear that the club might not reach another one for the next 20 years. You have to treat it like a unique chance to win this trophy."

Barcelona were not only quietly confident, they believed that if they followed the coach's instructions and hit their normal level of form then nobody in the world could beat them.

Estiarte tries to explain the evolution of that bullet-proof self-confidence. "First of all, we have the best player in the world. That's incontestable. Plus, he understands what it is to play for Barcelona. The Catalan players have made sure of that.

"Messi has humility – you can see it when he plays. He accepts that the core group is the life and soul of the club. Meanwhile, his team-mates are happy to recognise him as the best player in the world. There is no jealousy – that's very difficult to achieve.

"I was the best [water polo] player in the world and for many years I was a disaster in terms of my leadership skills. I was arrogant, I didn't understand enough, I thought it was all about me. You often find that with sportsmen who are at the top of their profession, who are considered the best in the world. They have a level of personal ambition and selfishness, but then you grow and you mature a bit, you become closer to your team-mates.

"But it's not something anyone has had to think about with Messi. Leo doesn't think for a minute that his team-mates have given him this authority. It comes totally naturally and that's the real miracle. That's what makes the difference. It is not forced or contrived.

It's not about self interest. It doesn't come from fear. That is a powerful combination: the best player in the world, who is comfortable working alongside a core group which has such a strong emotional sense of what it means to play for FC Barcelona."

Guardiola's assistant, Vilanova, explained the process of briefing the players on how to beat United. "We try to prepare the same way for every match. There's not much difference whether we're playing Hospitalet or a final at Wembley. We work on tactics and strategy in the same way and give the players the same amount of information. When we play league games the guys have played them 20 times already and know them inside out, but if it's a foreign team we give our players a little more information about who they'll be facing."

Estiarte describes a gear change in Guardiola that takes place as the season reaches its climax. "Pep is very clear about the fact that playing well is a means to winning. It's innate, this belief that the only thing that matters is winning. He says, 'I want to win and I'm going to transmit that to my team,' but if they lose, he is the first to say, 'Don't worry about it, let's start thinking about the next game.' However, from April to May he changes, his message changes to: 'We have to win. We are going to win'.

"In this team you have the best player in the world, who only thinks about winning. His whole world revolves around that ball and winning. But this is a very competitive team. We have three or four extraordinary players. Three or four who have a natural ability to take on the big occasions. You know you can always depend on them in the important games.

"Every single player gives it everything they've got

but some of them have a certain quality that tran-
scends sport. It goes beyond simply winning or losing.
It's about those players who remain constant, who are
not affected by the pressure or stress. It's the symbiosis
of their football sense and their human spirit which
means that they are always 'present'. There are very few
sportsmen who have that quality. It's sport in its purest
form. There are a lot of players who get fired up, but
who go too far and lose the plot. They end up doing
stupid things. They fight with the referee or other players. Not in our squad, though."

Wembley, London. May 28, 2011

United were significantly better than in Rome – until
just before Pedro scored, at which time Xavi and Iniesta
were beginning to hypnotise the United midfield. I
suspect that when Pep Guardiola saw the United team
sheet, with Ryan Giggs and Michael Carrick in midfield, he was delighted that Darren Fletcher's recovery from a virus had come just too late and that his
extremely mobile players might well find the centre of
the pitch increasingly spacious as the match wore on.
So it proved.

United's goal was sensational. Rooney produced a
mature, proud display and deserved more, but even
at 1-1, anyone who watched Barça often knew that
once they look 'in the zone' there's no way back for the
opposition.

I suspect that it wasn't only those of us who have
dedicated their working lives to studying Barça
over the last few years who knew, absolutely knew,

that while the scoreline said 'parity' the match flow screamed 'superiority'.

First of all the pattern changed. United's pressing subsided and Barcelona found space in midfield. The gaps appeared larger and Xavi or Iniesta appeared in them more and more regularly. Secondly, it was clear, even before he scored, that Messi was buzzing with energy.

United began to look ponderous, a product of the lightning-fast movement of the ball produced by Guardiola's men. Edwin van der Sar might not have been overwhelmed but he was working, hard.

The final game of his distinguished career was a sad one and the explosive nature of Messi's shot exposed him at Barça's second goal. But look how and where Messi picks the ball up – the goal was coming. If you want to put up a barrier against Barça it has to be very mobile and very intelligent. Before the goal there is space and time for Barça to shuffle the ball about at will and when Messi, who has dropped away from where the central striker would normally play, picks up the ball he has an ocean of room into which he accelerates.

Messi's wonderful little jink away from Nani to help set up Villa's sublime goal, well, that was the mark of a player who wanted the final 'owned', business taken care of and superiority translated into goals. Messi sank to his knees when Villa's curving shot whizzed past Van der Sar. He knew, just as we did, that Barça had performed exceptionally.

Abidal collected the cup and, afterwards, was utterly exhausted. Little wonder the Barça players had given Dr Josep Fuster, Abidal's surgeon, a standing ovation the first time they saw him after the Frenchman's tumour operation.

The victory was the culmination of three years of hard work. The Barcelona system had been redesigned; talent had bloomed into genius and an almost constant wave of appreciation was now crashing down on the Camp Nou from all around the world.

After a dazzling performance, their manager revealed that he had been worried that this kind of level might have been beyond his players that season.

"We had no idea how the team would be after having won so much, including the World Cup," Guardiola later reflected.

He was thinking of the impact on Juventus after the 1982 World Cup and the Barcelona Dream Team which crashed and burned in the USA World Cup in the hot summer of 1994. In fact, he had pitched up in the hotel Spain used around the 2010 World Cup final, at Sandton, to speak to his players in anticipation of them going on holiday.

Guardiola briefed them about his plans for the pre-season and was shocked that all his footballers were determined to play in the Super Copa against Sevilla in August 2010. They deserved more rest time and he was offering that to them. Puyol, Xavi, Iniesta, Villa and the rest said: 'Forget it boss.' The hunger never left them.

Guardiola said: "After winning so much, there is a natural temptation to lose that competitive edge, to stop striving for excellence, but they haven't lowered their standards for a second. They have gone to every stadium in Spain and given of their very best. I can't express in words how much they have achieved or my pride in them. They are an outstanding example of fair-play and passion for the game."

Estiarte can sum up what the three-trophy 2011 season tells us about the achievements of his friend, Guardiola, and where the group stood in its aftermath.

I asked him whether there was a secret or a way for outsiders to understand it better. I asked him to take us inside the training ground. He told me: "We're talking about an exceptional team. I have seen a lot of things in my life and have had a long career in sport, but in these last three-and-a-half years I have witnessed something exceptional, both in terms of sport and in human terms.

"And the most amazing thing of all? In three years and a handful of months there has not been a single argument in the dressing room. You could actually see that as a negative thing. With 22 people together like that, the most natural thing would be for there to be the odd falling out. One day one player tells the other to 'f*** off' and the next day apologises. That would be totally normal. From time to time that happens in every club in the world.

"But in all this time there's not been a single incident here where you have to worry about a personality clash or religious tensions or arguments between different age groups. I reckon that's down to us having that nucleus of homegrown players.

"Very, very few teams, perhaps Manchester United, have what Barça has. It's the men, the Catalans, the Spanish or guys who were born elsewhere but grew up here, who give our club its unique power. We've always had Dutch players and Argentinians or Brazilians who are great players, but are not natives. The Dutch are fantastic professionals. The British, too – Mark Hughes, Steve Archibald. I'm not saying for a minute that they were inferior in any way, but the others I'm talking about have an emotional attachment. Their hearts are in the club and that makes all the difference – and we're not just talking about a couple of players.

"There's Xavi, Busquets, Valdés, Messi, Iniesta, Piqué, Puyol, Pedro, Fàbregas, Thiago, Fontàs, Cuenca and dozens of kids in the teams below that. The captains are from here, they are Catalans. It is they who transmit this special dedication to the club to the other players. It's them who set the bar in terms of professionalism and the serious attitudes they have. Xavi and his ilk can come to work every day with the pride of knowing, 'I'm from Barcelona, and this is my club'. Guys like him are so proud of their country, Catalonia.

"Very few clubs have that engine driving them on. Don't underestimate it."

There you have it, skill, leadership, fun, flair, hard work and pride in the club they believe belongs to them – crucial elements in building the greatest team in the world. Let's find out how they achieved it.

DAVID VILLA: EL GUAJE

I LIKE DAVID VILLA BECAUSE he's old school. Old school about scoring goals. Old school about training. Old school about concepts like respect and professionalism.

Whether you are an opponent, a coach, a fan or a journalist, if you win his respect he is also old school in his reliability, directness and honesty. You can see the evidence of all of this on the pitch, too.

Villa is famous for his goals but for the big picture, look beyond that and draw on what his Spain and Barcelona colleagues think about him. They know they can rely on him. He's never found wanting, whether in terms of football intelligence or athletic hard labour.

Goal-getters are supposed to be selfish, but David Villa improved this Barcelona team upon arrival and became Spain's record goalscorer despite a willingness to do other players' work for them, to play wide on the left and accept that there is a price to pay for the privilege of partnering the world's greatest footballer, Lionel Messi.

But this son of an Asturian miner (his nickname, *El Guaje*, is Asturian for The Kid) is tough. He tells the story of breaking his leg as a young kid and continuing to play football so often, so intensely with his right leg in a plaster cast that his weaker left leg became equally good. It is an experience he would draw on later in his career, after another leg break, at the World Club Championship in December 2011.

He also has a bit of devil-may-care in him. I saw him opt to have a spin in a double pilot Formula One car up at the Montmelo circuit in Catalonia and exit the vehicle with jelly for legs. Whether his club at the time, Valencia, would have been delighted is a different story. A few weeks later he had become top scorer at Euro 2008 and steered Spain to their first title in 44 years.

Villa told me in South Africa, the evening before that torrid Soccer City final against Holland: "I have never, ever cried on a football pitch, and I don't intend to, but if there has to be a time then I suppose it better be tomorrow." I like that thought.

I claim no special acuity in having reported for several seasons that Villa was, pound-for-pound, the best signing any club in the English Premier League could make. Based on age, ability and availability, it was blindingly obvious he should have been bought. For Villa and Pep Guardiola, frustration at Barcelona's unwillingness to pay the sale price asked by Valencia and bring this exceptional, all-round goalscorer to the club one year earlier than they actually did was a reminder that constructing the greatest team in the world is not without its obstacles.

If the Champions League victory at Wembley in 2011, and the manner of it, was the icing on a cake three years in the making for Guardiola, then Villa's beautiful third goal was the daddy of all maraschino cherries. He's got the lot: intelligence, power, attitude, skill; he is ambidextrous, hard-working, and deadly; he scores with free-kicks, penalties, headers, inside the box, long-range finishes – hell, what more do you want?

All hail *El Guaje*. In fact, no – ¡*Viva Villa!*

2 – THE MAKING OF MESSI

"I believe Leo comes from a marvellous
planet, the one where exceptional people like
violinists, architects, and doctors are created.
The chosen people."
— Josep Maria Minguella

DISTINCTLY REMEMBER the first time I saw Leo Messi play football. One of us was patently off-form that day. I came away thinking that Joan Verdú, who was playing in what we would now consider Messi's best position, completely out-shone him and that the genius acknowledged as the greatest footballer of modern times had a bit of a stinker.

It was autumn 2003 at Barça's Mini Estadi, the 17,000-capacity arena a few hundred metres from the Camp Nou. My friend, Rob Moore, had asked me along to watch the Barça B captain, Arnau Riera, because he was considering representing him. Messi's name, of course, already had a buzz surrounding it, but that day he played on the left wing in a 4-2-3-1 formation and, although there were one or two of those delightful dribbles, he looked sluggish and disinterested.

The next time I saw him was the night he scored his first goal for Barcelona – against Albacete at the Camp Nou in spring 2005. No-one who was there doubted we were witnessing the arrival of a special footballer.

I'd taken my daughter, Cara, to the game and we were sitting high up in the 'Lateral' stand at the Camp Nou – closest to the Gol Nord.

Messi is 17 and has only accumulated 69 minutes of La Liga football, starting with his debut at Espanyol, six months earlier. He replaces Samuel Eto'o, and 107 seconds later has put the ball in the net. Ronaldinho gallops away from a couple of markers in midfield and scoops his foot under the ball in order to lob it forward to Messi. The Argentinian kid takes a touch and stylishly chips the keeper.

The goal is incorrectly ruled offside. The Albacete keeper, Raúl Valbuena, patronisingly pats Messi on the head: 'Tough luck, wee man.' The crowd of 80,000 roars its disbelief at a decision which has robbed them of a magical goal. There are 18 seconds left of normal time. Enough for the Brazilian sorcerer and his little apprentice to produce more magic.

Thirty seconds after the disallowed goal, Ronaldinho sends Messi down the left and his cross is very nearly converted into a goal by Andrés Iniesta. The little genius has only been on the pitch for two-and-a-half minutes. Albacete break up the pitch looking for an equaliser. Instead, Gio van Bronckhorst robs Rubén Súarez and Deco hits a pitching-wedge pass to Messi. The teenager controls with his head, holds off his defender and lays it back to Ronaldinho, who conjures up the same, scooped pass as before, over Gaspar Gálvez at centre-half. Messi lets the ball bounce before chipping Valbuena for a second time.

The Camp Nou erupted. We were yet to discover exactly how much Ronaldinho, a generous, lovable guy, already adored Messi, but here was a clue: the maestro fed the new boy two assist passes so that Messi could show the crowd his stuff. As they celebrated, Ronaldinho gave the youngster a piggy-back so that he was elevated to the crowd's adulation. A couple of weeks later, Messi explained: "It was curious because I could hear 80,000 people chanting my name, but everything was blank. I don't know if I sort of fainted or whether it was just the rush of emotion at scoring my first goal at the Camp Nou, but I couldn't see anything."

No-one could know how enormous the Messi phenomenon would become, but anyone who saw his cameo that night knew Barcelona had a precocious, nerveless new talent.

My initial verdict at the Mini Estadi remained a thorn in my side. Was I the only guy in the world to catch Messi early but be blind to his talents? That's the way I always told the story, against myself, until coming back to research this book.

Chatting about that game with Arnau Riera, he told me that, by then, Messi's impatience to move on from the Barça B group and his preference for playing just about anywhere except on the left wing meant that, from time to time, he would wander through a game. Not quite sulking, but not at his electric best.

"We knew as soon as he joined the squad that he would not be with us for very long," said Arnau. "He was a great team-mate, good company and he trained well – but he absolutely knew that he was ready for the first team at 16 and he didn't particularly like being stuck out on the left wing."

Thank heavens for that. I caught Messi on a quiet day. Reassuring.

He has said that he "hated" being made to play on the right or, worse still, the left wing, when Frank Rijkaard promoted him to the first team, but Messi also admits that it was vital for him to learn from playing along-side one of the most gifted modern centre-forwards, Samuel Eto'o.

Even at that early stage, I was not the first to mis-judge the player who would become the greatest in the world. Such mistakes nearly redirected him away from Barça completely.

The hormone deficiency with which Lionel Andrés Messi was born in Rosario, near Buenos Aires in Argentina, in 1987, would never have stopped him reaching his adult height. It would, however, have slowed his growth to the extent of denying him a career in professional football, had it not been treated. That much is quite well known, but the level of doubt and the lack of commitment shown by Barça to the young Messi because of his size is an underexposed story.

It got to the extent that Charly Rexach, then football advisor to Barça president Joan Gaspart, had to secretly commit FC Barcelona to contracting Messi by writing his personal promise on a napkin at the Pompeya tennis club; Messi's father was also forced to write strenuously to the Barcelona board, asking them when – if ever – they would fulfil their subsequent promises, because the money needed to keep body and soul together, having arrived in Barcelona from Argentina, was running out.

Messi's physiology is interwoven in the story of how he was spotted by Barcelona.

His initial specialist in Argentina, Dr Diego Schwarzstein, recalled: "Some people around the football club [Newell's Old Boys, where Messi first trained] came to me and told me, 'We have this little lad, he's a phenomenon, but he needs to grow'. He was missing a hormone which we can genetically recreate to give the body precisely what it is lacking. The only problem is it is expensive."

Messi was eight when the process began, but his family understood that their youngest son had a special talent and found money for the hormone injections. However, the cost wasn't the only problem. The injections were a deeply unpleasant experience for a boy so young.

However, he refused help from neighbours and family. "I'll always remember those nights, sat on my bed, having to inject myself in each leg," he said. "It wasn't fun, believe me, but I had such desire to be a footballer that I knew I could and would do it. But it was very expensive and although my parents tried everything we just couldn't afford the treatment on our own."

Matías Messi, one of his elder brothers, explains: "He would prepare the process, load the syringe and inject it himself. It was tough for the family, even though he never made a fuss about it; you knew that each night before he could go to sleep he had to go through this process, which wasn't a lot of fun for him at that age".

In Rosario he'd been unstoppable in the *fútbol sala* which is predominant in continental Europe and South America. The ball is smaller and heavier, the goals are narrow and high, rather than the letter-box goals which are the norm for small-sided games in the UK and Ireland. Whether he was the same size or smaller than his opponents he still had that anticipation of when to intercept, when to accelerate and possessed a version of the mesmeric dribbling which makes him unplayable today.

The local team in the barrio was called Grandoli. At times, his father, Jorge, coached him there. His late grandmother first took him when he was just over five and Messi's first experience was when one team was missing a player and he made up the numbers. It is that grandmother, Celia, to whom he still dedicates his goals with arms pointed to the heavens.

The club was about 4km from the Messi home, on Calle Estado de Israel, which meant an hour's walk if someone wasn't available to drive him there or the bus was too expensive. Soon enough, his ability meant that Newell's Old Boys took him to train with their junior sections. To this day, Messi says that he'd like to end his career with the club.

Their stadium was about 6km from home and when young Messi went there to watch the senior team it must have seemed like heaven. He saw his country's idol, Diego Maradona, play one of his five games for Newell's in late 1993 when his dad took him uptown to watch the great man. Set in the Parque de la Independencia, just above the hippodrome and Rosario Jockey Club, there is an artificial lake, rose gardens, impressive historical sculptures – a far cry from downtown Rosario.

Newell's' training facilities for kids, Instalaciones Malvinas, were far nearer his home and also far more basic. He thrived there but neither they, nor River Plate, who coveted his signature, could afford the approximate $1,000 per month it was going to take for a couple of years of hormone treatment to allow Messi to attain his natural height at normal growth rate.

Jorge Messi had persuaded his employers and another local business to sponsor the initial cost of treatment, but that became unsustainable after two years, partly because of the downturn in the Argentinian economy.

Then, in 2000, a little miracle happened. This diminutive 12-year-old found his way into Barcelona's field of vision, moved with his family to the other side of the world, continued his treatment, overcame his doubters within the Camp Nou and grew to be one of, if not the greatest footballer ever.

Two Argentinian intermediaries in Buenos Aires heard about this amazing kid who couldn't grow properly. They phoned a contact, Horacio Gaggioli, in Barcelona, who brought into this drama a central character – Josep Maria Minguella, an ubiquitous figure in the modern history of FC Barcelona and an extraordinary man.

Minguella was taken on at FC Barcelona as a translator to the English coach Vic Buckingham back in 1970. He became a coach, the manager's assistant, a youth-team organiser, a scout and a player agent. He's also the man who brought Diego Maradona, Romario, Hristo Stoichkov and, finally, Leo Messi to the Camp Nou.

On the subject of signing Maradona, Minguella explained to me: "It was a very long and difficult negotiation. I spotted Diego for the first time in 1977 and I tried to quickly bring him to Barcelona.

"I was scouting a player for the No 7 position at Barça and during the third match I'd been to in Argentina, to watch a guy called Jorge López, some kid with short shorts and dark curly hair started playing. As soon as he started to take the ball he took my attention, too. He was different to anyone I'd ever seen. When I asked the president of Argentinos Juniors he told me the members would kill him if he sold him and, at that moment, Barça didn't want to sign junior players from other countries.

"In the end it took until 1980 to sign a contract between Maradona, his club and FC Barcelona. We returned to Catalonia and it was still all completely secret. Fifteen days later, the Argentinian FA president, Julio Grondona, called me and told me it was vital to come back to Buenos Aires, because there were problems. Grondona said that I had to meet the sports minister in the government. He was one of the generals who ran the World Cup in 1978, and Argentina was still a military state. They decided that Maradona could not leave the country until after the 1982 World Cup.

"I wasn't aware what was happening between the military and the people in that country, but at that time they were killing people indiscriminately, perhaps as many as 40,000. I'm not sure that I'd have been arguing with them so vociferously had I known at the time.

"The deal was that Diego signed for Boca Juniors, but would then come to us after the World Cup."

Maradona is, and always will be, important to Messi. When he was first called by El Diego to appear on his 'La Noche del 10' television programme in Buenos Aires, it reduced young Messi to tears and he spoke emotionally about not believing that he was receiving a call from his country's greatest ever sportsman.

Maradona coached Messi for Argentina and while there have been occasional glimpses of jealousy from the older man, he has also hinted that he believes the younger man is his better.

Minguella also recalls with great clarity the process of being convinced by Messi's talent and then trying to convince others. "Messi's case was even more difficult than Maradona's," he said. "I first saw him when he was 12 and he was not big. Physically, there were doubts whether he'd ever become a good footballer in Europe, but as soon as I saw the videos it was like seeing the light. I believe Leo comes from a marvellous planet, the one where exceptional people like violinists, architects, and doctors are created. The chosen people.

"He was instantly similar to Maradona. Left foot, No 10, same mentality. All kids like him wanted to be playmakers, to emulate Maradona, but I knew there were both serious possibilities and serious problems.

"Again, Barça were not too interested. They said, 'It will be 10 or 12 years before we see the benefit'. I was determined, so I paid his ticket across to Spain, him and his father, and installed them in the Plaza Hotel in Plaza Espanya.

"In the training sessions the coaches could see what he had, but there were weeks of discussions because some directors thought he was too small, some liked him, but no-one would take decisions. I called Charly Rexach, who had been my friend for years, and was a football advisor to the Barça president Joan Gaspart. Charly prepared a friendly match."

It was played on the outside pitches at the Mini Estadi, hard, flat artificial turf, and Messi, despite being underdeveloped for his age, played with kids of age categories above his – and he shone. Only a blind man could have missed it.

"Charly saw immediately what others had been scared to commit to," said Minguella. "But things had dragged on for so, so long by that stage that Leo's dad was frustrated and losing faith. So we went up to Pompeya tennis club in Montjuïc, where I was the president. I was confident in Rexach, but the Messi family had been here one month or more and they thought it was all going wrong.

"Therefore, famously, Charly took a paper napkin, laid it on the table and wrote: 'In Barcelona on the 14th of December 2000 and in the presence of Mr Minguella, Horacio Gaggioli (representing the Messi family) I, Charly Rexach, technical secretary of FC Barcelona, use my position, despite there being some whose opinion is against it, to commit to signing the player Lionel Messi so long as everyone sticks to the financial terms we agree on.'"

However, time was running out. Jorge Messi was tired of being messed about.

He had ended up in a similarly frustrating mess with River Plate a few months previously and now, on the other side of the world and separated from the rest of the family, Barça appeared to be making fools of themselves and the Messis.

By this stage – although Minguella swears he would never have contacted Real Madrid – Barça's great rivals were aware of this phenomenal prospect, and of the slow progress being made with the Catalan club. Messi didn't have a professional contract in Argentina and a coup would have been straightforward.

Had he and his father returned home that Christmas in frustration at Barcelona's ineptitude, the most likely scenario would have seen Messi, under Argentinian FA contractual rules, sign a professional contract (most likely with Newell's) and the chance for Barça to make a simple deal would have disappeared.

Taking on faith that the weird 'napkin-contract' was valid, the Messis re-committed to Barça, Jorge was promised a paid role (at around €42,000 per year) within the club's youth development and scouting system and his son's career at the Camp Nou began. Well, almost.

In my first interview with Messi, in February 2006, he told me what it was like to say goodbye to Rosario, now that he was to become a full-time FC Barcelona junior footballer.

"Even now I can remember when we left our neighbourhood and everyone came out to say goodbye," he said. "My mother and father and my two brothers and sister were all getting ready to go in a taxi to the airport and every single one of us was crying our eyes out. Everyone had told me that Barcelona would look after me and my family, but I was worried in case that had been a lie, so when we got to the Camp Nou and it was so impressive we all had to pinch ourselves to believe it."

It still took until March 2001 for a full junior (rather than professional) contract to be signed, during which another of the heroes in this story, Joan Lacueva, Barça director general at that time, also tired of the club's flat-footed ineptitude and began paying for Messi's growth hormone treatment out of his own pocket.

This is the testimony to that remarkable moment which he gave for this book, talking in depth about this pivotal moment for the first time, 11 years on.

"I was the director general, in charge of administrating youth football at Barça. I was aware there was a player taking trials at Barça, a certain Leo Messi. Josep Maria Minguella came to me and said, 'I've got this kid who's going to play for the first team one day. I like him a lot and we need to find out why his dad isn't happy and why things aren't progressing as they should be. I want to get this sorted out'.

"I went to the head of the sporting side of the *fútbol base* and said, 'There's a player we're trialling and I need to know everything about him so that I can decide whether to push this through or not.'

"The more I spoke to all the coaches – the guys who were at the training sessions – the more I heard the same incredible reports, so I insisted that we needed to sign this guy.

"Whilst all this was happening, a meeting had taken place, at the father's insistence, with Carles Rexach, the technical director. They met at the tennis club where they agreed the deal and signed on that famous napkin. It was obviously not a legal document, so Messi's father came to see me that afternoon. I was the one who would take charge of the contractual arrangements.

"I couldn't produce an official document immediately because the board had to agree it first, so I decided to copy the agreement on the napkin onto official club stationery, which I then signed. From there it went to the board, where it had a mixed response. Some directors were supportive, but others considered that, at 13 years of age, the lad was far too small and was more suited to indoor, five-a-side, or even table football.

"The proposal was that we pay this kid more than we had ever paid a player at his stage, but by the end of the meeting they had agreed to start the process of signing Messi to the club.

"I knew Messi had been receiving growth hormones in Argentina, so I spoke to Josep Borrell in Barcelona's medical team and told him about the treatment the player required. His advice was to start as soon as possible. That meant someone had to pay for the treatment and, as far as I remember, I paid 152,000 pesetas for the first round of injections. I wasn't motivated solely by the kindness of my heart, though. Given that Messi wasn't yet a Barça player, I couldn't justify paying for it out of the club's funds and later, when he was playing for the club, I was reimbursed."

The action taken by Rexach and Lacueva was fundamental in convincing Jorge Messi that Barcelona was the right club for his son, at a time when the Camp Nou board was divided on that subject and avaricious eyes were watching from Madrid.

Lacueva is one of those, like Rexach, Minguella and only one or two others, who can sit back in a privileged seat at the Camp Nou, or at home on the sofa, and watch Lionel Messi write footballing history with a sense of immense satisfaction in having participated in signing him in the face of opposition and with intelligence, honour and alacrity.

"He's definitely introverted and a bit shy. When he first came here I would often visit the family in their hotel and, for a couple of weeks, he was pretty scared and desperate to go back to Argentina," remembers Lacueva. "What turned things around was his teammates' reaction. When they played or trained with him they immediately realised how good he was and that affected him in a very positive way.

"Eventually if you said to him: 'Okay then, let's send you back to Argentina,' he'd refuse even to go on the Metro in case you tricked him and it was the start of a journey back to the airport!

"Now Leo is 24 I still think he's got a lot more to give in terms of his physical development, in his dealings with the media and the degree to which he is a sociological phenomenon. It wouldn't surprise me if someone makes a film about him one day. There's a sensational, human story there.

"Leo was a wonderful football talent, but his time in La Masia has made him a great team player. My memory is that they had to keep moving him up to the next category every three or four games. He came from a team where he was used to five, six or seven touches, dribbling with the ball, and they taught him how to play in a team and play one- or two-touch. The world can see the results when he plays with Iniesta or Cesc.

"Did I imagine that Messi would become the best player in the world? As far as I was concerned, we were signing a potential first-team player who was young enough to apply for Spanish nationality so that he wouldn't count towards our foreign players quota. I didn't think for a second that he would turn into the player that he is today.

"Even back then he was doing amazing things for his age but I was only too aware how much things can change between the ages of 12 and 18. You get kids who turn into bad-tempered teenagers and kick up a fuss every time they don't get a game."

So, despite ineptitude typical of that Joan Gaspart era, Barça somehow untangled itself and accommodated the kid who would earn them millions, power a trophy conveyor belt and become the best footballer in their history.

However, by July 2001 the situation had reached perhaps its gravest point. Jorge Messi wrote the following letter to Joan Gaspart:

Barcelona, July 9, 2001

To the President of FC Barcelona.

I write to you as the father and guardian of my youngest son Lionel Messi, current player with the FC Barcelona Infantil squad.

Last March we moved from our family home in Argentina with the aim of letting my son sign for FC Barcelona. At that time we signed all the documents pertaining to Lionel's sporting situa-

tion and they also made clear what would be the circumstances for me and my family (my wife and four children, including Lionel). That meant I could begin the process of obtaining my Spanish residency papers thanks to the labour contract I signed with you.

Beyond the original payments which I received, the start date for the contract we signed was July 1, which has now passed.

As of today, despite constantly being in contact with the appropriate departments of the club I have not been able to establish what my situation is. Every single person who has been involved in the operation so far, Mr Lacueva, Mr Hinjos and finally Mr Jaume González, tell me that they are now not able to give me any information at all.

As a result the current situation in which I and my family find ourselves is exceedingly grave. I made financial plans to keep us going independently until this month, at which point the contract we signed was supposed to start. Instead I'm currently without any indication of when I will begin to earn and nobody is willing to tell me how to proceed.

That is all and now I hope we can resolve the situation as speedily as possible – yours,

Jorge Horacio Messi.

As well as the Messi family's growing frustration with

the Barcelona board, the player was caught in bureaucratic red tape of the worst kind. For six months he was not registered to play competitive matches within the Barça youth system – only friendlies.

No competitive football, no formal supply of growth hormones, wages promised to Jorge Messi unpaid. The family would have been forgiven for feeling unwanted.

Minguella has his theory: "I believe that they didn't show a great deal of faith in this exceptional little player because, after 50 years in football, one thing is very clear to me. The only thing for football directors is to win the next match. What happens in a year, or three, or five … I don't know too many who care about that. Win this weekend, that's okay. Some people probably thought, 'When Messi gets to 20 I won't be here', so they didn't pay his subject proper attention."

It all culminated when Messi, finally cleared to play and in only his second league match, damaged his ankle so badly that he needed months of rehabilitation.

Gradually, after jetting back and forward between the two countries, his sister missed Argentina so much that she and her mother, Celia, returned home to Rosario. Soon after, Messi's two brothers, Matías and Rodrigo, followed them.

Messi told me that he hid his tears from his father, either when the hormone injections were too painful or when he, too, felt desperately homesick. He had reached a crossroads, however, and his father knew it.

Jorge Messi decided to give his son a clear choice. It was his call: they could reunite their family in Rosario, or stay in Spain and attempt to overcome the obstacles in their way. Messi, tough little guy that he is, refused to give in.

In 2006, he reflected on that decision. "It was me who asked to come and I'm not so sure I'd have the guts to allow my own son to do the same thing. It was tremendously difficult for them and I'm so grateful for all the encouragement my parents, brothers and other relations gave me. Without them I wouldn't be here. It's as simple as that."

Part of Messi's characteristic determination he owes to his older brothers, Matías and Rodrigo. When we spoke in 2006 he told me that, as the smallest of the three, he would often lose games of football and end up in tears – or, if he won, his siblings would tease him relentlessly, reducing him to tears.

"Ever since I was a little kid I always hated to lose and if I played with my brothers we would always end up fighting about something," he said. "Even if I won, my older brothers would always know how to start a fight with me by saying things they knew I hated. If I lost they would tease and pinch me until I cried. It's the kind of thing which happens amongst brothers in a family, but they taught me to hate losing."

Messi has outer layers of timidity, under which is tungsten. But he likes to smile, to laugh and, according to absolutely everyone I have spoken to who knows him, he is an uncomplicated, easily-liked character. For all those who returned to Rosario, that kid must have been hard to leave behind. However, Messi was finally in the right place at the right time.

He moved into a youth team which had Gerard Piqué, Cesc Fàbregas, Víctor Vázquez, Víctor Sánchez and Marc Valiente – a remarkable outfit. Winning became second nature to them and, as Messi grew, his football maturity outstripped even his now normalised growth.

Not that it was easy. The first day that Gerard Piqué saw Messi in the dressing room he said, "This guy's going to play with us? He looks like my little brother!" Fàbregas has often commented that, initially, they thought Messi was mute. Each of them, however, always adds that the instant Messi got the ball they were his servants.

All except Víctor Vázquez.

Vázquez was a sublime youth-team player who should have made it at Barça (he is currently with Club Brugge) were it not for terrible injuries. He and Messi used to compete to see who could score more goals for the *Juvenil* side and, according to Piqué, there were games when the ball was evenly divided between the two and nobody else, on either side, got a sniff of it.

As soon as I started interviewing Messi, I asked him about his playing style and the inherent risks. He's been taking kicks now for just about 20 years – some of them horrific. How often have you seen him retaliate? Lose his temper? Cower out of a game?

This is how he explains his style. "Something deep in my character allows me to take the hits and get on with trying to win. I've always had this ability to get up and get on with it. Long ago I just made up my mind that the fact people try to kick and foul you comes with the territory if you play the way I do. Usually the attacks are not malicious. However, if they are malicious then you do have to protest a bit. At the start of a match, when you are not properly warmed up, it hurts a bit more. By the time the game is in full flow, you are concentrating so deeply on winning that most times you barely even notice what has happened."

However, early in that spell during which the remarkable *Juvenil* side went unbeaten for nearly four years, Piqué lost his temper at one team, appropriately called Damm, which tried to kick Messi out of the match. Piqué took physical retribution with one or two of the opposition and was sent off, protecting his friend.

Growing up like this created a bond. When, in the summer of 2011, Pep Guardiola, reunited Cesc Fàbregas not only with his best friend in football, Piqué, but with Messi, he was adding something very special to an already great team.

Messi's adaptation to his new club and the physical challenges he faced was helped by something which Barça instituted for all its talented youth players: a strategy named the 'Individual Physical Development Programme'. Aged 13, when he began his first contract at the Camp Nou, Messi was 4ft 10in and weighed 39 kg. Three years later, the striker measured 5ft 5in and weighed nearly 25kg more. The 16-year-old Messi was closer to his current physique of 5ft 6½in and 69kg.

The programme also put heavy emphasis on gym work, diet and food supplements. Its aim was to 'improve the physical condition of some youth team players who have excellent technique but some physiological disadvantages'. The club doctor, Josep Borrell, along with a sports medicine specialist, a dietician, a physio and a fitness coach combined to progressively change Messi's physique and they actually decreased the amount of growth hormone which had been prescribed.

Most of the reportage of those early Messi years is focused on the hormone imbalance and the replacement programme. However, his family and Barça staff explain that strength and stamina were hindered by the treatment. As a result, his perpetually active playing style was draining for him; he could not possess the same resistance to fatigue normal for a kid of his age.

He was increasingly happy in his new life. He was popular at school, clearly the most talented footballer in his group and with a physical capability growing to meet his prodigious sporting talent. However, it wasn't all work and no play for young Messi.

Bright but disinterested at school, he'd often get caught listening to music at the back of the class and now he can only really remember the play-time football matches on the patio.

Although life in the old Masia next to the Camp Nou had more than its share of sniffling, lonely youngsters (amongst which have numbered Iniesta, Valdés and Messi himself) there was a good deal of high jinks, too.

Messi and pals used to sneak down past the security cameras and break into the single training pitch which used to sit between the southern wall of La Masia and the Gol Nord of the Camp Nou. For generations, it was the first team's main training ground and passers-by, usually headed to or from Barcelona's main maternity hospital, could gaze in from the pavement.

The groundsman must have been puzzled when he left a pristine pitch at night only to find divots and stud marks in the morning. Messi and company often couldn't resist a night-time kick-around, even though it was forbidden by the club and had to be played in the semi-dusk of streetlighting.

One night, the budding Barça basketball star, Asier Zengotitabengoa, joined in with Messi's gang and revealed his own competitive nature – but no great subtlety. Already about twice Messi's height, 'Zengo' was marking him in the gloom and realised that a long pass was about to land in the space in front of the Argentinian's run. The basketball giant lunged out with a sliding tackle which badly bent Messi's ankle and ended the game.

Disaster loomed, but Messi's Rosario street instinct took over. The rest of the gang sneaked him back into La Masia, distracting the security guard, and ice was applied all night. Messi arrived at the youth-team training session the next morning disguising his limp as best he could, walking slowly out to the training pitch and then, just as the first pass arrived to him, collapsed in a heap as if he'd just twisted his ankle at that very moment. The previous night's caper was obscured and Messi's recovery was complete when the swelling went down a few days later. Cute.

Minguella remembers how Messi's obsession with football remained during this time of his life. "When he arrived here he was quiet, discrete and one time we had a dinner here in my garden with Juan Riquelme and Thiago Motta. Leo was 14 and he was just gazing at these players like they were gods. My experience with him, from the beginning until now, is that he's literally crazy for the ball. He's addicted to football. He only ever thought about getting a ball and playing. That's what his life centres on. He's not a guy for nightclubs and a big social life. Everything he does is centred on his football life and how to play better."

The incident which best sums up Messi's meteoric rise from the kid who Barcelona weren't sure they wanted in December 2000 to first-team debutant less than three years later is the '*partido de la máscara*' – the face mask game.

He was playing for coach Alex García's *Cadete A* side that season and the team went undefeated all year. "He was like the little brother of the team during the week, everyone wanted to look after him," remembers García. "But come the weekends he didn't need any looking after. Piqué, Cesc, Víctor Vázquez and Messi stood out. They were extraordinary talents even then, with the football maturity of a 22-year-old despite only being 15 or 16. With respect to our rivals, this group of born winners competed all week so that they could treat the Sunday match like a training session while the others all trained so that they could compete on match day.

"The only real problem was that they all wanted to be top scorer and, if a penalty was awarded, these four would all go forward to take it and argue amongst themselves until I had to take the decision for them and shout across from the touchline. Even then, nobody could compete with Messi. I think he scored close to 40 that season."

Speaking from Tbilisi, where he now coaches, García added to his memories of a gifted former pupil. "Leo was shy and introverted. Very sensitive and not a lad who enjoyed publicity. He was never the joker and was a good listener. In fact, you wouldn't have noticed him until you saw him on the pitch.

"I never imagined that he was going to turn into the best player in the world, but I could always see that he had something very special. Whenever I see him he's exactly the same, still that 16-year-old boy I used to coach. He's a born winner, like the other guys of his generation, Piqué, Cesc. They were all 16-year-old boys who already thought like professionals. They competed in the training sessions but then used the matches as training. There was just no other team who could match them."

Come the end of the season there was a league title decider with Espanyol. Barça won, but Messi collided with an opponent, was knocked unconscious and suffered a serious cheekbone fracture. He was taken to hospital immediately. Eight days later, Barça were to meet their city rivals again in the final of the Copa Catalunya for the *Cadete* age group. There should have been no chance of Messi making that game, but he begged to play.

"After he broke his cheekbone it seemed sure Messi wouldn't play in the final," admits García. "Other players were beginning to worry: 'The final without Messi ...'"

Carles Puyol had suffered a similar injury earlier that season and the face mask specialist who had prepared the protective plastic for 'Puyi' still had the mask. Messi was allowed to play on the strict condition that he wore the mask – and even then it was a tremendous risk. One more collision and he could suffer far greater damage.

Seven minutes into the first half of the final on Sunday, May 4, 2003, Messi trots over to the bench, claims he can't see properly because the face mask is making him sweat too much and throws it to García and his assistants. All the rules, all the warnings are also tossed aside and, before he can be substituted, Messi has scored. Then he gets another. By half-time, Piqué has made it 3-0 and coach García manages to persuade Messi to be substituted for his own safety. Barça win 4-1 despite Piqué being sent off along with the Espanyol coach for a second-half falling out. It ends a season when that team won every trophy, remaining unbeaten throughout, and in which Messi has scored 40 times. The victorious final is also Messi's last game with Cesc Fàbregas until winning the Supercopa at the Camp Nou seven years and some €40m in transfer fees later.

García recalled the risk-filled adventure. "Messi seemed happy to wear the mask during training and said to me, 'Honestly boss, there's no problem'. Typical Messi. But then, during the match, he came over to the bench and tossed it over to me telling me that he couldn't see properly. I told him, 'No way, it's not safe!'

" 'Let me play 20 minutes more,' he begged, 'and then you can replace me.'

"In those 20 minutes the guy scored two goals. There was always a risk that he would be badly injured without the mask, but even though he was only 16 we trusted him completely.

"His dad was very worried when he went on to play without the mask because he'd been present throughout the process and had attended the medical meeting so he knew what was at stake. Thank God nothing went wrong. We were 3-0 up at half time when he came off, but I would have substituted him no matter what – even if we were losing 3-0."

"I remember having to play the final wearing Puyol's old face mask because I had a facial fracture," Messi recalled years later. Puyi hadn't seemed to mind wearing it, but the minute I touched the ball, I looked down and couldn't see a thing. I just turned around, took it off and threw it down on the bench."

Fàbregas was off to Highbury and Messi was on the road to superstardom and unrivalled success with Barça.

Promoted up to Barça B with Pere Gratacós as his coach, the Flea, as an Argentinian journalist had begun to call him in print – having heard that Matías and Rodrigo Messi had nicknamed their brother *Pulguita* (Little Flea) – was only a couple of months away from his first-team debut.

Gratacós echoes Arnau Riera's opinion that Messi quickly saw he was ready to vault the Barça B stage and go straight to the first-team squad. "He needed new challenges; he needed to be training with people like Ronaldinho, Eto'o and Deco – players who are obliged to be better than the rest and who would push Messi's development onwards.

"Every week when we had our technical meeting I would go on and on about Leo to Frank Rijkaard. Finally [in November 2003] they came to me and asked for some academy players to fill up the squad which was going to Porto to inaugurate their new stadium."

Messi was 17 years, four months and 23 days old. He had just scored a hat-trick for the B team against Granollers and, as it was an international break, was taken to the Dragon Stadium in Oporto and came on with 15 minutes left.

Although a very weak Barça side lost 2-0 to José Mourinho's Porto, Messi produced three good scoring chances in his 15 minutes on the pitch and, when Gratacós got his player back, it was with the news that "you were right, he should be training with the first team – you can have him back at weekends for games".

It was around this point of the season that Rangers fans came closer than anyone knows to the extraordinary prospect of Lionel Messi, or indeed Andrés Iniesta, playing on loan at Ibrox.

2 — The Making of Messi

Alex McLeish has always had an adventurous outlook on how to add quality to his squads. He has always loved European football and his early managerial success, at Hibernian in Scotland, centred around his imaginative recruitment of the former France defender Franck Sauzée and Russell Latapy, a magical midfielder from Porto – this when Hibs had been relegated from the Scottish Premier League.

As Rangers manager, he succeeded with Mikel Arteta, a La Masia graduate, Jean-Alain Boumsong and Dado Prso. However, during season 2003-04 he came closest to the greatest coup of his career.

McLeish recalled: "Jan Wouters was my assistant at Ibrox at the time and I asked him whether or not he knew Frank Rijkaard and if he'd be willing to get in touch to check if there were some quality youngsters who might benefit us because of their talents, but who could gain experience in Scotland before returning to Barça.

"Jan told me that he was slightly friendlier with Rijkaard's assistant, Henk ten Cate, and our scouts had already been aware of Leo Messi's growing reputation at youth level.

"We didn't have much budget at the time and the previous season we'd taken some bigger-name players on free contracts or low transfer fees but higher wages. This time, we thought that the fans might be a little bit more understanding if we brought younger or less experienced players, but who were evidently of good quality.

"Ten Cate and Jan Wouters had chats about us taking Messi on loan, but the guidance from Henk was that he was probably too young and possibly too slight to get benefit from Scottish football. Our view was that Barça were probably hedging their bets at the time. Even then, they knew how good he was and they must have thought that letting him go to British football might be a risk because of the tough tackling and the physicality, but they were also obviously unsure about how quickly he might actually make the Barça first team. We caught them just in the middle of that process of working out what they wanted to do with Messi, but during the discussions Henk said to Jan that we should do ourselves a favour and take Iniesta on loan instead.

"I think his exact words were, 'This boy is going to be a world beater,' which he proved against Holland in South Africa. Henk told us that Iniesta 'sees the picture in front of him' earlier than anyone and that he's got a great pass and an ability to beat people.

"Eventually we made a formal enquiry; I think it would have been towards the end of season 2004-5. But Messi played brilliantly in the Youth World Cup and Barcelona were sure that they wouldn't loan him. Then Iniesta scored in a big pre-season game which meant that the club couldn't really loan him out without losing face. It was a pity nothing worked out because I'd been really excited at the idea of one or other of them coming for a season.

"The other thing about Messi was that my kids were into that Championship Manager game and they'd told me about him when he was only 12 or 13, that he was going to be a superstar."

Ferran Soriano was one of Barça's two vice presidents at the time and well recalls the fierce debate galvanised by Rangers' determination to take either Messi or Iniesta on loan.

"At the time of the Rangers interest there were lots of discussions about Iniesta. I remember Henk defending his logic saying, 'The guy's small, he doesn't have the strength, maybe we send him elsewhere for a couple of years and then we'll see.'

"He liked Marc van Bommel, for example, a symbol of which is the Champions League final in 2006, where they [Rijkaard and ten Cate] started with Van Bommel and the game changed when Iniesta came on for him.

"In those discussions about whether to loan to Rangers, history and tradition played a role. I remember Begiristain, Laporta, the old guys, the local guys, defending Iniesta very, very strongly and saying, 'No, this guy has talent, he has to stay,' and they were proved right.

"It wasn't easy to argue because the guy is small and at the time our rivalry was with Chelsea. We had several Champions League games against them. He was playing against guys like Essien, who is three times bigger than him. So, it was a tough debate. Now it wouldn't be an issue, but it was tough then."

In the space of 16 months across 2003-04, Messi had risen five levels, from *Cadete* through both *Juvenil* teams, Barça C, Barça B and now into the first-team squad. Such accelerated promotion could have left him out of his depth, particularly given his timid nature, but, even though he was Argentinian, the Brazilians were about to come to the rescue.

Deco quickly started warning people that there was a new midget in training who could beat him in foot-tennis. Sylvinho, Edmilson, Juliano Belletti and Deco welcomed and protected him, but he owes a special debt to Ronaldinho.

"Ronnie has been massively important for me – I was so young when I started to come into Barça's dressing room, but he made a point of being first to step up to me and look after me," Messi told me, not long after he broke into the team.

"In my case there was no jealousy at all to cope with – in fact, it was quite the opposite. Ronaldinho led the way and everyone else, without exception, supported me and made me feel welcome. Of course, I could have run into another kind of team-mate but all that makes me feel is very lucky.

"As a senior colleague, Ronaldinho looked after me and protected me but as a team-mate it's a privilege to play beside him. There's a 'Brazilian' table at meal times and they often make me sit with them, but they always tell me I'm the only Argentinian they'll ever allow to join them! I try to copy little things Ronaldinho does, but more fundamentally I just try to play for the joy of it. Look at the way he always has a smile – that's how I feel. Playing football has always meant joy and happiness to me and that's why I do it."

All of which brings us back to the beginning of this chapter: Ronaldinho setting Messi up twice in the last seconds of the Albacete game and the little prince finishing both chances with divine style.

"My debut was about the same age and I know exactly how difficult it can be making your way in a dressing room full of adults as the talented kid," explained Ronaldinho. "So, to take the pressure off him, I treat him like a kid brother and we try to joke around with him to make it all as natural as possible. I'm just showing camaraderie."

That was that as far as Messi's season in the first team

went – no more competitive or friendly appearances, but most certainly a part in Barcelona's first celebration of a league title in six years. However, his work during summer 2005 meant that, within the space of a couple of months, he was both champion of Spain and world champion with Argentina at Under-20 level. All just a couple of days past his 18th birthday.

For anyone who loves football to be beautiful, unpredictable and anarchic, it's a great sadness of this story that Ronaldinho, having shepherded Messi into the flow of first-team football, began his decline just as the kid was ready to become a fully-fledged genius. Imagine the two of them sharing their best years together in this team? But *azar* – fate or luck in English – struck again. The Brazilian's time had been sensational but short. The Argentinian was about to rip up the record books.

MAKING-OF MATCH:
SHAKHTAR DONETSK 1 BARCELONA 2
CHAMPIONS LEAGUE GROUP STAGE, OCTOBER 1 2008

For many people, this match will become lost in the memory. Probably is already. But this was the moment when Guardiola's Barça not only showed that every bad habit of the previous two years had been shed, but that they were now the kind of football team you wouldn't want to meet down a dark alley after a couple of drinks on a Friday night. Lean, mean and not to be pushed about.

This was the kind of week which would have required brown trousers for the Barça faithful over the previous couple of years. Espanyol away (which proved to be a last-gasp, hotly controversial 2-1 win up on Montjuïc); Shakhtar in Donetsk, where Barça had lost last time out, on Leo Messi's Champions League debut in 2004, and then Atlético Madrid at the Camp Nou. Buy the paracetamol, draw the curtains, hope for the best and avoid Real Madrid fans at work. That's the way it would have been.

"What we've done up to now means nothing compared to what will be asked of us this week," the Barça coach warned before it all began.

Guardiola knew Mircea Lucescu, Shakhtar's wily old Romanian coach, from his time in Italy, and he knew his adversary would instruct his players to give Barcelona a physical pasting. A phrase Andrés Iniesta used to Luis Martín of *El País* the day before the match caught my eye. Lu, a journalist the players revere, asked about the kind of spirit which Samuel Eto'o had often referred to – the idea that 'nobody will have it easy against us ever again'. Iniesta replied: "Exactly, there is a commitment which goes way beyond playing well now. It might not be our day, but we will never lose for a lack of trying to make it our day."

When good players know, deep down, precisely what they are capable of, they have a steel core of confidence, and that's what champions are made of.

Okay, to business. Guardiola rests Messi, Sergio Busquets and Éric Abidal, tests Thierry Henry at centre-forward and Barça play pretty poorly. One-nil up from just before half-time thanks to Ilsinho, Shakhtar reach the 87th minute with that lead, before something which came to symbolise this incredible season occurs.

Barça still believe there is something to be taken from the match. One Shakhtar player, Brandão, tries to time-waste by feigning injury. Darijo Srna hoofs the ball out, but referee Howard Webb not only waves away the Shakhtar claims for treatment to Brandão, he waves play on. Guardiola's players are alert. From the throw-in, Rafa Márquez puts Bojan away down the right; his cross is fumbled horribly by the Shakhtar goalkeeper, Andriy Pyatov, and Messi, who has replaced Thierry Henry, scores.

In the fourth minute of added time a sweet, seven-pass move ends with Xavi slicing open the home defence with a ball inside Srna at right-back and Messi finishes, just brilliantly, from an acute angle.

Dead and buried at 1-0, seven minutes later they are leaving Ukraine with three points. I focus on it because it was crucial. New fitness, new mentality, new cutting edge, and an away victory snatched from the jaws of defeat. An absolute turning point.

On the equalising goal, Lucescu claimed that: "It was shameful. If this was Italy you wouldn't get out of the stadium alive." But Srna admitted to Barça players that they had done the right thing in playing on and he hauled his Romanian coach away from his confrontational raging against Guardiola and his team.

That season, Barça would score nearly 30 goals in the last 10 minutes of matches. No fluke and a massive weapon which stemmed from physical fitness and a hunger to play through to the whistle, win lose or draw. This was the night when they dug deep, found what they were capable of and earned a victory which propelled them towards the greatest glory in the club's history later that season.

Barcelona (4-3-3) Valdés; Alves, Piqué, Márquez, Puyol; Xavi, Touré, Keita (Gudjohnsen 80); Eto'o (Bojan 74), Henry (Messi 59) Iniesta.
Shakhtar Donetsk (4-1-4-1) Pyatov; Srna, Chygrynskiy, Ischenko, Shevchuk; Hübschman; Ilsinho (Willian 85), Duljaj (Lewandowski 89), Fernandinho, Brandão; Luiz Adriano (Seleznov 71).
Goals Ilsinho 45; Messi 87, 90 + 4
Bookings Xavi, Srna, Fernandinho, Chygrynskiy, Keita, Brandão
Referee Howard Webb
Attendance 18,000, Olympic Stadium, Donetsk

3 – THE EXILE RETURNS

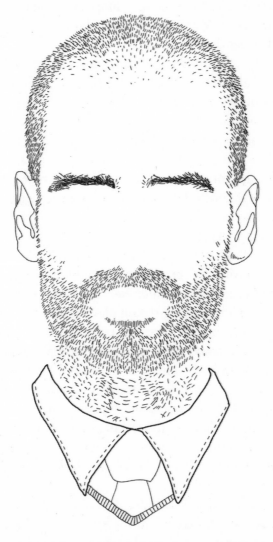

"That fantastic spark of inspiration, the joy of
that single instant, is why I'm a coach."
— Pep Guardiola

THE DEAL TO PROMOTE Pep Guardiola to first-team coach, although long since agreed, was signed in May 2008, the very day Guardiola's third child, Valentina, was born.

By then, Guardiola had known for a few months that he was likely to succeed Frank Rijkaard. However, he hadn't been a shoo-in for the position. Far from it. President Joan Laporta asked his experts to cast about for ideas and inspiration when it came to replacing Rijkaard.

Marc Ingla, recently appointed vice president in charge of football, was charged with recommending a new coach. He mounted a forensic search for a candidate to stand the fierce cross examination of the Barcelona board.

Txiki Begiristain, director of football since 2003, would prove an exceptional guide for Ingla – a football fan whose expertise lay in marketing and entrepreneurship. Begiristain played nearly 500 games for Barça during the glorious Cruyff regime and is an alert, modern and communicative football brain.

Begiristain had realised from around October 2007 that placing faith in Rijkaard for a second season after the 2006 Champions League victory in Paris was a brutal error. He'd begun working on ideas even before Laporta summoned him to demand a managerial beauty parade. This is where simple hard work and diligence paid off.

Begiristain and the admirable José Ramón Alexanco, the man who lifted the European Cup for Barcelona in 1992 and then the head of Barça's *Fútbol base* had made a habit of attending the B team's matches.

They were entranced.

Even though Barça B were then in the third division,

Guardiola ensured that every future opponent was filmed so he could study them on his DVD screen with all 20 players, excluding the two goalkeepers, in vision all the time.

In the words of an interviewee for this book, who'd rather remain a source than be named, "he worked, from the first minute, as if he were training the Champions League winners rather than a third division side. It was as if he was a vastly experienced coach who was going to be facing Milan, Arsenal or Bayern Munich every week".

Alexanco and Begiristain saw that Guardiola was a box of tricks. If the other team played long ball football, if they liked roughhouse, if they switched, mid-match, from 3-5-2 to 4-3-3, Barça B would always be prepared with counter-measures. Guardiola not only put on a masterclass of tactical analysis and coaching, he had already convinced his new pupils to both assimilate and apply his ideas. His former Dream Team colleagues were buzzing with excitement.

Ingla takes up the story. "Immediately after I took office in October 2007, Txiki's point of view was that Frank Rijkaard's 'cycle' in the club was definitively over – he must leave irrespective of whether the team did win a trophy or not.

"We needed a clear agenda about what kind of man to appoint, and we needed privacy."

In Lyon, they began to plan what would become the most successful era in the club's history. Ingla says: "I asked Txiki who should replace Rijkaard and he wouldn't specify names, so I pushed him and he admitted, 'I'm thinking of Pep Guardiola'.

"In retrospect it was impressive that he didn't say, 'It's

Pep, it's got to be Pep'. His mind was very open, but he had a clear vision. He believed that a coach with Pep's profile – education, experience, credo, understanding of the club's inherent values and coaching style – was our future.

"Txiki told me, 'I like the way the B team plays, how it reacts, how he makes tactical changes, how he trains the team – everything.' It was an influential moment."

Ingla decided that they needed to look at other candidates and ensure that they didn't miss an ideal contender, but if Guardiola continued to impress and, crucially, felt able to accept the challenge, then the outside candidates would need to demonstrate that they were superior to the 36-year-old Catalan.

Ingla again: "The other names were Laurent Blanc, Michael Laudrup, Arsène Wenger and Ernesto Valverde, and again they emanated from Txiki. We started the process of sounding people out and assessing them, but then came Christmas."

From Jornada 8 until Jornada 16 there had been a series of flaccid performances. Rijkaard's team lost to Villarreal and Getafe and drew with Espanyol and Valladolid. Next up was the Camp Nou Clásico.

Bernd Schuster was coaching the reigning champions and arrived as the first Real Madrid trainer who was also a card-carrying Barça *socio* or member. His *culé* past obviously didn't cut Barça any slack. Madrid dominated a paper-thin Barcelona and won 1-0, via a lovely Julio Baptista goal.

Rijkaard's team that night, two days before Christmas, was: Valdés; Puyol (Zambrotta 76), Milito, Márquez, Abidal; Touré, Xavi (Bojan 81), Deco (Giovani 57); Iniesta, Eto'o, Ronaldinho.

Which, with relatively little tinkering, became the core of a treble-winning team under a new coach the following season. Madrid started the New Year seven points ahead of the Catalans and, of course, it meant commotion in the corridors of power at Barça.

Ingla recalls: "The results were bad, Frank was not reacting, he was low. We prepared for the scenario where Frank didn't want to finish the season, at which point several people thought of Johan Cruyff taking over. Now I'm a massive fan of his, but I thought that putting 'God' on the bench of a club in this state wasn't a good idea, because the problem we had was not uniquely the coach – it was some of the players, too."

Football, traditionally, operates on the idea that sacking the coach is a bloodletting of almost ritual significance. Make the sacrifice to the great god of football and the crops will grow again. Ingla, his fellow vice president Ferran Soriano and Begiristain thought differently.

Joan Laporta was toying with the idea of placing Cruyff in caretaker charge, perhaps with a view to full control at the end of the season. The president also became seduced by the early information coming up the command chain that Guardiola was a Dauphin. Laporta even began to push the idea that, if Rijkaard were sacked immediately, Guardiola could be parachuted into the first team mid-season. Ingla, Soriano and Begiristain were horrified.

"I warned everyone that the coach wasn't the only issue," recalls Ingla. "My view is that coaches can transform things, but players have a very high percentage accountability for what kind of football is played and what trajectory you have.

"You could have put another coach in there at that time, be it Cruyff or Guardiola, and he'd have failed. We wouldn't have won the title and we wouldn't have made the Champions League final in Moscow. Looking back, I'd say thank God we didn't put Cruyff in; thank God we didn't parachute Pep in. Because there was a moment in March when we started to kiss goodbye to the league, but the Champions League was still a live possibility and some of the board wanted to replace Rijkaard with Pep immediately.

"You can't imagine the fight I had to defend the option not to put him in. Looking back, I'm sure that this is one big favour I did for the club and for Pep – fighting hard to make sure that when he took over it was to work with a clean slate and without Ronaldinho and Deco."

Laporta even asked Cruyff whether he would come back as coach to mentor Guardiola, who would be his assistant. Cruyff told Laporta no, that he wouldn't ever come back to full-time coaching again, and also emphasised Guardiola was ready. Later, in September 2008, the Barça president confirmed: "Cruyff knows very well that I'd have loved him to be the coach to take over from Rijkaard, with Pep at his side."

So, by May, Guardiola signed on and the entire deal was made public a month later. History was about to be written, but the theme of Guardiola being too easy to undervalue, a recurrent one in his story, took over briefly. Many, including me, worried that Guardiola was too inexperienced.

His football vision wasn't in question, or the fact that his Barça B work showed promise. Guardiola had always demonstrated leadership, strategic insight and a remorseless will to find a winning edge as a player, but where was his man-management experience? Most footballers often find this a major obstacle when they take over a squad.

Guardiola was 37; he had played with Xavi, Puyol, Piqué and Valdés in either the Barça first team or the Catalan 'national' team, and was now to be their boss. Also, the Barcelona dressing room was riven with jealousies, laziness, and superstar, multimillionaire players who had grown entrenched in their flawed ways.

I wondered how a 37-year-old could manage a squad with such demanding personalities as Ronaldinho, Deco and Samuel Eto'o, having had such little experience of man-management on a daily basis. I was very far from alone. There was a less than ecstatic welcome from the Spanish media. Spain were on their way to winning the European Championship, but *El País* relegated their report of Guardiola's accession to the 13th page of their sports section.

El Mundo Deportivo used a clever graphic trick on their front page. The words "YES" and "NO" were either side of Guardiola's photo from the waist up so that, graphically, it represented the debate in Catalonia about whether he was the right choice. Their 'get out of jail card' was that under the "YES" they said: "It's yes to playing with three strikers; keeping Rafa Márquez and yes to signing a new centre forward." While under the "NO" headline there was: "No to Ronaldinho, Eto'o and Deco; no to a 100-day honeymoon state of grace for his work and no to moving to a semi-ready training ground."

La Vanguardia chose their double-page headline as "I Don't Think I'll Fail". Hardly a sign that the Catalan newspaper wholly believed in the project.

The media mood was mixed. One well-regarded Catalan journalist, who later went on to become a successful agent for players at the Camp Nou, warned me, "Without experience to fall back on, this place could burn Pep out before the end of the season".

Nevertheless, Joan Laporta possessed a great talent: the ability to take an important decision promptly and with firmness, irrespective of risk.

Before handing the keys to the club over to Guardiola, Laporta said: "Pep has managed to find the ideal balance between modern, serious football and the traditional style which we at Barcelona love – attack. The Guardiola era has begun".

And how.

In sporting terms, Barça had become flabby; training lacked intensity, several players had lost both a mental edge and the ability to either press the ball as hungrily as in the prime years under Rijkaard or succeed in the risky but devastating final ball which opened defences.

The training-ground culture needed to be changed, but that wasn't the source of my personal doubts. Where the situation looked grim was the entrenched, hard-nosed attitudes of the dominant dressing-room personalities – Ronaldinho, Deco and Samuel Eto'o.

Guardiola made it clear to the Camp Nou board that, rather than deal with Ronaldinho's issues, it was time to cut the cord, put the football gain ahead of the financial loss (you could estimate the Brazilian's 2005 World Player of the Year worth in excess of £40m and he moved to Milan for less than £15m) and send a message to the rest of the squad.

So, in June 2008, Guardiola had no compunction in answering questions about Ronaldinho, Deco and

Eto'o with a tone which matched his funereal black suit and tie. On his first day in charge, Guardiola said: "These three are not in my mind for the future; in fact we will be going onwards without them.

"My view is that it's all about performance and what players can give to my squad. Such decisions are based on intangible sensations. For example, if I could be guaranteed that Ronaldinho and Eto'o could score me 60 goals between them then I'd keep them, without doubt. But I don't 'know' that.

"It is time for a 'restart' in this dressing room. I don't know if there are bad habits in there yet because we haven't started work, but the past is gone.

"What I can promise is that I will not tolerate a lack of effort put into this project to rebuild the success of the team. Sure, you can be guaranteed my players are going to run and run, but my primary intention is to convince the players with my words. I want their involvement in my plan, I want to inspire their faith in what we are doing and above all I want even the talented, inspired players to understand that, individually, they are worth much less than when they invoke team values."

Ronaldinho (Milan), Deco (Chelsea), Edmilson (Villarreal), Gio dos Santos (Spurs), Santiago Ezquerro (Osasuna), Marc Crosas (Celtic), Oleguer (Ajax) and Gianluca Zambrotta (Milan) were all shipped out and Lilian Thuram retired.

At Guardiola's behest, Laporta bought Dani Alves, Aleksandr Hleb, Henrique, Seydou Keita, Gerard Piqué and José Martín Cáceres.

Under the new manager, fighting weight became an issue. Where, previously, a kilo or so here or there was overlooked, now it was clamped down upon.

It turned out that, like Sir Alex Ferguson, Guardiola was normally first to the training ground every morning – usually not long after 8am. Punctuality, as a representation of being mentally prepared, became equally strictly enforced. One guy who should have known better, having been schooled under Arsène Wenger – whose rigid adherence to time-calibrated training sessions became famous – was Hleb, who signed from Arsenal that summer.

Guardiola's rules were simple, but not for Hleb. First, the team arrived in time to breakfast together. Not everyone was forced to eat together in the morning, although lunch was almost always regarded as a part of the training day and thus obligatory. However, the players had to sign in by a specific hour, usually 60 minutes before training began. If training started at 11am then that was when you were expected to be on the training pitch, fully kitted; ready, physically and mentally, to put everything into the session, or you were fined.

The fine for lateness started at €500 per five minutes, up to €6000, and whoever was late had to start training on his own. Tying up your laces on the training pitch, arriving at 10 seconds past 11, any breach, no matter how small, was forbidden. Latecomers were greeted with ironic applause from absolutely everyone else involved in the session.

Monday to Friday, the players were expected to be at home by midnight at the latest and they could expect a late-night call from Guardiola or one of his assistants. If a phone call to the house went unanswered and was not properly explained, another four-figure fine was on the way.

3 — The Exile Returns

When and where players were allowed to film commercials or work for their sponsors was tightly controlled and only one man, Pep, held the final decision.

Use of mobile phones and headphones were both controlled (as at many clubs) and players were told that taking their place in the rota for press conferences and signing autographs for fans on away trips were obligatory.

There was also an incentive scheme based on a system Guardiola had developed when he was in charge of the young bucks of Barcelona B. If the team won four straight Liga matches or two consecutive Champions League ties, Guardiola would pay for either a lunch or a dinner for the entire squad plus staff.

Why didn't the fines pay for the dinners? Yes, that's the norm. A football team has a system of fines imposed by the boss and at the end of the season the money is used for a big dinner or, more likely, a good party.

Guardiola thought that to be self-defeating. If your fine eventually goes to paying for an alcohol-fuelled team night out, then how have you been penalised? Instead, all fines collected were sent, at the end of each season, to a charitable cause, often associated with hospitals.

Hleb, who moaned about Guardiola not having faith in him as a footballer, was repeatedly late for the signing-in book, and often claimed that he'd arrived on time but forgotten to sign in; he regularly traipsed onto the training pitch unprepared, if not physically then certainly mentally.

Guardiola showed understanding; here was a talented but immature player, a Belorussian who needed help to adapt to life in Spain. Please learn Spanish, he was told. How can we help you learn Spanish, he was then asked when no progress had been made.

On the pitch, Hleb too often tried his trademark dribbling and didn't pass and move like his team-mates needed him to. He was chided, coaxed, and warned – then dumped at the end of the season.

No ceremony. No mercy. No great loss. Guardiola would apply the same ruthless standard to Samuel Eto'o and Zlatan Ibrahimovic in subsequent close seasons.

Back to that first, crucial, summer and the preparation for the new manager's first season in charge.

St Andrews, on the east coast of Scotland, had been chosen as a training venue – partly because the facilities and climate were suited to the training schedule, partly because the Scottish government offered a financial incentive and partly because two of the club's power brokers, Begiristain and Cruyff, are golf addicts.

On the playing fields of Fife, one of the most important, most impressive dramas of Guardiola's entire reign was played out. It was the summer of the Beijing Olympics and Argentina had long indicated that they would pick Leo Messi for the tournament, which started on August 8 with obligatory training camps before that.

Under Rijkaard, Barça had finished third in La Liga, only three points off joint fifth, and they had a Champions League qualifier in August against Wisła Kraków of Poland. So nervous was president Laporta about the possibility of not qualifying that he embarked on a slugfest with the Olympic movement, the Argentinian Football Association (AFA) and FIFA over Messi's involvement with his national team. He claimed that Messi could not be co-opted by the AFA as the Olympic tournament was not part of the FIFA calendar. Sepp Blatter, the president of FIFA, held in favour of the Olympic football tournament and the AFA, and it was only when Laporta ordered the case be appealed to the Court of Arbitration for Sport that a final resolution was found. CAS backed Barcelona and it was game over for Messi, Argentina and the Olympics.

Or at least it should have been.

The CAS verdict came through on the 16th anniversary of Spain's victory in the semi-finals of the football tournament of the 1992 Olympics, when a young Pep Guardiola steered his team into the final, in Barcelona. Their gold-medal victory at the Camp Nou was a huge landmark in his playing career and as Barcelona awaited the judgement of CAS, there were now gentle indications that the new coach's thinking on the Messi situation differed to that of his two bosses, the club president Laporta and the director of football, Begiristain.

Begiristain warned: "If CAS backs us then Messi will just have to fly home. We respect the rules and we will apply them."

However Guardiola's version was: "When we hear the verdict the club will decide. But we have to listen to the player. He's the most important in all this."

Guardiola's second big decision, having effectively kicked Ronaldinho and Deco out of the door without waiting for the club to find buyers, was sown in Scotland.

The training sessions in St Andrews were tight and demanding. There were mere seconds between changeovers, there were short drinks breaks, which were timed, and the entire process was filmed so that

Guardiola, his assistant Tito Vilanova and fitness trainer Lorenzo Buenaventura could review them.

Gerard Piqué recalls: "Initially, he kept stopping the training sessions to tell us exactly what he wanted us to do, but thankfully we got our act together quickly and put his ideas into action on the pitch."

But the new coach quickly discovered that Messi had a stone in his shoe.

Guardiola took a very short time to ask, firmly, what the hell was wrong. Messi is not a sulker, but his already reserved demeanour was augmented by the expectation that he would be denied a shot at an Olympic gold medal. When he finally confided in his new coach, Guardiola told him to buck up, train hard, go with the Olympic squad and then await developments, like everyone else.

But Guardiola revealed to Messi that he was a potential ally. He explained how important the 1992 Olympics had been to him personally and indicated that if Messi shaped up in training he might have a vocal supporter in Guardiola, if it came to it. When the CAS verdict was announced on August 6, Guardiola had already fought, and won, a huge battle.

He told Laporta and Begiristain: "You've appointed me, I'm the boss, I know how the boy feels about the Olympics and I say he stays in China, misses the Champions League qualifier – and that's that."

How did it play out?

An unbelievably talented Argentina squad which included Messi, Javier Mascherano, Sergio Agüero, Pablo Zabaleta, Ángel di María, Ezequiel Garay, Ezequiel Lavezzi, Fernando Gago and Éver Banega, naturally emulated Guardiola, Kiko and Txapi Ferrer by winning Olympic gold. Barça turfed Wisła Kraków out of the qualifier 4-1 and Guardiola won a debt of gratitude from the world's greatest footballer.

How might it have played out?

Guardiola won implacable enemies in Laporta and Begiristain, Messi broke a leg in Beijing and Kraków drew at the Camp Nou then (as they, in fact, managed) won 1-0 in Poland. Disaster after disaster and more of an end than a beginning to Guardiola's reign.

The third enormous decision of Guardiola's early reign was to backtrack on the announcement that he "didn't count on Eto'o for the future".

With Ronaldinho, whom he envied, gone, with Thierry Henry, a friend, now 'the other' striker and with Guardiola setting new standards, Eto'o refused to take rejection lying down and worked brutally hard to convince the new coach to change his mind.

That summer, Eto'o kept his mouth shut, trained like a dervish, scored 11 goals in 11 games for club and country and, crucially, not only got a goal against Wisła Kraków, but led the team in workrate.

On his presentation day, the new coach had added, sotto voce: "If any of the three [Ronaldinho, Deco and Eto'o] stays next season, I won't be prejudiced against them and I'll push them to find their previous levels."

Only the African fitted that category. Long before the market closed, Guardiola sat Eto'o down and told him: "I like your workrate, I value your pressing. If you play and train like you have been, then you stay. But I've spoken with the team's captains [there is one captain, Carles Puyol, plus two vice captains] and they say there must be no more disruptive behaviour. No more warnings, one strike and you are out."

Eto'o agreed readily and the decision proved inspirational. Eto'o scored 30 times in La Liga, got a goal every other game in the Champions League, including the crucial opening strike in the final against Manchester United, for a total of 36 goals. However, when the normally patient Guardiola says 'one strike and you're out', he means it.

But pre-season had gone very well. There was no question who was in charge. Xavi, returning with his fellow Spain internationals from winning the European Championship, explained the impact Guardiola had from the first moment: "The pre-season had already started when I joined the training and the squad were working their butts off. The coaches, the physical trainers, Pep, they were on us like hawks, pushing for repetitions, pushing for intensity of training.

"Puyi [Carles Puyol], Andrés [Iniesta] and I all kind of looked at each other with the thought that, 'Woah! What's going on here, these guys are absolutely full-on'. More importantly, I thought to myself, 'This is one of those moments where you either jump right on the train or it's leaving without you'."

Guardiola's first league game, away at Numancia, is both uplifting and shambolic. For the record he uses: Valdés; Alves, Puyol, Márquez, Abidal; Xavi, Touré (Hleb 56), Iniesta (Keita 65); Messi, Eto'o, Henry (Bojan 61)

The team is hungry, creative and looks fit, but also disorganised and naive. Once defensive mayhem allows Mario to score there is a slight lack of self-belief, no matter how many chances they make (27 attempts at goal, six of them on target, two off the woodwork). Barça are humiliatingly beaten by the new boys of La Liga.

3 — The Exile Returns

"There are rules of positional play. We all know them and all summer, until now, we have applied them, so I'm surprised that we played like this," Guardiola said. "We should have won, we played poorly. It was our own fault, but we can correct the errors."

Next morning, the papers were full of wounded, angry emails and texts from readers. One reader survey that week wanted Messi to be ordered to stick to the right wing, Iniesta converted to a left winger and, at all costs, the signing of Andrey Arshavin, one of the stars of the European Championships of that summer.

Guardiola's view about corrective therapy was 100% correct. The players' day off was cancelled and a tactical session was brought in the next morning. Unfortunately for him, there was an international break immediately and he kissed goodbye to the majority of his players for the next 10 days. Because of Guardiola's belief that he had a 'short squad' and because the artificial pitch they used might have been damaging, those first teamers who remained (Alves, Eto'o and Sylvinho) were not called to the Copa Catalunya match at Sant Andreu, just north of the city, where a mix of B team and youth players lost 3-1.

A decent handful of fans who made it up to that game shouted and gestured abusively at Joan Laporta, but also at Guardiola, for what was starting to look like paper-thin football identical to that which had cost Rijkaard his job. When those away defeats were followed by a 1-1 draw at home to Racing Santander, there were howls of dismay from around Catalonia – from fans and media.

Messi's return from Peru, where he played for Argentina, meant he was left on the bench but he came on to score a penalty with 19 minutes left. In front of only 54,678 fans (meaning over 40,000 empty seats), Racing equalised three minutes later. With one point from six, Barça were 15th and there were alarm bells ringing everywhere – except Casa Cruyff, where the man of the house was deaf to the noise, but keeping his eyes open.

"I don't know which game you saw," he asked his readers in *El Periódico*, "but I saw one of the best Barça performances for years.

"Okay it means two games, one goal, from a penalty, and both the chances from the opposition have gone in. But those are only numbers. Football-wise, Barça were of the best. Positionally excellent, moving the ball with speed and precision and pressing well. You draw your conclusions but, to me, this season looks very, and I mean very good."

That week, Barça won twice – 3-1 at home to Sporting Lisbon in the Champions League and 6-1 away to Sporting Gijón in La Liga. Guardiola's players had been unleashed.

Betis came to the Camp Nou and recovered from 2-0 down, only for Eidur Gudjohnsen to score a winning goal which had total determination written all over it. Having shown that they now had a rock-steady chin as well as a devastating combination of jabs and hooks, Barça were unstoppable.

From 1-0 down away from home, they won the Catalan *derbi*, Messi's last-minute penalty giving them a 2-1 victory over Espanyol. Now, they were just one victory away from testing Guardiola's wallet.

However, an away Champions League match in Donetsk was a brutal challenge. Barcelona's performance in Ukraine, where they remained a goal down as late as the 87th minute but left with all three points, revealed new depths of determination and belief. It was a milestone for Guardiola's team.

Big victories followed over Atlético Madrid and Athletic Bilbao, plus a 10-0 aggregate in two matches against Basel and Almería. Guardiola's team was on a roll.

After the Almería game, during which Eto'o scored three by the 23rd minute, the fastest hat-trick in Barça's 109-year history, Guardiola opened up to us in the press conference: "The key to all this is that we have fantastic footballers," he argued. "No coach, least of all me, works miracles.

"Even in pre-season I couldn't believe how many chances we were capable of making. Then came the two slip-ups at the start of the season, against Numancia and Racing, which actually did us good. Up in Numancia we had the same amount of chances as today, but this time we took five of them.

"And I like the atmosphere too. Look at the subs on the bench, celebrating the goals as if they'd scored them. That's not something a coach can order them to feel. Either the players are totally up for one another or not – it's within them. You can see that ours are."

It was the point at which Xavi, again, underlined that the players wanted credit pushed back to their coaching team. "Little details matter a lot now and, psychologically, we are undergoing a Masters degree with Pep. Everything is controlled and well prepared. We spend a lot of time on strategy, tactics and how the opponent is going to play against us. We are loving this."

But Piqué, not short of confidence, was the first in the squad to really tell it as it was. "We've got a team which is capable of winning the league, the cup and the Champions League," he said.

Then, with their 11th straight victory in all competitions, Barça put four past Málaga, away, and went top of the league outright.

Guardiola's assistant, Tito Vilanova, retrospectively put it like this: "Barça had two bad years and although we had an excellent run during the pre-season, our first few results in La Liga weren't good. The Camp Nou was half empty and people weren't coming to the games. Week by week, we managed to lure people back, a thousand here, a thousand there. Now we've made the fans proud of us."

From that night, week nine of La Liga, until the title was won, Barça never moved off top spot. New coach, failing team, one point from six and 52 matches since Barça last led the title race, but top by November 2 and leaders from then on. Not bad.

It was that night that the father of Guardiola's goalkeeping coach, Juan Carlos Unzué, died aged 84. The funeral happened to be on the afternoon of November 4, a day before Barça played FC Basel, when a win would assure a place in the Champions League knockout stage. Pep Guardiola immediately put it to his players, those who were injured, too, that he felt the entire squad should attend the funeral 500km away, just outside Pamplona. This is Guardiola, the guy who wants to minimise player travel and tiredness; Guardiola, the guy who treats tiny details of preparation as if they are the moment the atom is split. All agreed and off they went. Perhaps it was not heroic, but it was impressive and helped foster a genuine 'one-for-all-and-all-for-one' spirit amongst staff and squad.

This was the breakthrough moment, the crucial season. This was when Guardiola established his norms, learned at lightning speed, laid down markers for his team, his assistants, the board, opponents, the media and even for his loved ones.

The players all talk about how Guardiola takes care of their boredom levels and guards their quality free time. In return for hard work and victories, Guardiola instituted a new and often controversial policy. Once the players are fine-tuned, focused and briefed, Guardiola wants them as far away from tension, pressure and needlessly burned energy as possible. So, for home matches he did away with the much-hated *'concentración'*, the popular continental idea that the team needs to be taken from their homes and put in a hotel the night before every game so that they can concentrate.

Some players, particularly those with a house full of young kids or a wife who doesn't fully understand the demands of top-level football, actually like that night in the hotel, where everything is done for you and you are mixing with team-mates. But 90 per cent of players regard the practice, at best, as a nuisance.

Guardiola also instituted an unusual match-day training session which, in fact, is training-lite. It's a warm-up, a chance to perfect last-minute details for the coming match and to focus players' minds.

Then, at about midday, players are sent home and not expected at the Camp Nou until 90 minutes before the match. If it's a 9pm Sunday night kick-off, that's seven-and-a-half valuable hours away from work on a 'family' day. Players love it.

Then there is the away match. The normal practice in

Spain is to fly or take the team bus the night before the game. It means another night of boredom in yet another hotel. For the players of Barça and Real Madrid, like Manchester United, Internazionale or Bayern Munich, these trips come on top of regular Champions League excursions, domestic cup ties deep into the season and international travel to represent their countries.

This wasn't for Guardiola. He well remembered his boredom and frustration at the endless travel, the time wasted in hotel restaurants and airports. So Barça's domestic policy is to take an early flight on the morning of the match, arrive, take a siesta in the team hotel, play (win!) and then, if possible, leave between 90 minutes and two hours after the match.

The squad often arrives back at El Prat airport in Barcelona between 2am and 4am the next morning and they will train again at 11am, but the net gain, for staff and players, is enormous.

Across a season, Messi, Xavi, Iniesta and the rest will save hundreds and hundreds of hours when, previously, they would have been stuck – at the stadium, in a hotel, watching TV, sitting on a bus or waiting in an airport. A team like Barcelona not only needs to be physically tuned, but mentally sharp in order to complete their lightning-fast passing movements game after game, and this is one of the great innovations of the Guardiola era. Prevent boredom, prevent rust, keep the players fresh and in your debt, show them the carrot as well as the stick. The conclusion that Guardiola's time management has been brilliant is inescapable.

November and December brought a sequence, thanks to the random selection of the Liga Nacional de Fútbol Profesional (LFP) computer, which both thrilled and fascinated anyone who was into Spanish football. I witnessed some of the most brutal, skilful, stunning football I have seen.

We called it the mini-league in English, the Spanish did too – *La Liguilla*. All of the key title rivals had to play each other in sequence. Guardiola's team faced, in order, Sevilla away, Valencia at home, Madrid at home and Villarreal away.

Madrid faced Sevilla at home, Barcelona away, Valencia at home and Villarreal at home (fixtures which would cost Bernd Schuster his job as the coach of Los Blancos). Sevilla (who would finish third) played Valencia, Barcelona, Real Madrid and Villarreal. You get the picture.

Guardiola's team won 3-0 at the Nervión, hit Valencia for four at the Camp Nou, defeated Madrid 2-0 in the most brutal of kicking matches, sponsored by Madrid's new coach, Juande Ramos, and then inflicted a 2-1 defeat on Villarreal at El Madrigal. Twenty-two days, 12 points, an 11-1 aggregate and one of the most resounding declarations of intent I've ever seen in football. It was scintillating and it was merciless.

The match at Villarreal saw two red cards, for the ex-Manchester United team-mates Piqué and Giuseppe Rossi. *El Submarino Amarillo* actually led, but Keita and Henry turned the tables. In fact Henry, never massively popular at the Camp Nou and now something of a footnote, was actually sensational in that mini-league. Beyond a couple of assists, including one for Messi against Madrid, he scored four times.

"We knew that Pep's work ethic would change the team, but it's happening much sooner than we imagined," Begiristain, Barça's director of football, observed.

Landmarks at this time included Pep sanctioning the move from the single training pitches of La Masia and the mini stadium to the Ciudad Deportivo (Sports City) which is between the Camp Nou and the airport. When the ground was originally bought, in 1989, Guardiola the teenager had been asked by then president Josep Lluís Núñez to accompany Cruyff at a 'flag-planting' ceremony. The project was finally completed after years of indecision, dispute and financial uncertainty.

The move to this state-of-the-art facility was complete by the middle of January, just before Barça faced Osasuna. José Antonio Camacho, a Real Madrid legend who was then coach of Osasuna, got it right. "Barça are a team of stars who work like navvies."

Mid-season, Guardiola's team was scoring precisely three per game, 51 in 17, and led La Liga by 11 points. It was the best half-season in the club's history.

And then came the genesis of another of the huge decisions that would define the evolution of Guardiola's team. At training on Tuesday, January 20, the morning before Barça were to play Espanyol in the Catalan *derbi*, up on Montjuïc's Olympic Stadium, in the first leg of the Copa del Rey quarter-final, Guardiola ordered some lengthy stretching exercises. Samuel Eto'o's mind was not on the job. He was not stretching properly and Guardiola told him so. The striker replied that this is how he always did it. The manager told him to do it as instructed, Eto'o argued back and was immediately sent to the dressing room.

The next night, Eto'o was not involved in the game and Barça drew 0-0, having previously scored in their last 28 games and won 13 straight. Asked about the absent player, Guardiola only said: "I've got nothing to say. He's an exemplary player. These things need to stay on the training pitch."

A couple of weeks later, Eto'o told *Sportsweek* in France that: "I hate those players who score and kiss the badge. If a multi-million pound offer came in the next day, they'd take it.

"I've decided whether I'll be staying or not for the last year of my contract next season, but I can't say anything yet. I wasn't very welcome at Barça last summer because some people didn't believe in me, but that's all forgotten now. I've proved myself."

Eto'o was restored and scored in the 4-1 win over Numancia, but by the end of the season he was turfed out. Explaining this shock decision, one I have always believed was a mistake, Guardiola said in the summer of 2009: "I understand perfectly that people want to know why this is happening, because he's a marvellous footballer.

"In fact there aren't 'football' reasons. It's a question of 'feeling'. On and off the pitch he's been fine all year, the decision is exclusively mine."

Eventually, Eto'o is pushed out the door, a court case ensues, he is part-exchanged for Zlatan Ibrahimovic and in no sense, football or financial, do Barça come out of the deal better off.

The second leg of the quarter-final against Espanyol is won 3-2, Bojan scores twice, and, after eliminating Mallorca in the semi-finals, Guardiola is in his first cup final as a manager – against Athletic Bilbao at the Mestalla, an historic ground for Pep the Olympian.

February brings an international break and Piqué and Busquets make their debuts for Spain; within a year-and-a-half both will start in, and win, the World Cup final.

Meanwhile, Guardiola's team has lost a bit of sharpness and are grinding things out.

They draw at Betis and lose at home to Espanyol for the first time since just before the World Cup in 1982.

Then, after a harum-scarum game at Atlético Madrid that they lose 4-3 – having led 2-0 and also 3-2 with 18 minutes left – some might easily have considered that Guardiola was wobbling.

Post-match, amid *Colchonero* euphoria at the Calderón, he said: "First of all, when others were talking about how superb we were and how the league was 'won,' I was the one warning that that wasn't true and that many obstacles remained.

"In this game, at 2-0 we had two or three chances to kill it off and failed. Then our positional play failed us and, when it was end-to-end, we didn't defend properly. There were errors but they are correctable."

Once again "positional play" was the weakness, once again Pep knew best.

Barça won eight and drew two of their next 10 matches, which included the reverse *Liguilla* fixtures (Sevilla, Valencia, Real Madrid and Villarreal) and, in particular, an awesome 6-2 win at the Bernabéu.

Consider Barcelona's schedule in April and May:

April 22: Barça v Sevilla.

April 26: Valencia v Barça

April 28: Barça v Chelsea, Champions League semi-final

May 2: Real Madrid v Barça

May 6: Chelsea v Barça, second leg

May 10: Barça v Villarreal

3 — The Exile Returns

May 13: Barça v Athletic Bilbao, Copa del Rey final

May 16: Barça confirmed as champions of La Liga

May 27: Manchester United v Barça, Champions League final

Now, I don't have to put a fake 'build' on the suspense. You know that they won all three competitions. But just consider the tension, the energy expended, mental and physical, the travel, the celebrations after humiliating Madrid in the Bernabéu, the 'pinch me did that just happen' feeling after the manic match against Chelsea at Stamford Bridge, the suspensions and the injuries.

I cannot swear to you that there has never been a more testing, more impressive way to win three tournaments in the space of less than a month. But here's my pitch. What this team, which was flaccid and dull the season before, achieved under a rookie coach against all but one of the top five Spanish rivals, plus Chelsea, Athletic Bilbao and then Manchester United to win the treble is the single most impressive month in football history.

Of course, in the middle of that examination of character and stamina came what probably remains the most controversial game of Pep Guardiola's reign, perhaps of modern Barcelona history: the second leg of the Champions League semi-final tie against Chelsea, at Stamford Bridge. In the context of this run, let's just remember how physically and emotionally draining it was; the comeback, with 10 men, and the accusations that followed them back to Spain.

Immediately after that test of fire, following a 3-3 draw against Villarreal, Barça faced their first Guardiola final.

That six-goal thriller against Manuel Pellegrini's team meant that this Barça side had scored more goals in a league season than any of their predecessors. They had registered the most wins in the club's history, the most away wins too, they had scored the most away goals in the history of La Liga, and the most all-competition goals of any team in any season in the history of Spanish football. It had been a jamboree.

Yet the 3-3 draw had come at a cost. A win would have clinched the title and Barça were 3-1 up at one stage and winning 3-2 in the 92nd minute – but still conceded.

Poor old Iniesta had suffered a small tear in a thigh muscle and was out of the Copa del Rey final, struggling badly to make the Champions League final. Éric Abidal, sent off in London, had received another straight red and was now suspended for both cup finals.

The first final is a 4-1 victory over Athletic Bilbao. By the Saturday, Guardiola had won the double.

Pep's first 'full' title as a player? Madrid lost 3-2 to late goals in Tenerife in 1992.

First as a coach? Same scoreline, different venue, just as dramatic a finale – Villarreal 3 Real Madrid 2, last-minute winner for Joan Capdevila.

Guardiola keeps his players on a tight leash all season, but when he says 'right, let's let our hair down', he means it. Just over a week before his first European Cup final as a coach, Guardiola told his players he'd hired a restaurant, that girlfriends or wives could come if they wished, but that this was a squad night out, it would be liquid as well as fine dining and that they could party a bit.

3 — The Exile Returns

I had a player interview the next day, about mid-morning. The player texted me about 45 minutes before we were due to meet (it's not one of the players you might expect) to say, "Look, our interview is going to have to be put back a good few hours, I've just got in."

For this coach, it's a big deal that the players should let off steam once objectives are achieved, especially if they do so together, enjoy it and come out the other end with strengthened bonds and a sense of having been rewarded by the boss.

Within nine minutes of the Champions League final in Rome starting, it was evident that the big night out had had no ill effects. It was a triumph of substance, style and skill.

Sir Alex Ferguson's remarkable admission that a goal in the ninth minute, from Eto'o, "killed us" and Leo Messi's stunning header – this was one hell of a pink ribbon to tie around the perfect season. No Alves, no Márquez, Puyol at right-back, Touré out of position at centre-half, 35-year-old Sylvinho at left-back, Iniesta far from match-fit and about to do himself an injury which would cost nearly five months of recovery time – and still Barça played United off the park.

Before any of it, Guardiola had a surprise for his players. Having come back in from the warm-up they were intrigued to find a large screen against one wall. The lights were dimmed and the screen filled with images of their dynamic season, inter-cut with music and action from the Russell Crowe movie Gladiator. How Barça put Manchester United to the sword that night in Rome speaks for itself.

I don't want to ignore the epic nature of Guardiola's

second La Liga title, but I think these first 12 months still serve to explain as much about the man, his management, his vision and his decision making as anything we've seen since.

Guardiola, the 37-year-old rookie, inherited a disaffected group of superstar egos and talents and got it right immediately. He won their trust, demanded their utmost every day and inspired them to better what they thought was their upper limit. It is a managerial achievement of gargantuan proportions.

To inspire, galvanise, and command this group of men while handling the brutal pressure of managing this particular club – that has been his signature of brilliance.

Guardiola broke down in the most unexpected attack of racking sobs in Abu Dhabi later that year when, having added the Spanish Supercup and the European Supercup, Barça also beat Estudiantes to become World Club champions.

The more his assistants tried to console him, the more his shoulders heaved up and down. It was a telling moment – the master of diplomacy, control and preparation melting with emotion in front of the television cameras. His assistants went to him, Thierry Henry put an arm round his shoulders … then something happened which I'm suspicious about, but have no proof of whatsoever.

The only other player who came up and put an arm round him was Zlatan Ibrahimovic. The Swede said something, a joke it seemed, and Guardiola shrugged him off and almost instantly lost the emotion, before giving his player an old-fashioned look. What was said? Did that have a slight impact on the pair's relationship, which we now know was approaching breaking point? In this instance I'm speculating.

Because of various disappointments, skirmishes off the pitch and failed signings, some people look upon Guardiola's second season as a little disappointing. It's not a view I share.

Four of his first seven trophies were won in 2009-10 – and each of them came via a brutal struggle. Beaten in Sevilla in the first leg of the Supercup, Barça needed a magical Messi night in the return leg for a 5-3 aggregate. The European Supercup was a sweaty, torrid evening on a bumpy pitch in Monte Carlo. Shakhtar Donetsk played hardball, Messi very nearly headbutted Darijo Srna and it was Pedro to the rescue in extra-time.

Then came the third, and most vital, trophy. Madrid had been crowned World Club champions on three occasions; Barça had lost their two shots at that title, once with Guardiola in the Dream Team in 1992. This was a big deal.

The World Club Championship was yet another game which they could, and probably should, have lost. Before the game, Guardiola had tried to defuse a bit of tension. "The most important day of our lives? I hope not, because we all have wives, children or other family at home. But the future is bleak, because there is no way we can improve on what we have achieved so far."

If that struck an odd note, then his pre-match speech to his players was right in tune. His words were: "If you lose, you will still continue to be the best team in the world. But if you win you will be legendary."

Juan Sebastián Verón's team played roughhouse, but

they also parked the bus once they went 1-0 up. The pitch wasn't the greatest, the Argentinians pressed, tackled and harried as if they might be jailed if they returned to La Plata without the trophy. With two minutes left, Guardiola's dream of completing a clean sweep of his first six tournaments was, if not dead, then in intensive care.

But he'd thrown on Pedro and Jeffrén to stretch the pitch horizontally and vertically with their pace and wing play, the back four were free to get forward to win knock downs. And it worked again.

Pedro, one of the smallest men on the pitch, headed an equaliser with the clock ticking down to disaster. Then Messi – who else? – scored the winner.

I defy you not to be moved by this glorious team, led by an icon of the Camp Nou, winning the first World Club Championship in its history via the greatest player of modern, perhaps any, times, when he stoops to steer home a cross, realises that neither his head nor his boot will be absolutely assured of making clean contact, and so dips his chest, like a sprinter going for the line, and knocks the ball into the net with the Barcelona club crest.

Through his tears of stress and joy, Guardiola said something telling. "My players are like the best old-fashioned amateurs," he sniffed. "They already have everything, but they keep on playing because they love it and because they have a simple, driving hunger to win and win again. Without them, I'd be nothing."

It was a triumph he would repeat without the tears in 2011, this time in Yokohama, Japan, after a 4-0 victory over Santos.

3 — The Exile Returns

The 2009-10 season had much that was sweet for Guardiola, but was also much more sour than the previous one.

The Zlatan Ibrahimovic deal, in which Guardiola participated, was ultimately ruinous. His first half of the season was productive, professional and may even be said to have won Barça the title. He scored a glorious volley to win the first Clásico of that season, 1-0 at the Camp Nou from an Alves cross. That was worth three points and that was the distance between the great rivals at the end of the season.

Initially, Ibrahimovic and Leo Messi clicked. The goals and the assists flowed.

When he scored that volley on November 30, Ibrahimovic had nine goals in all competitions, six assists and had scored the opening goal in five of the 12 La Liga matches to that point.

By the end of the season, the Swede had scored 21 times in all competitions, had nine assists, and won four trophies. Pretty powerful stats.

In the only one-on-one interview we did that season, Zlatan told me: "When I left Inter I told them I would only move to Barcelona because this is the most beautiful football, the style that people will be trying to replicate for the next century."

That was winter. By April, he was saying: "In many matches I've been a bit static because my role here is so different from Inter, where I had total liberty to move where I chose. The coach chooses a tactic, but in the end that tactic depends on how the players interpret it on the pitch. From early in March I was both confused and questioning myself about all this and for that reason I stopped making so many runs. Eventually, I just decided to stop thinking about it and, sadly, then came my injury."

It was both ridiculous and sad that Zlatan signed up for Guardiola's "beautiful" football, then once he arrived started to question why it was he who had to convert his anarchic play to the very system which produced the football which had seduced him.

After Christmas he was fined by Guardiola for using a snowjet while on holiday – this was prohibited by his contract.

Ibrahimovic began to work less, move for the ball less, press less and it wasn't only Guardiola but Messi who became frustrated.

The Swede's autobiography has laid down the bones of the breakdown from his point of view, revealing that he confronted his manager about having to run so much, moaned about being used inappropriately in the tactical scheme and accused Guardiola of losing his nerve in the face of the threat of José Mourinho and Inter Milan.

Then, after giving Barça all three points on week 29 with the only goal at Mallorca, Zlatan pulled up with a calf injury in the warm-up before playing Athletic Bilbao at the Camp Nou. Bojan stepped in and scored twice; he hit six in nine as Barça pushed on to win a viciously tight title race.

It was clear that the Swede felt extremely miffed, once fit, that Bojan had staked such a claim to start and it demonstrates what Guardiola thought of Zlatan's reaction to Bojan, a La Masia boy and a popular kid in this dressing room, if you examine the Swede's playing time after he recovered from the injury. Returning against Espanyol on week 33, Zlatan then managed 8, 90, 6, 65, 0 and 11 minutes in six crucial matches. An average of 30 minutes per match in a title race which Barça only won on the last day thanks to their 4-0 home victory over Valladolid and Real Madrid's draw at Málaga. Not exactly the dictionary definition of what you need from a €70m purchase.

Guardiola felt that Zlatan had overstepped so many boundaries (mostly sporting, but some personal), despite warnings and encouragement to change his ways, that the relationship withered and died.

At the end of the season, the Swede announced that: "The coach is sacking me. We have no relationship. He's only spoken to me twice in six months."

After he was booted out, to Milan, Zlatan spent a lot of time moaning about Guardiola, calling him "the philosopher" and, generally, painting himself as a victim.

What he didn't admit was that at a time when relations were strained, Ibrahimovic's agent had plenty to say for himself. In May, he said: "If [David] Villa wants to come and try to take Zlatan's position then it's better that he stays at home. If he wants to come and accept sitting on the bench, then he's welcome to."

Then, at the end of that month: "It was Guardiola who signed Zlatan, if he wants to sell him at the end of just one year then he should head off to a mental hospital."

While all this was going on, the Barça coach was applying his, perhaps mistaken, elegance and outward calm to the situation. "I don't regret signing Ibrahimovic," he said. "Zlatan has been professional in training, but there is also the individual and that always counts more."

Originally the deal cost Barça €46m, plus their valuation of the last year of Eto'o's contract, €20m. But when a deal to loan Aleksandr Hleb for a season collapsed, that added another €2.5m to the price. So €48.5m in cash, the €20m value of Eto'o (plus the emotional cost of watching him lead Inter to a treble) in exchange for a player who performed only in fits and starts after the turn of the season and was then forced out of the club. Disastrous.

The salary outlay over the five years of Zlatan's contract was to be an astonishing €75m. Some fault lay with the player, but also with the original research conducted by Guardiola and Barça. People such as Ronald Koeman and Ruud Gullit had been consulted and the word was that Ibrahimovic, who carried a reputation for trouble in the dressing room, had matured and changed.

The sadness, for David Villa, Guardiola, the Barça coffers and Joan Laporta is that other mistakes were made. Villa was buyable from Valencia, but Laporta went public that he wouldn't pay "that price" (€50m) for David Villa. In actual fact, purchasing the brilliant, hard-working and much-loved striker would have avoided the Ibrahimovic debacle and, I believe, brought Barcelona another treble.

Guardiola eventually pushed the button marked 'eject'. Zlatan was 'loaned' to AC Milan with an obligatory purchase clause of €24m at the end of season 2010-2011. It meant a minimum loss on the one-year contract of over €24m.

Sports director Andoni Zubizarreta explained:

"Guardiola told us that the problem started on the pitch and that he saw that Ibra was unhappy at not being a guaranteed starter, which he has always been in other clubs, where the team plays for him. I told the board we had to find a solution."

Vice president Josep Bartomeu put it like this: "We had a problem of how much loss there was on the deal, but we are also saving €60m for the four years of salary we won't be paying."

But volcanoes. Don't talk to Guardiola about volcanoes.

Leaving early for London because of a second Icelandic explosion of volcanic ash worked fine in May 2011 – because they had enough notice and enough choice, so they flew. But when Eyjafjallajökull fully erupted on April 14, 2010, with the plumes of ash and smoke reaching nine kilometres in height there were only seven days before the first leg of the Champions League semi-final against Inter and there was a Catalan *derbi*, at Espanyol, before that.

It was a roughhouse match in which Barça had their least domination of the ball all season and Dani Alves was sent off after an hour. By the end of the season, Guardiola would say: "This was the match which won us the league." However, at the time it seemed to be a point gained at high cost.

They couldn't move until Monday at the earliest and by then the relevant airspace was closed. They waited and waited for wind currents to clear airspace, but it didn't happen. So a bus journey to Milan, via an overnight stop in Cannes, was mooted and Guardiola, with little option, approved it.

Barça's staff and players set off at 2.45pm that Monday,

and arrived for the night in Cannes, at the Hotel Martinez, at about 10.55pm. From 10am on the Tuesday, it took until well after 2pm to cover the 380km to the Meliá Milano Hotel. They arrived nearly 24 hours after leaving the Ciudad Deportivo in Barcelona.

"Better most of a day in buses than sitting at home watching other people play on the television," was Guardiola's dry verdict. But the game was disastrous.

Despite leading 1-0, Guardiola's team is roughed up, with Inter playing both within and outwith the rules. José Mourinho's team play old-style Wimbledon 'Crazy Gang' football – but with total clarity of purpose. It is one of Mourinho's smartest triumphs.

The ball is lumped long to make Piqué and Puyol turn and they never get time to settle; Inter chase and harry like Barça at their best and they get a little lucky with a couple of fouls not given at crucial times, plus an offside goal. However, Barça are pallid and look like they are wading through mud. The demands of the season, the Catalan *derbi* and then the interminable bus journey have caught up with them.

The second leg was conditioned by intense Inter defending, Motta's controversial red card for shoving his hand out at Busquet's face and the lack of cutting edge which haunted Barça a little that season.

Piqué scores, Bojan has one ruled off and misses a sitter of a header, possession is 78/22 in Barça's favour and Julio César produces the save of that season, from Messi, at a time when Barça are threatening to score three or four. Tracks are laid for the following year when Mourinho runs up to yell at Guardiola, while he briefs Zlatan as Motta is being sent off: "You think it's all over, but it's not!"

3 – The Exile Returns

At the end, Mourinho does his famous victory run to the Inter fans high in the gods of the Camp Nou's third tier, despite Víctor Valdés first verbally and then physically attempting to dissuade him.

Inter worked brutally hard for their win and Barça lacked a killer touch. End of story. What the defeat served to do was underline the massive resilience Guardiola had instilled into his players.

The four remaining Liga matches were won by an aggregate 15-3 goal margin, when the squad might have had a negative reaction to the traumatic European exit. The first game post-Inter was at Villarreal. It was a must-win. In fact, it was also a horse whipping – 4-1 at El Madrigal. This was the win which surpassed their own record for a number of victories in a season (28), beat the record number of points any team had gathered in a 38-match season and was an enormous blow to Madrid, who had been relentless, implacable pursuers all season and who must have believed that Inter had done damage to Guardiola's squad.

I recall the tone and content of the pre-match press conference – if he spoke that well to his players after the Inter defeat and ahead of a test like Villarreal away, then little wonder his players paid him back with excellence. Guardiola argued that: "This season has already been exceptional. I've been making the point for a long time that we are not invincible, so it's logical that, occasionally, we'll lose. I think even the LA Lakers lose one now and again! [They won their 16th NBA title that year and most of Guardiola's players are obsessed with basketball].

"Our Champions League season was a great success and there were many small details which prevented us reaching the final again. Last season, we sneaked in via the top corner in the last minute, this season we lost out by the same tiny margin, but I'm very happy with my team's performance. I wouldn't be surprised at all if we get at least that far again next year."

The four wins, culminating in a 4-0 home drubbing of Valladolid, made Barça record-breaking champions. Spain dubbed it, pound for pound, the best title fight in La Liga history and we discovered a little bit more about our protagonist.

The first thing Guardiola said when he sat down to face the media as champion of Spain again was what dignified rivals Real Madrid had been. Contrast this with the heat and anger and pettiness which José Mourinho's arrival at the Bernabéu subsequently generated. Guardiola opened with: "I'd like to congratulate the coach and players at Madrid because I admire their attitude this season. Without them, I don't believe we'd have registered 99 points, and without us they wouldn't have won 96 points. Their play and the way they've competed for this title has dignified the institution of Real Madrid. I want them to know that there are people at this club who admire what they have been attempting to do, it's been exemplary."

He then had a firm blast at the way his club had been treated by the Madrid-based media, but took care to separate his view on them and his respect for Manuel Pellegrini's Madrid. And he returned to a favourite theme. "There is something truly 'amateur' in my players' spirit. They love to train, they love to come to work and they love to compete. That sustains us in a hard year when we've only been able to lose one game all season if we wanted to win the league."

In those first two seasons, Guardiola often showed the personality which he has to subdue slightly now that he is coach of the best club in the world. Those who knew him well as a player report that he was always massively inquisitive, open-minded, bright and fun. His life has always been controlled – diet, night-life, alcohol. But he has a sense of the ridiculous, a dry sense of humour and an interest in people.

Partly because he felt some in the media betrayed him during the darker seasons towards the end of his Barça playing career, and partly because he knows that the voracious media machine could swallow up all the time he spends making his team excellent, he has made it a public rule never to give one-on-one interviews while in charge at Barcelona.

There have been a handful of exceptions, to my knowledge – twice he has allowed me to join him in his office for an interview which then became a Guardiola article in the Champions League final programme. It's a privilege gained because I've been representing UEFA, the tournament organisers. Each time, I've found the experience both fascinating and frustrating. Fascinating because when he starts talking on a subject he's passionate about, you have no idea where it might lead because his mind is quick, chock-full of information and he has a unique interpretation of football matters. Just a bright, thoughtful man on top of his game. Frustrating, because time is immensely short and we have to move at a clip.

Television get face time from Pep, particularly around the Champions League, but largely our route to understanding him comes via his press conference appearances. The deal is this: before and after every match, the Barça manager will give generous chunks of time in press conferences, where you will often see a minimum of four languages used: Spanish, Catalan, English and Italian (he's fluent in all of them). With Barça's level of match commitment, that can very often mean six press conferences in a seven or eight-day period. Given that most pre-match conferences will last up to an hour and most post-match appearances last about 20 minutes, we can be talking about four hours a week, most weeks. Inevitably, some journalists, some repetitive questions which he can't or won't answer and some agendas tire him. But get him on football and it can be a wonderful education. What's more, he can be funny.

Over the last three years he has broken into a bit of 'Rehab' mid-sentence when somebody's phone went off and the late Amy Winehouse was the ringtone. There was one particularly funny incident where a Catalan journalist was being paid by a Gulf television channel to ask a question in English. He had a few shots at it, broke into Catalan to explain to Guardiola that he'd been practising all morning and, after suffering a good bit of teasing from the 'Mister', Guardiola changed sides and told him sympathetically: "Don't worry about all these smart guys who are laughing at you – the next press conference is completely in English and anyone who doesn't do it properly won't get an answer."

After Spain won the World Cup, prompting Piqué, Puyol and Pepe Reina to ambush Cesc Fàbregas and pull a Barça top over his head live on television, Guardiola was asked about it by a BBC reporter. "Okay, Piqué can be a funny guy," Guardiola said, laughing and causing more laughter in the press conference because he was already tapping the side of his forehead to signify what was coming next, "but sometimes he's got a screw loose".

There will always be someone, irrespective of medium or language, who has been sent in by their editor with a question they don't particularly want to ask but are ordered to. I'm guessing David Ibáñez of Telecinco was in that situation just before the Spanish Formula One Grand Prix in Catalonia, when he asked Guardiola: "Who do you want to win this weekend, Alonso, Massa or Hamilton?"

The great man was a bit stumped but asked: "Who do our fans like? Alonso supports Madrid, right? Well, I'm up for Hamilton then!"

It wouldn't bring the house down at Jongleurs, but his quick mind and neat way with words lightens what can be one of the great burn-out sections of his work. All of that contrasts with how fed up Guardiola got with the ancillary nonsense during the 2010-11 season.

The tension is obvious when he is on the side of the pitch. His row with Ståle Solbakken – in November 2010, in Denmark, after Copenhagen gave Barça what Pep called "the hardest, most intense, most physical game in my years in charge" – spoke volumes. It was a precursor to the Mourinho row. Solbakken had asked for a four-game suspension for José Pinto after the first game because the keeper imitated the referee blowing for offside via his own ability to whistle loudly and sharply. Copenhagen were clean through on goal and manifestly lost a scoring opportunity because of it.

Guardiola reacted with fury at another coach specifically asking that one of Barça's players receive a long ban. Out came the claws. But as the two men locked horns all the way down the touchline post match, bumping each other chest-to-chest, looking like it might all go off if they had another 50 metres to walk, something else happened.

Sergio Busquets is the team's 'enforcer'. He ran across to have a pop at Solbakken, but as soon as he did, his manager hauled him back by the shoulder; not so much 'keep out of trouble,' more 'I can fight my own battles'.

And think about this: losing at home to Hércules in the second game of the season, humiliating and annoying though that was, caused Guardiola much, much less grief than signing a contract extension at the club he loves and has made truly great once again. With his deal running out in June 2011, but a new 'rolling' contract all but agreed as far back as the summer of 2010, Guardiola extended until June 2012. Typically, he insisted on new, extended terms for all his backroom staff such as Domènec Torrent and Carles Planchart, who scout matches and prepare short, sharp video presentations for him and his players; Tito Vilanova, his right-hand man, and all the staff who, each season, get something special from him, a big slap-up meal, a personalised gift, but of whom much is demanded.

Still, for all that, there was little *alegría* (joy) in his body language or energy when he finally talked about the news. In mid-February 2011, prior to a hard-fought draw in Gijón, he spoke like a tired, not particularly happy man – a thousand light years away from the guy who took over in 2008.

"It just seemed like a moment not to put things off any more. More than a one-year extension? This already seems more than long enough to me. If I could, I'd only renew for six months at a time.

"It's not my idea to be here a long time. If everything goes well then after the end of this fourth year that I've signed up for, we'll see what happens. When I quit it'll be because these things happen in football – time wears everything down in this life. If I see that I'm in the way, that I'm running out of strength or passion, that's the time.

"There are really just two ways in which you leave a job like this – when you are sacked because you ain't winning any more or when you know it's just the right moment and you seize it. Either we'll be happy to stay on with you, or we'll see the moment and take it."

Many of the ups and downs of season 2010-2011 are touched upon in other places in this book – it was a very special time for Leo Messi, David Villa, Éric Abidal and Andrés Iniesta in particular. But it's the season during which Guardiola endured the most stress and became most troubled.

José Mourinho often annoyed him over those first 12 months as Madrid coach, but what Mourinho did which got under Guardiola's skin most of all was to put winning the Champions League and Spanish title under threat.

No matter how you evaluate the choice of tactics and the fact that, in the end, Barça lifted two trophies and Madrid only one, Los Blancos were breathing right down the neck of Guardiola's team during that epic, manic, full-on 'world series' of Spanish football – four Clásicos in 18 days that decided La Liga, the Copa del Rey and which club would face Manchester United in the Champions League final.

Pep Guardiola is not a bad loser, but he lives to win. His desire to stick to the team's philosophy was incredibly intense. When I interviewed him in 2009, in the first flush of success, he talked really passionately about the importance of playing with style and verve, partly to give fans something back. Speaking for the Champions League final match programme that year, he explained: "We live in a world where everything is spiralling in cost and many people need to make a big sacrifice in order to go and watch a game of football. So, for me, it all makes sense, the effort, the work, the planning, the concentration and the discipline if you do it for the people. The manner in which we have played this season is a demonstration of the respect we have for the people who pay for a ticket or pay money to watch matches on television."

After winning that 2009 Copa del Rey final, he also said: "You know what? With all the stuff that's going on in the world right now, the absolute minimum we can do is leave our guts out on the pitch every single game. I've got friends who are suddenly on the dole now and living with fear. A lot of Barça fans are pretty screwed because of economic circumstances, but they are proud of how we defend our playing style and won't abandon it. If, at the end, we also win then the best thing we can see is their joy."

Then, when I asked him in 2011 if he and Sir Alex Ferguson shared a general philosophy of attacking and entertaining he was much more prosaic. He said: "When you train a massive club, or a little third division outfit, when you go out to play football in any situation, it is always about winning. Full stop.

"If Manchester United and Barcelona share a

philosophy about how to play football, it is simply because we both think that attacking football is the best way to win. The only thing which interests us is achieving the victory. If that wasn't the case, if that wasn't what drives me every day, then I wouldn't be here."

Both of his statements are true to what he believes, what he works for. They do fit together and aren't contradictory, but they differ in tone. The first season was a rush, pure joy – testing, but like surfing a wave of absolute and total self-confidence. Latterly, all the things which, over the generations, have always grabbed at the ankles of champions are taking a toll on the coach and one or two of his senior players: Xavi's Achilles tendon, Puyol's knee problem, and the brutal news of Abidal's sudden discovery of a liver tumour. The joy of victory is possibly even sweeter, but it also comes at a greater cost.

Guardiola and all his players take tremendous nourishment from people telling them how special this brand of football is, how it lights up a dull, or troublesome life. But they have an undimmed hunger to win. It takes you far, but there is a bill to pay.

Pep's father, Valentín, told his local paper up in Santpedor that Cristina Guardiola often has to drive in to pick her husband up at 11pm at night when he's still poring over videos and working on a playing system for a coming match; in around 8am, often home at four or five in the morning after away matches, after 11pm on normal working days; media, stress over matches, signings and sales, injuries and presidential relations. Little wonder Guardiola's mother, Dolores, admitted: "He looks older, he's losing his hair and losing lots of weight because of the stress."

Success has come at a cost, but it is addictive. The incredible jag of adrenalin, joy and satisfaction at winning the most thorny of La Liga titles in 2011, the utter brilliance of the performance at Wembley to become European champions at the end of that season; these both renewed Guardiola's energies and called out to him to keep on achieving while he still has this remarkable bunch of players at his disposal.

After receiving the Catalan Parliament's Medal of Honour in September 2011 Guardiola explained:

"I want to let you into a little secret. Ahead of every match I head down to my little office in the basement of the Camp Nou and I lock myself in for a couple of hours. My guys give me a couple of DVDs of the next team we face.

" 'F***!' I say, "their left winger is quicker than their right, their centre backs aren't of the same quality, they really use the long ball … etc.' I note their strengths then I look for weaknesses.

"That always starts me thinking: 'Ok, if I use these players here … if Messi goes here and somebody over there, maybe we can see them off.' It's the 'Eureka!' moment.

"That fantastic spark of inspiration, the joy of that single instant, is why I'm a coach. Everything else is part of the daily grind, the stuff we all have to do.

"It can last a minute, or sometimes 90 seconds. Some days I have to watch two DVDs, but however long it takes, I always get to the point when I can say, 'I've got it – we're going to win tomorrow!'

"I don't know where it comes from but I get a mental image and that's always enough to convince me. Tomorrow we're going to win."

Pep Guardiola, the man of vision. Unchanged by power. Still fighting for the idea that playing beautiful football can not only win you great prizes, but define your club, your cultural identity and your position in the world.

MAKING-OF MATCH:
ATHLETIC BILBAO 1 BARCELONA 4
COPA DEL REY FINAL, MAY 13 2009

If football was predictable and theory ruled over talent, then this very special cup final should probably have unfolded in reverse.

Guardiola's team limps into Valencia on the day of the game. Their schedule in the previous few weeks has been utterly brutal. The previous weekend, they tossed away the chance to win the title, despite leading 3-1 at home to Villarreal, and in the process Andrés Iniesta was added to the lengthening injury list; Barça also have Thierry Henry, Rafa Márquez and Gaby Milito all ruled out and Éric Abidal suspended. Athletic Bilbao, meanwhile, are in good nick and have won four and drawn one of their last five matches. This is Nirvana for them.

Athletic had become powerful and attractive – well coached by Joaquín Caparrós and with future World Cup winners Javi Martínez and Fernando Llorente, both of whom scored in the semi-final humbling of Sevilla, already prominent.

What's more, it looks like Athletic are taking the Copa del Rey way more seriously. Their 25,000 fans come down long before the Catalans – some spending Monday to Thursday drinking, singing and proclaiming Basque pride.

Barça's fans have more prosaic things on their mind – work, family, early bed. Remember, these are neither your most raucous nor your most defiant of football supporters.

Guardiola's players have not practised for penalties "because it takes a bit of arrogance to want a penalty after extra-time and under pressure. You can't train that". So keen is he on the players getting rest that they take an 11am flight down to Valencia on the day of the final.

Athletic's last couple of training sessions have been open and attracted vast crowds – this is a fiesta and the final is there to be enjoyed, before being won. What's more, the Rojiblancos go 1-0 up.

Caparrós' team lead Spain in set-piece goals this season and, naturally it is a back-post header by Toquero from David López's corner, with Xavi and Keita totally out-jumped, which puts the Basques ahead, a goal met by a wall of noise inside the stadium. Barça could be forgiven for being stunned, but when Yaya Touré frees himself from centre-back for a long, meandering run which ends with him thrashing the ball past Gorka from distance, the Basques shrivel and we watch what will become a typical sight – Xavi and Messi, in his first cup final for Barça, six years after his debut, taking over the game.

But I go back to my point. Barça should have been on their knees, not gaining in strength and running Athletic ragged by the end of the game. Things went in reverse and while a comparative lack of world-class players in the Athletic squad was a factor, it was also the case that Guardiola's players felt that having come this far, having been to hell and back the week before in the semi-final of the Champions League against Chelsea in London and knowing, for sure, that they were fitter than anyone in Spain, no way were they going to let this cup escape them.

There was one amusing postscript; at least I found it funny. The state television station, TVE, had the game live. Given that this was Basques v Catalans, the arrival of the King and Queen in the stadium – followed by the national anthem – was greeted by jeering and whistling. TVE somehow managed to cut away from all this, to scenes in San Mamés.

They were deluged with complaints from the rest of Spain. They then apologised and played the national anthem – edited, with the whistling almost inaudible – at half time instead. The less funny side was that poor old Julián Reyes, TVE's head of sport, was fired the next day as the channel furiously denied censorship.

One trophy down in Pep's first season. Two to go.

Athletic (4-4-2) Iraizoz; Iraola, Ocio, Amorebieta, Koikili; Yeste, Martínez, Orbaiz (Etxeberría 62), López (Susaeta 59); Toquero (Vélez 62) Llorente.
Barcelona (4-3-3) Pinto; Alves, Piqué, Touré (Sylvinho 88), Puyol; Xavi, Busquets, Keita (Pedro 87); Messi, Eto'o Bojan (Hleb 83).
Goals Toquero 9; Touré 30, Messi 54, Bojan 57, Xavi 64
Booked Touré, D. López, Koikili, Keita, Messi
Referee Luis Medina Cantalejo
Attendance 55,000, Mestalla

4 – THE MACHINE

"I must have at least 100 touches of
the ball every match. If I had to go back to
the dressing room with only 50 I'd be ready
to kill someone."
— Xavier Hernández Creus

I T IS JUST OUTSIDE the FC Barcelona dressing-room door at Wembley, about an hour after Manchester United have been defeated 3-1 in the 2011 Champions League final. The dancing, singing and beer drinking in the Catalan quarters have only just died down. I've been charged with interviewing two of the winning players, with the trophy, for the final Champions League Weekly television programme of the season and there is now a desperate need for a player to emerge from the fiesta, never mind agree to the damn request.

The producer has a spare dressing room set up and ready to go. Our guests can't be the man of the match or one of the goalscorers, who have already had to give interviews after showing the cup off to the Barça fans.

Éric Abidal has stopped, surprised the life out of me by giving me a big bear hug, but said he'd prefer not to speak because he's too tired and emotional. He has played despite the liver tumour operation which was supposed to keep him out until August. What's more, he has been given the captain's armband and told to hoist the cup by his captain, Carles Puyol.

Thiago, once my sixth-floor neighbour in our Pedralbes apartment block, also pauses for a quick chat, beer in hand, but he's en route to the mandatory UEFA drugs test.

Barça's reliable, friendly and hard-working press staff have been inside the dressing room trying to entice one of the victors out while the songs get louder and more raucous. Time drags on, deadlines are being stretched like United's back four and it's not looking good. Other players are whisked away by high-ranking backstage officials for television rights holders, who have paid handsomely for access.

4 — The Machine

Gerard Piqué, tired and hefting a big cardboard box full of I don't know what (it wasn't the goal net which he cut down to keep as a souvenir, because I asked that one) agrees to a nice piece to camera – enjoying being with the cup for a moment. We have been allocated a neighbouring, empty dressing room, and it's a weird moment – the trophy, a Champions League winner I first met when he was still a kid in the *cantera* and an empty, clean, atmosphere-free changing room – but his joy radiates like a cloud. However, while he is filmed, all the other players skip past, leaving just one – Xavi Hernández.

"Five minutes Xavi, not a second more," is my pitch as the two ranks of television reporters about 50 feet away growl and will him to say 'No', so that they can get their last hit of a glorious night. Also, he knows that everyone else is waiting for him. Not only is a big party at the Natural History Museum in South Kensington waiting for him, but the last one on the coach, especially if the rest have been held up, will know all about it. "Ok, I know you're good to your word, let's do it." Joy.

We sprint down the corridor, relieve the UEFA official of the trophy he's quite legitimately removing in the belief that the second interview has as much chance of arriving as a Christmas card from José Mourinho, knock off a quick piece and prepare to rush the great man to the sanctuary of the bus. For no better reason than residual excitement, I mention to him, as we trot out of the dressing room, "I thought Messi's movement across your run was outstanding and it opened up Pedro's space for your assist pass". (Take a look on You-Tube. Xavi's forward run has him poised like a quarterback on the move; Pedro has Nemanja Vidic tight on him, but as Messi goes towards Xavi's run, Patrice Evra follows him, Pedro backs off into the vacated space, Xavi finds the pass and his team-mate finishes, bottom corner). Which is enough to make him stop dead and say: "Man, I love the way you enjoy your football," and then walk me through Barça's first goal.

It was magical, just a fractional glimpse of what we all miss out on – reporters, fans, officials, sponsors – when the winning players stop to dissect and enjoy what it is they have just done.

As for Xavi, it was typical that he was compelled to stop and talk about football. He's as good at analysing it as he is playing it – which is why so many believe he'll become Barça coach. It wouldn't be the first time he has followed in Pep Guardiola's footsteps.

That chat was one of the best moments of a long career in sports journalism, and it could scarcely have been more different from the first time I tried to get an interview with Xavi. It was 2002 and I'd just moved to Barcelona. The press office had 'Okayed' an interview, but needed clearance from the player. In those days, the set-up was different. Sometimes you could see the request from the Barça staff taking place and, unbeknownst to Xavi, I witnessed him listen to the press officer, Chemi Teres; I saw him mull it over for less time than it takes him to find a cute pass before saying, "Nah, never heard of him, don't fancy it".

Poor old Chemi had to come back to me with the reply, "Sorry, something's come up and the player's too busy. Let's try again another time." No harm done. Chemi is paid for that work, Xavi probably managed not to lose too much sleep over his side step and I viewed it as an incentive to win his trust.

4 — The Machine

Wembley 2011 was different. Xavi and Barça were exhilarating. That first goal against Manchester United typified Xavi, Messi and Barça under Guardiola. When Iniesta slips the ball to Xavi, he's 'between the lines' (a pocket of space between the opposition's midfield and defence in this case) – nobody has picked him up.

During the dribble, he switches body position in case he has to pass in either direction, but there's a given point when Messi is static and Pedro is sandwiched between both Evra and Vidic. No goal chance is looming. The very second Pedro decides to take a couple of steps backwards, Messi spots it, darts three or four metres towards Xavi, dragging Evra and opening a channel for the pass. Vidic, thinking Evra is still behind him, doesn't notice Pedro stealing a few yards and getting ready to give Edwin van der Sar 'the eyes' and bury the ball past him. It's poetry.

Football is full of little ironies and quirks of fate. Consider this: When Xavi was establishing himself in the Barcelona first team, the chance to join Manchester United came up. He thought long and hard about it, but decided to dig in and fight for his chance at the club he has always supported.

Just imagine Xavi supplying his laser-guided passes to Andy Cole, Dwight Yorke, Ruud van Nistelrooy, Wayne Rooney or Ole Gunnar Solskjær.

Xavi is now the venerated, brilliant, visionary, all-time great Spanish midfielder but, between 1998 and 2002, he was an under-rated, misused and unfairly judged young player. Ironically, his first problem was Pep Guardiola.

Xavi followed up his Barça debut against Southampton in the summer tour of 1998 with a competitive debut, under Louis van Gaal, in the Spanish Super-cup that August. His chance came because Guardiola and Albert Celades were both injured. Xavi had been on holiday, lying on the beach, only to get the urgent call to take a flight back to Barcelona that afternoon. Destiny calling.

The Supercup first leg was a horrible defeat at Mallorca, but Xavi scored and received rave notices. Guardiola was one of the quickest to praise his "awareness" and "maturity" but promised to make it hard for Xavi to take his place. He would deliver on that promise.

All of this happened as Van Gaal's team stumbled without a single victory, competitive or friendly, from April 19 the previous season until they defeated Rafa Benítez's Extremadura on September 13. Things weren't going well for Spain's champions. By mid-September, Xavi made his Champions League debut, at Old Trafford in a frenetic 3-3 draw against a United side which would win the treble that season. His first La Liga start came in an imperious 3-1 win at Valencia the following month.

By this time, he seemed established as not only a *canterano* (youth team product) of major promise but a first-team regular. That season, he played every Champions League group game and made 27 appearances in all competitions – the 10th most-used footballer in Van Gaal's squad. However, Guardiola's return to full fitness from another calf injury, just before the half-way stage of La Liga, resulted in fewer appearances for Xavi.

It is no disaster for an 18-year-old to be relegated by Phillip Cocu, Luis Enrique, Rivaldo, Ronald de Boer, Pep Guardiola and Geovanni, particularly when you score a goal that is vital in the successful defence of the championship. Xavi's strike at Valladolid brought victory in a poor display and sparked a run of one defeat in the next 16 matches until the title was retained. "Of course, when I scored in Valladolid, I was really saving Van Gaal's bacon," he recalls. "He had so many detractors at the time, people wanting him kicked out of the club. That goal was the catalyst for us then going on to win the league".

Xavi had some important business of his own in the April of that first season as a Barça regular. He, Iker Casillas and Carlos Marchena became world youth champions in Nigeria, winning a tournament which featured several players who would play a part in his story at Barcelona: Ronaldinho, Seydou Keita, Gaby Milito, Rafa Márquez, Ashley Cole and Julio César. At the same competition were players who would go on to represent countries in every corner of the football world: Robbie Keane, Damien Duff, Danny Invincible and Brett Emerton; Joseph Yobo, Roque Santa Cruz, Aldo Duscher and Mahamadou Diarra; Simão, Diego Forlán and Idriss Kameni; Peter Crouch, Andy Johnson and Matthew Etherington; Junichi Inamoto, Shinji Ono, Carlos Bocanegra and Tim Howard; Mancini, Juan, Dani Aranzubia, Pablo Couñago, Fran Yeste and Gabri.

The following year Xavi, with Marchena, Joan Capdevila and Carles Puyol steered a wonderful Spain squad to the final of the Sydney Olympics tournament; he scored in the final, a 2-2 draw with Cameroon, and tucked away his penalty in the shoot-out, only to lose to opponents inspired by Samuel Eto'o. So, in those two breakthrough years, Xavi won the Spanish title, the FIFA Youth World Cup and picked up an Olympic silver medal; a Catalan, schooled in the Barça *cantera*, evidently gifted and a high achiever. Life should have been sweeter than Turkish Delight dipped in Nutella.

Yet the Camp Nou not only didn't take him to its heart immediately, he remembers hearing its disapproval if he came on as a substitute for Guardiola, reading fans' letters to papers, hearing them on radio phone-ins, objecting to the young pretender trying to 'oust' King Pep from territory that was rightfully his. The club's managing director, Javier Pérez Farguell, had briefed at least one agent that Barça were 'open minded' to the idea of selling Xavi – largely because he didn't have 'great marketing cachet'. Iniesta they liked. Iniesta was untouchable. But Xavi, well …

"People initially drew constant comparisons between me and Guardiola – I struggled to shake that off," Xavi admitted when he celebrated his 10th anniversary in the first team in 2008. "To be valued and respected for the way I play was a real battle, especially when Van Gaal used us in the same position and compared the two of us at press conferences. It was hard having to compete against my idol. I worried about robbing him of his place, about whether we would get on or not. I idealised everything about Pep – how he talked, his leadership on the pitch. So, psychologically, it wasn't a great beginning, despite the fact that in terms of my own football, I felt great. But either you're man enough to meet the challenge or you have no place in this club."

Xavi hadn't known that Martin Ferguson caught his debut, in his role as head of European scouting for Manchester United, nor was it more than fate that paired the two clubs in that Champions League season. Ferguson recommended that his club keep a very close eye on this Catalan midfield metronome, so when United were alerted to the fact that Barça were not only in the doldrums, but Xavi was at a stage when he had to decide whether to cut the strings and establish himself elsewhere or fight for a life at the Camp Nou, there was real interest.

When I raised the episode with Xavi just before Wembley in 2011, he explained: "There was a long time when I genuinely thought about accepting United's offer. I needed a change of scenery and things were not going well for me at Barcelona. I don't know, perhaps the club thought about selling me, too.

"I have always felt a real attachment to English football and Manchester United would be my club in England. For a long chunk of my career, when it looked like I was the successor to Pep in midfield, I was made to feel like an outsider – a bad guy for taking over from the legendary captain.

"We are not good at handling change here. I hated all that debate about me and Guardiola and Van Gaal wasn't particularly tactful to put an 18-year-old kid through it."

The truth is that his father and both his brothers, Alex and Óscar, at various times shared their feelings that Xavi might have to go somewhere else just to be appreciated. "What eventually made the difference is that I'm as stubborn as a mule," he recalled. "I thought about going to United, but I dug my heels in. I said to myself, 'I need to prove myself here'. The lucky break for me came when Pep left.

"As a player, I needed him to go, but then I loved it when he came back to take over as manager. We've always got on well, despite the fact that we had been set up as rivals. Pep gave me advice and tried to help the situation. Now I know exactly what he expects of me, because he's so good at explaining things. It's all worked out in his head and he communicates his ideas brilliantly.

"I'm a *culé* – this is my club. I'm in the third Champions League final of this Barcelona generation and I wouldn't swap anything that I missed for what I've had here."

Others took different decisions. Cesc Fàbregas comes to mind and his repatriation was a long and thorny issue. Marc Crosas encountered similar obstacles. But there was also Mikel Arteta – a real La Masia product. Basque-born, talented, formed at FC Barcelona, but with quite a queue ahead of him.

"I left Barça because Xavi had just been promoted to the first team and Pep was still there playing, too, so I didn't really see a way forward," said Arteta. "Luis Fernández called me to try life at PSG on loan and I went. He had played in my position, I learned massively from him and it seemed like a good decision."

Xavi's decision to stay has seen him become the most gifted, consistent and visionary player Spain has produced. The stats help make that argument – six league titles and three Champions Leagues with Barça, Euro 2008 winner, a world champion with Spain's Under-19s and with the senior team in 2010. He's also the club's all-time appearance holder and has more than 100 caps – some feat at only 31.

However, it is his complete package of vision, style, steel, technique and will to win which makes him stand alone in Spanish history.

4 — The Machine

Xavi's love affair with the ball began on the concrete covered Plaza del Progreso in Terrassa, about an hour outside the city of Barcelona. It's where he still lives to this day.

Smallest of the gang, the Catalan kid nonetheless ran the show, never letting the ball get away from him on to Galileo Street, which runs alongside that town square where a thousand games were won and lost during a golden childhood.

He was so good that Antoni Carmona, Barcelona's scout in 'the Valleys', not only spotted him aged six, but pestered Barcelona remorselessly until they signed him five years later. It took that long because Xavi was particularly small, although according to his coach, Joan Vilá, "already had that amazing ability to never give the ball away".

By the age of 11 he was in, initially driven to and from training (a two-hour round-trip) by his father, then taking the local train from Terrassa to the Camp Nou. His first pay packet, still aged only 11, was 4000 pesetas (around £20) – he took his mum down to the Rambla in Terrassa and bought her a toaster.

Today, that same Plaza sports a sign which shows a red line through a soccer ball and reads: '*Fútbol Prohibido*'.

"They've made it very nice, very modern, but they've screwed it up for the kids who are like I was – no chance of playing football there now," Xavi told Canal+ when they filmed a documentary. It all constitutes another little reminder that time never passes more quickly than during a golden age. If you blink your eyes and rub them, when you open them again, Xavi will be gone.

He turned 32 in January 2012; he had what Barça's medics called a 'chronic' Achilles tendon problem the season before that and still played nearly 60 times for club and country. He thinks there are four or five more good seasons left in him. This is the time to savour an absolute gem of a player.

From Terrassa town square to Wembley 2011 was a journey filled with learning, intelligence, great passes and good laughs. "In our house, when I was a boy, we lived and breathed Barça," he recalls.

Signing for the youth team meant he got into the matches free, but of course it also meant he wasn't assigned a particular seat. He and the other trainees would turn up 10 minutes before kick-off and find somewhere. "I'd be delighted with myself that I'd found an empty seat and then just before kick-off, some guy would turn up and say, 'That's my seat, kid'. So I'd have to go and find somewhere else and for the really big matches I often ended up sitting on the stairs."

Xavi's home life gave him valuable back-up. "The worst time for a young footballer is between the ages of 15 and 18. That's when all your mates are going to clubs and dating girls and you're stuck at home. My dad played professionally in the second division and a little bit in the Primera and that helped me. He was on top of me all the time – 'Get home by 10! You've got a game tomorrow!' Diet, timetable, attitude – he taught me about professionalism very early. You need to make sacrifices to succeed, but I've also had a lot of luck."

Which is not to ignore his misfortune. Louis van Gaal was his first important senior coach. The Dutchman had the courage to promote the saturnine, intense youngster. However, it was the era when things were falling apart and the dog-days of Van Gaal's reign were so flawed that Barcelona would enter a fallow period of five years without a trophy, in heavy debt and with a badly-structured salary system.

While Van Gaal possesses immense abilities in many areas of football training, he is also brash, stubborn and difficult to be around if he takes against you. He lived off what is called in Spain his *libreta* – that little notebook you could see him scribbling into during the entire match. Xavi reported that: "He used to mark us with stars and show us the book with what it said about us in it."

The two had a turbulent relationship, including a period when Xavi, having established himself as a first-team regular, was made to do hard time back in the Barça B team. "Some of the worst weeks of my career," is how the player has described it. But the absolute worst thing which Van Gaal did to this talented, creative passer was insist that he was, solely, a *pivote*.

Xavi was made to play the defensive role in front of the back four and, while his ability to pick up possession and restart the creative flow for Barça was of a high level, it was shiningly, screamingly obvious that he had to play further forward in the 4-3-3 formation. Coach after coach missed this until the wind of change blew right through the club in 2003, when Joan Laporta was elected president and the Dutch, or Ajax, philosophy was reinstated.

"Until Frank Rijkaard arrived I was a *pivote* for six or seven years," Xavi confirms. "They asked me to try to get up and down and provide assists, but it's difficult from that position. Ten or 15 metres further up the pitch, where I play now, makes it much easier for me.

"I am never afraid of receiving the ball in any situation, I have to get it and pass it 100 times a match. It's a need."

Just think about how obvious his move towards the danger-zone looks in retrospect. Xavi's predecessor was Guardiola – taller and much happier hitting longer-distance passes, but not as nippy across short distances. Since Xavi has been unleashed higher up the pitch, the *pivote* position has been the exclusive territory of tall, strong, tackling players like Edmilson, Rafa Márquez, Yaya Touré, Thiago Motta and Sergio Busquets. Spot the difference between them and the 5ft 7in Xavi? Then why couldn't Van Gaal, Lorenzo Serra Ferrer, Charly Rexach or Raddy Antic before Rijkaard took over?

Stranger still is that Xavi was so inculcated in his *pivote* designation that he even told Frank Rijkaard that he didn't really see himself moving further forward in the team. "I've learned a lot from every coach, but perhaps what will stay with me forever is him convincing me to change position, because he told me he envisaged me giving the final goal-pass much more often."

Xavi is the light and shade of the last 10 years. He is the same outstanding product of the FC Barcelona *cantera* which is now being lauded as football's great, cure-all production line. A product of the La Masia system? Well there's nothing shinier, prettier, more fashionable or sexy. But let's not forget that system's flaws and failures.

Xavi was mistreated, almost sold, played in the wrong position and left brutally frustrated by a lack of standards, vision and direction at the club. I recall Rijkaard's master-stroke in bringing the Ajax-trained Edgar Davids to Barça in the winter market of 2003-04. He made his debut in a flaccid 1-1 home draw against Athletic Bilbao, was patently out of shape but still shone. The link-up play with Ronaldinho defied the Dutchman's reductive 'Pitbull' nickname.

Davids and Ronaldinho were on the same level of understanding. I could see Xavi looking to one side each week and realising, 'So that's what it takes for us to be a winning, hard-nosed team again. And that's exactly how I could be playing'.

Rijkaard's team would have gone eighth that night if defeated and they were already 16 points behind the Liga leaders, Rafa Benítez's Valencia. They were a shambles. But after losing to a David Villa-inspired Zaragoza in the Copa del Rey, Xavi, Davids and Barça then lost only once in 20 matches, 1-0 to Henrik Larsson's Celtic. That was enough to finish second and if Rijkaard's team had won, rather than lost, two of their last three games they'd have been champions.

Another of the strokes of luck which Xavi mentions is that Rijkaard fervently wanted his former Ajax team-mate, Davids, to stay on a permanent deal, but was rebuffed because Inter offered better terms. Rijkaard held a grudge and, when Davids latterly wanted to return, it was he who was rebuffed. Davids' departure allowed Xavi, albeit from the other side of midfield, to take up the attacking, creative link play with Ronaldinho and then Eto'o.

Tucked away in that 20-match run was a win at Madrid, in April, which undoubtedly helped Xavi metamorphose into what he has become. Ghosts were exorcised at the Bernabéu, a marker was laid down and Xavi grew in confidence – putting one over a close, but competitive, amigo.

Los Galácticos – David Beckham, Zinédine Zidane, Luis Figo, Raúl and Roberto Carlos (Ronaldo was injured) – were joint top, seven points clear of Barça. A Real victory would have turned blowtorch heat on co-leaders Valencia and would have cut Rijkaard's surging team adrift. Santi Solari put *Los Blancos* ahead, a very young and floppy-haired Víctor Valdés played unbelievably and eventually Patrick Kluivert equalised.

The exorcised ghost was Figo, who had caused enormous haemorrhaging of self-respect and confidence at the Camp Nou by defecting to Madrid four years previously. A vindictive, shin-high foul on Puyol got the Portuguese sent off and when Xavi played a delightful one-two with Ronaldinho, it allowed him to volley a lob over his buddy, Iker Casillas, for victory.

Barça went on to finish second, Madrid's golden Galáctico idea began to corrode irrevocably. Following that Xavi-inspired defeat, Madrid lost sequentially to Deportivo (2-0) Mallorca (2-3), Murcia (2-1) and Sociedad (1-4). The result, but more importantly the absolute self-belief displayed that night, marked a shift in power, an augmentation of confidence which would be constantly repeated over the next seven years.

"That win, that late goal having been one down, changed the winning mentality with which Madrid had dominated Barça for a few seasons," recalls Xavi.

Before losing 2-0 to Barcelona in April 2010, Iker Casillas admitted: "People ask me every year who I'd take out of their side to give us a better chance of winning and every year I tell them: 'Xavi'. Apart from being my friend, he's just fantastic – his control and use of the ball make him their best player."

The relationship between Casillas and Xavi has been a defining point of Spain's growing football maturity and recent domination of international tournaments. Clearly, Spain's excellence is a product of many factors, but that Casillas, a die-hard *Madridista* who would be behind the goal on the Curva Sur if he wasn't a professional footballer, could be truly close friends with Xavi, a dedicated Barça man and symbol of their modern excellence, has helped mend relations and encouraged Catalans, particularly, to feel differently about the national side.

Xavi is first-generation Catalan, proud of his 'country' but not a radical (his father, Joaquín, is Andaluz). He happily wore a Spain flag while cavorting through the post Euro 2008 celebrations in Madrid – knowing he'd be criticised for it in Catalonia and not giving a stuff.

The two youngsters first met in the build-up to the 1997 Under-17 World Cup in Egypt, where Spain would finish third. In 1995, 15-year-old Xavi had impressed the selectors during the three-day trial for the squad; Casillas was then only 14, but also just a year away from his first call to the Real Madrid first team, when he travelled as reserve goalkeeper for a Champions League match against Rosenborg in Norway. Two extreme talents, two polar opposites in terms of their football sentiments – there could easily have been sparks. Instead, they shared a common enjoyment of pranks, card games (which Casillas always wins) and a hunger for excellence, even perfection.

Xavi's view is this: "In the youth ranks for Spain you

talk more, your goals are identical, but you've done nothing, so I think that fear of not achieving and the drive to succeed makes you share more and thus brings you closer."

Their personalities are complimentary, not identical. Casillas isn't quite as happy-go-lucky as Xavi, but slightly more intense, slightly more driven. I've often heard Xavi admitting that he can be a little lazy about his work initially, but can also be unstoppably determined when he gets his teeth into training, a match or, indeed, any other personal objective.

Casillas, however, has a remorseless work ethic, a need to set an example and hates losing.

However, the Catalan explained to me about the Castilian: "Don't be fooled into thinking that Iker is super-serious, he's a joker and a prankster, but I've been privileged to have been his friend and team-mate since we were 16.

"Iker's a complete *Madridista* and I defend Barça's colours to the death, but it does give off a good image to people that we are friends and team-mates. Ordinary, humble, working-class people get behind the national team when they see our bond; we are just guys who don't know about business or politics, only how to play football well."

Xavi often says: "If we [Barça] had more of Madrid's basic philosophy we'd have won the Champions League far more often. I don't know what exactly that club has, or that badge has, but they have always shown an ability to win even when they don't play well." Or he'll say, "Real Madrid players always have loads of *jeta* [cockiness]". In Casillas he found the former attitude, but an absence of the latter. He liked it and learned from it.

4 — The Machine

The pair of them can also be stubborn when they want to. I was invited to attend the FIFA refereeing supervisor's briefing to the Spain team in their World Cup training camp in Potchefstroom, South Africa. Horacio Elizondo, the Argentine who sent Zinédine Zidane off in the final of Germany 2006, lectured and quizzed Vicente del Bosque's players for an hour while Cesc Fàbregas and Gerard Piqué pinged people's ears, threw rolled up balls of paper at team-mates and held true to the norm that the 'bad lads' sit at the back of the classroom.

At the end, he asked for feedback. Casillas, Spain's captain, ceded to Xavi, a vice captain, who gave it to the official, hot and strong. "We've sat here and listened to you for an hour telling us about how the rules are going to be interpreted, which is fine but you go back and you tell Sepp Blatter this. Tell him that because FIFA aren't watering the pitches anything like sufficiently and because they aren't cutting the playing surface short enough, they are handing a huge premium to defensive football [Spain were one of the last to kick off and there was already a furore about how few goals and how little entertainment the world was watching]. If he wants good football and he wants exciting games, tell him that; tell him to sort the pitches out."

Elizondo took an involuntary half-step backwards as Xavi smouldered. It was a valid message, too.

Casillas and Xavi as shop stewards – the seeds were sown in Nigeria in 1999, when Spain became world youth champions. Despite a massive fever which cost him four kilos and saw him sleeping in a track-suit in 39-degree heat because he was shivering with cold (Xavi hasn't had the best of luck in Africa –

conjunctivitis in Egypt at the FIFA Under-17 World Cup and a horrible animal-hair allergy in Rustenburg in the Confederations Cup) the Barça midfielder had been stellar during Spain's tournament victory. Óscar Tabárez and Michel Platini visited the Spanish camp towards the end of the competition and, according to the Spaniards, gave them the explicit understanding that Xavi had won the vote for the Golden Ball (for best player) and that his team-mate, Gabri, was second. However, at the FIFA gala, not only did Seydou Keita win the Golden Ball, neither Xavi nor Gabri made the podium and Pius Ikedia of Nigeria (who were hammered in the quarter-finals) won silver. The Spain team walked out of the gala and ate in a pizzeria.

Xavi's participation with Spain merits focus in order to understand his success at Barça because it has been central to topping up one of the few under-nourished parts of his game: self-belief.

He was always determined, brilliantly talented, athletic, articulate, visionary – but by no means arrogant. Finishing third, first and second in his first three major international tournaments not only helped him develop and ride out the tough years at Barça, it showed him what he was capable of.

"Winning the [Under-19] World Cup in 1999 was the catalyst for an entire generation of young Spaniards who saw that we could win the biggest prizes; it was a massively important achievement for all of us," he told me during the 2010 World Cup.

Guardiola knew innately what it took to win big prizes. Xavi had the abilities from the outset and initially performed precociously, but suffered from not being coached by a genius, as Guardiola was by Cruyff, and needed to assimilate hard-nosed confidence before not only emulating Guardiola's achievements, but surpassing them.

Celebrating his 100th cap for Spain, Xavi explained: "As soon as I started playing for the youth international sides I could see and feel the difference. You are regarded differently within your own club, opposition coaches take more notice of you and it's more demanding to play against opponents. It's prestigious and it spurs you on – just ask anyone who's not an international but should be. You feel the difference."

Playing for Spain has moulded Xavi and it's only just and proper that he's given back so much happiness and pride to the country. Development at international level has vastly improved what he's been able to do for his club.

Xavi had been outstanding during the title win in 2005 – Barça's first trophy for five years – but the severity of the knee damage he suffered in training early in December that year, when he ruptured cruciate ligaments, would restrict him to a place on the bench for the Champions League final against Arsenal in Paris. By the time the 2006 World Cup came around, he was still not at peak fitness.

There were those who were beginning to think that Xavi was a continuation of an old problem for club and country: talented but fragile. Instead, he was the solution; only circumstances were conspiring to delay it. By the time Euro 2008 came along he was ready to dominate, irrespective of the absolute decline of his club's domestic form.

One interview I did with him at the time spoke volumes about his pride in putting the old 'never mind the quality, feel the width' maxim to the sword. It was the first time that the 'wee men' were beginning to dominate under Luis Aragonés. As soon as I arrived at the tournament, one of the Spanish FA staff told me: "Now that Guti and particularly Raúl are not here, the atmosphere is a million times better – something big could happen this summer."

Iniesta, David Silva, Cesc, Santi Cazorla, Xavi and even David Villa were the relatively diminutive talents who were lifting Spain to quite new levels of performance and reliability. Not one of them is above 5ft 9in, some considerably shorter.

In Spain's group were Russia, coached by Guus Hiddink. Andrey Arshavin had been banned for the first two matches because of a red card during qualification, but returned in the decisive group match against Sweden. The little Russian destroyed the Swedes, helping to make the first goal, hitting the post, scoring the second and claiming the man-of-the-match prize. In the quarter-final he surpassed that performance, again with an assist and a goal, as Holland were pulled apart. Before the Spain v Russia rematch, I sat down to film an interview with Xavi – he was buzzing.

"Another little guy who can rule the world!" he reminded me, half joking, half thrilled. "Do you know, I'd never even heard of Arshavin before this tournament and he's absolutely superb? He's just one more example of how football is for the smart guys, not the big guys who can run all day." Then Xavi ruined poor old Arshavin's day (not for the last time) with a goal and a star performance as Spain romped through the semi-final 3-0.

My point is this: from that day to this, Xavi's

determining performances during the key matches of Barcelona and Spain have been historic. In the Euro 2008 final, in Vienna, he is by far the best player and gives a gorgeous goal assist for Fernando Torres to defeat Germany.

For the first Clásico of the 2008-09 season, it is Xavi's corner Puyol heads down for Eto'o to score. In the second Clásico, Barça go to the Bernabéu and win 6-2 – Xavi walks away with four goal assists. "I've played Madrid many times and never felt so superior to them in any game," he said later.

In the 2009 Copa del Rey final, he runs the midfield and scores the fourth goal against Athletic Bilbao. Against Manchester United later that same month, he's UEFA's man of the match in the Rome Champions League final, sending that delicious, curling cross over for Messi to head the ball past Edwin van der Sar.

In the Spanish Supercup first leg in Bilbao, he makes one for Pedro and scores one in a 2-1 win. Four months later, it's Xavi's chip into the box from which Piqué sets Pedro up to score in the World Club final with two minutes left and Barça are about to win their sixth trophy in a year. The Bernabéu Clásico that season is also a Xavi masterwork – 2-0 and both goal assists are his, one for Messi, one for Pedro.

At the World Cup, he's twice Spain's man of the match and produces a couple of goal assists – the most crucial of which is his corner for Puyol's match-winning header in the semi-final. He not only made the most passes in that tournament, 669, but the most accurate passes, 599, for an 89% success rate.

So good is his tournament that Michel Platini, UEFA president, asks the president of the Spanish FA, Miguel

Ángel Villar, to request Xavi's No 8 shirt from the Soccer City final as a memento. "I couldn't say no!" recalls Xavi.

"I'm delighted that he gifted it to me," Platini replied the day before Wembley 2011. "His football intelligence, his comportment on and off the pitch make him the ideal footballer. I love watching him play."

Perhaps his big-game mentality is a shade more discreet in 2010-11, but he still produces a goal in the 5-0 Clásico win, an assist in the Supercup victory, two more in the Copa del Rey semi-final and that wonderful pass for Pedro's opener against United at Wembley in the Champions League final.

Skip forward to the final of the 2011 Club World Cup in Yokohama and, again, he rises to the moment, with a goal and an assist against Santos.

After that remarkable 5-0 Clásico victory at the Camp Nou on a rainy, freezing November night in 2010, the Casillas-Hernández alliance was still strong enough for their mothers, Carmen and Maria Mercè, to dissect the remarkable result live on Ona FM radio. Maria Mercè Hernández and Carmen Casillas competed to establish that the other woman's son was lovelier, more dignified or more humble than their own. Which is an indication of how sour things eventually became that season when, six months later, Casillas and Xavi were openly disrespecting one another on the pitch during the epic but poisonous four-match Clásico series.

They stopped chatting and texting on their phones and Casillas's version of a peace gesture was to tell the papers: "I shouldn't have gestured to him the way I did, but when we see each other I'll just call him a 'silly bugger' and that'll be it all forgotten."

4 — The Machine

Casillas is one impressive, straight-talking fella – a sulker he is not. It's no coincidence that his promotion to Spain captain has coincided with a time when, irrespective of tournament victories, the squad is both harmonious and perpetually hungry to win the next match.

However, Xavi's stance in the midst of the mayhem struck me much more firmly. As Real Madrid and Barcelona exchanged insults and made claim and counter claim, culminating in each club presenting written complaints to UEFA, he spoke out, firmly.

He called Madrid's claims against Barcelona "lamentable" but he spoke clearly about "these complaints to UEFA", and said it was pathetic that "all these things were going on in the world of football". It seemed clear that he included the Barcelona board in his criticism. Their moaning to the governing body had not impressed him either. What's more, he had the nerve to say so.

During my working time in Spain, Xavi has been a generous, fascinating subject for a number of interviews; someone whose work on the pitch and attitude, or intelligence, off it makes writing and broadcasting about football a joy. He is up there in the pantheon of all-time great European midfielders and, probably, pound for pound, the greatest Spanish footballer.

However, he doesn't even consider himself to be the most talented Spaniard at the Camp Nou. He'll often say that Iniesta is "the most complete Spanish footballer I've played with", which is why Xavi was disappointed, but not bitterly so, to miss out on the Ballon d'Or in January 2011, when he and Barça's other two musketeers were shortlisted, with Messi winning.

Firstly, he thinks Messi is the greatest footballer in history. Secondly, not only does he stress that Iniesta possesses gifts he doesn't have, but 'Andresito' scored the World Cup-winning goal in the time-frame of that award. Probably most importantly, the occupation of the podium by three La Masia products thrilled him.

"What makes me happiest is that players like Leo, Andresito and I prove that talent remains more important than physical power in modern football.

"I'm a team player. Individually, I'm nothing. I play with the best and that makes me a better player. I depend on my team-mates. If they don't find space, I don't find them with the ball and I become a lesser footballer.

"I don't think Leo is in a position to comment on this out of respect for those who have gone before, but I believe he's the best footballer ever. Leo was brought up here. He's Argentinian, but it's like he's from here. Barça is a football school, but it's also a school of life, where you get taught the values that I think are correct and Leo is an alumnus of that process. Here, the players are educated how to behave, to demonstrate respect and I'm very proud to belong to this school."

Xavi has earned a couple of nicknames. The late Andrés Montes, an eccentric radio and television commentator, called him 'Humphrey Bogart'. Some viewers thought it was because Bogart and Xavi shared saturnine looks but, really, it was for Bogart's misquoted 'Play it again, Sam' line from Casablanca. Montes reckoned that, for Spain and Barça, it was always Xavi who would 'play it again, and again and again' as that ball flew from boot to boot.

Most of the players call him 'Maki', which is short

for *maquina*, machine in Spanish. It's such a prosaic, industrial nickname for such an inventive player, but there is a warmth and positivity attached to it. Xavi is always working, always smiling, and always having a playful verbal dig at someone. Perpetual motion. His passes come off an incessant production line. He's always prompting and prodding team-mates into movement and into situations where they can damage the opposition.

Xavi's movement is like a kind of reverse sheepdog trick – instead of penning a flock in to an enclosed space, his darting, nipping and barking is about spreading them around the field, into unexplored, unpredictable spaces. Why no-one came up with 'Shep' before I can't explain.

"During a match, most of the other guys shout 'Maquina' or 'Maki' when they want me to pass them the ball, apart from Messi and Alves who just shout 'Xavi'," he said.

"If I don't get the ball for two minutes, I'm like, 'Hey! Guys! Look for me! I'm free!' There would be no point playing otherwise. I'd be happier staying at home. I must have at least 100 touches of the ball every match. If I had to go back to the dressing room with only 50 I'd be ready to kill someone."

So, there you have Xavi – fun to watch, fun to be around. Sublime player, top man. A footballer who epitomises what has gone right at FC Barcelona over the last couple of decades.

"I've been a Barça fan since I can remember being alive," he reflected. "What's happening right now, how we are playing – it's just a permanent fiesta for anyone who supports this club.

"Over the years I've bought my mum watches, jewellery ... all sorts. But she loves football, so probably the best thing I've ever bought her is her Barça membership and season ticket so that she can watch all this happening.

"I am a romantic about football and I agree with Johan Cruyff's argument that we are fighting a battle for the soul of beautiful football. I have a lot of respect for José Mourinho, but the coaches who'll go down in the history books are Guardiola, Sacchi, Cruyff and Alex Ferguson. These are the guys who have gone that bit further and reinvented the game. They're the winners."

DANI ALVES: STYLE, INC.

WHEN BARCELONA BOUGHT Dani Alves for €30m in 2008, a Greek chorus dissented at the price. What immediately became apparent was that, above and beyond his evident football skills, there was extra value in his joie de vivre, which would have a major impact in the dressing room.

He is irrepressible, funny, full of the joys of life – things that were conspicuously absent from the Camp Nou by the end of the Frank Rijkaard reign. Obviously, none of the money they paid Sevilla was originally intended to go on witty repartee, dance moves or that infectious smile – they were bonuses.

Barcelona fought off Chelsea and other clubs willing to outbid them for the right-back. They did so because their analysis told them Alves was a player who could mesh perfectly with the speed of thought and movement that Lionel Messi was beginning to demonstrate. They have been proven correct. It is hard to argue that there is another footballer in this squad who links better with Messi than the Brazilian.

Alves' marauding runs down the right get all the attention, and then the focus is often on whether the cross or shot at the end is productive enough. That risks under-estimating other parts of his game.

He loves inter-passing in tiny spaces, particularly if it becomes a test of who has the quickest feet and minds. He and Messi frequently play this game of 'do-you-really-think-you-can-box-us-in?' against three or four defenders, and usually win. The tighter the space, the more the two little entertainers relish it.

Dani Alves: Style, Inc.

They also sometimes cut through opposition teams covering massive swathes of the pitch and one of the best examples of that came in Barça's 5-0 demolition of Real Sociedad in December 2010. Messi and Alves move the ball between them from near halfway to just outside the six-yard box, from where Messi scores. They exchange passes three times in the tightest of situations. Hordes of Sociedad defenders can't stop them.

The two of them produced another knife-through-butter move when Barcelona beat Madrid 3-1 from 1-0 down at the Bernabéu in December 2011. For their side's third goal, Messi breaks out of midfield and feeds the overlapping Brazilian, who crosses expertly for Cesc Fàbregas to head home at the back post.

Everything about the Brazilian – his pugnacious attitude, his physique – is as if he had been scouted and developed within the *fútbol base* system at Barcelona. He is the same size and shape as Xavi, Iniesta and Messi. He has the same belief – shared by everyone at the club – that small, talented footballers are better than bigger, stronger automatons.

Even after the game is over, Alves delivers. Sometimes he'll pitch up in the mixed zone to talk to media wearing a sensational velvet smoking jacket, winkle-pickers, a white-on-white shirt and pencil-thin tie. Style, Inc. He's also the guy who, when I asked him about Xavi, produced this fantastic quote: "You and me, we live on the same planet but Xavi's from another world."

Pep Guardiola's team would have been less adventurous without the purchase of Dani Alves – and the rest of its players would have had a lot less fun.

5 – THE THEORY OF EVOLUTION

"When Cruyff and I arrived to take over at Barça, we decided to install the football which inspired us. The football of Rinus Michels. Make no mistake — it cost us to achieve."
— Charly Rexach

I F THE 175,000 FC Barcelona members, or *socios*, queued up in an orderly line, night after night, to massage his tired feet, cook his dinner and tuck him into bed; if they carried his golf clubs round Montanyà's hilly 18 holes; if they devoted 50% of their annual salary to him … it still wouldn't be anywhere near enough to repay the debt those who love this club owe Johan Cruyff.

Without him, there would be no Pep Guardiola, no Messi, no Xavi and no Andrés Iniesta. They would have been judged to be too slow, too small – table footballers.

The genius from Amsterdam created the conditions which allowed these incredible players to be recognised and to become central to FC Barcelona's values. Without Cruyff, this story simply wouldn't exist.

Even the latest, greatest, Barcelona era has his DNA running through it: the way they train and play, how they recruit players and staff and why entertainment falls only slightly behind victory in their list of priorities. Therefore, it seems utterly remarkable how many modern Barça fans say such derogatory things about the man who was born Hendrik Johannes Cruijff.

Cruyff gets so much grief from the kind of Catalans who, historically, have claimed vociferously that they ached for FC Barcelona to overhaul Madrid and conquer Europe but were content to continue underachieving so it would fuel their loser's mentality and allow them to keep on moaning.

Perhaps a man who counts "If I wanted you to understand I'd have explained it better" among his maxims can neither complain nor care much about the fact that so many people misunderstand him and maul his reputation. Perhaps. Usually, it's those who know less than nothing about football, or who are jealous, that are snide or hysterical about him.

One example of how Cruyff inspires this baffling ill-feeling is the relationship between the Dutchman, a footballing genius in both playing and analytical terms, and Barça's current president, Sandro Rosell. They are like cat and dog, if the cat is a hungry panther and the dog is a bull-mastiff trained to attack on sight.

Early in Rosell's reign, Cruyff commented in response to a deal to make the Qatar Foundation Barça's shirt sponsor that: "He and his board are demolishing the respect in which FC Barcelona was held around the world. Creating is hard work, destroying is easy."

Feelings had been pushed to boiling point when, almost as soon as Rosell took over, his board announced that the club's statutes didn't provide for the position of honorary president. Joan Laporta had given Cruyff that role – as Real Madrid had to Don Alfredo Di Stéfano, Cruyff's equivalent at the Bernabéu – in March 2010, just before departing the presidency. He did so in full anticipation that Rosell, his one-time ally, but now critic and opponent, would sweep the coming presidential elections.

Just a couple of weeks after winning a landslide victory, Rosell's board made it high-priority business to propose stripping Cruyff of the title, so that general elections for the 'new' position could be held. The very next morning, while Rosell conducted a press conference, Cruyff marched into the Camp Nou offices and handed back the badge of honour which had been in his possession since April. "These things take a long time to earn but cost little to hand back," said the

Dutchman. "If this position is so important that it took priority in the new board's first meeting, then it's obvious that I'm a thorn in someone's side, so I'm getting out of the way."

Rosell commented: "Obviously anyone would do the same. If you find you are in a non-existent position then of course you hand the insignia back. Nobody wants to be in a position which doesn't actually exist. I guess he's looked the whole thing over with lawyers."

However much the two men are at 'daggers drawn' – a few months later Cruyff raised the issue of what he claimed were unpaid fees to his foundation to help disabled kids – it was an undignified chapter in recent Barcelona history.

I believe Cruyff's contribution to FC Barcelona dwarfs that of any other individual. Twice the Dutchman has made a big splash at the Camp Nou, in 1973 and 1988, first as a player and then as a coach.

His playing time at the Camp Nou was less spectacular than his time as a coach. However, it did contain one remarkable, enduring moment which again suggests that *azar* – fate, chance or fluke – has an enormous influence on how the greatest achievements develop.

On February 17, 1974, Cruyff inspired Barça to a historic 5-0 win over Real Madrid at the Santiago Bernabéu. In the last year of the life of El Caudillo Franco, the despot who had ruled Spain with an iron fist since 1939, this match was, for many Catalans, the final nail in his coffin and that of their subjugation. Real Madrid had a strong association with Franco throughout his reign, during which time El Clásico became far more than a game.

How important was Cruyff to that achievement?

The first league match between the sides that season, at the Camp Nou two weeks before Cruyff made his full debut for Barça, ended 0-0; the Copa del Rey final at the end of that season, again not featuring Cruyff, was a 4-0 thrashing in favour of Madrid. Except for the only time the Dutchman played against them that season, Madrid patently had the measure of their Catalan rivals.

Schoolboys such as Joan Laporta and Sandro Rosell were transfixed and inspired by the 5-0 match and it remains a sore point between the clubs today. Cruyff only played in it because of his singular vision of how things should be handled. Firstly, Ajax had tried to sell Cruyff to Madrid and had agreed a price, but the player just said 'no'. "I don't like things being done behind my back … and, to be fair, I've always liked a little battle," is his explanation of what happened.

Then, midway through that first title-winning season with Barça, came Cruyff's first Clásico. His first child, Jordi, was due to be born on the matchday – February 17. Cruyff explained: "I'll never forget that game as long as I live. It was the date that Dani [his wife] was supposed to give birth, but she and I agreed to bring the birth forward by a week and that she'd have a Caesarean section so that I could play.

"I honestly hadn't fully realised how much the Barcelona sentiments were influenced by a game against Madrid until that day, but the impact of winning by that scoreline taught me a lot about Barcelona and probably involved me with this club for the rest of my life."

No Caesarean section? Almost certainly no 5-0. Without that, would Cruyff have been so irrevocably tied to the club? Would Laporta or Rosell have followed their current paths?

While he played and coached, trophies were won, but it's almost as much for the ripples as the splash that Cruyff should be venerated instead of moaned about and, in some extreme cases, loathed in Catalonia.

His great achievement has been to install not only a mentality at the Camp Nou, but a backbone. No matter who comes and goes – players, coaches, presidents – it's the case that if FC Barcelona select players (of whatever age) as they do now and train them as they do now, they won't be far away from being attractive, successful and hard to play against. And make no mistake, the world is still watching the fruition of seeds planted in 1988.

No Cruyff, no Dream Team. No Cruyff, no coordinated and prolific *cantera* trained to play thrilling 4-3-3 football. No Cruyff, no Joan Laporta (the club's most successful president, as I write). No Cruyff, no Frank Rijkaard and the resuscitation of a club suffocating in its own stupidity. No Cruyff, no Guardiola. The player-turned-coach maintains he wouldn't even have been given the chance to stake a claim for a first-team spot had it not been for the visionary faith of the Dutchman and his lieutenant, Charly Rexach.

FC Barcelona is stocked with Cruyff disciples at coaching, development and administrative levels: Guardiola, Andoni Zubizarreta, Guillermo Amor, Eusebio Sacristán, Juan Carlos Unzué, Óscar García, Tito Vilanova and Rexach are key examples. Another, Sergi Barjuán, left in July 2011.

What about the repeated criticisms of the Amsterdammer? Cruyff has often confronted the idea that he cares too much about money. The concept is surely risible and hypocritical, given that footballers with a tiny fraction of his talent are paid £100,000 per week and more. Moreover, all of the Dutchman's critics, put in his position, would probably profiteer with still greater abandon than he does.

There is an anecdote from his playing career to sum him up. He has a healthy regard for his own worth, not an over-inflated one like many modern footballers. And he can be innovative when it comes to benefiting from it.

In the early 1980s, after spells in the US and at Levante in La Liga, Cruyff returned to Ajax as a director, but then pulled on his boots again. He led them out of decline to trophies, notably the 1982-83 double. However, Ajax president Ton Harmsen thought 36-year-old Cruyff was past it and refused to give him a new contract.

Cruyff opted for the ultimate two fingers. He debunked to Feyenoord, Ajax's most bitter enemies. They didn't have the finances to pay his existing wage, so he thought up the ingenious scheme that Feyenoord, who had been averaging crowds of 10,000, pay him a proportion of any extra attendance once he joined. Cruyff proposed that income from the first 1,000 extra fans who paid to come and see the team would stay with the club. From then on, for every 1,000 extra fans who came to De Kuip, he and Feyenoord would split the ticket money down the middle. If 20,000 fans came, 4,500 paid their ticket money to Cruyff.

He loves the punchline that, "We normally filled the stadium with 40,000 people and it was an economic success for both the club and me. Better still, we won the cup and the league, so I enjoyed myself quite well that season".

As for charging media for his time, the practice started when he was a player and bombarded with interview requests. He instituted a system where he would fend off the majority of the requests – which came from organisations with little interest other than piggy-backing on his fame for their own financial gain – by asking for interview fees. Those people or organisations he knew, liked or needed would be treated differently – put in the request, wait your turn and then have immense fun (and sometimes an immense test) speaking with the great man. No charge. To a great extent, that system continues – normal access if you are a credible, known football medium, or if his Johan Cruyff Foundation to help disabled children via sport can be publicised.

During the Laporta era, Cruyff was offered a position as what is called an *asesor* in Spanish football. It is the equivalent of a consultant. Cruyff turned it down and explained in his *La Vanguardia* column: "Laporta offered me that post, but I said that it's a thankless one. You work at it, but in the end all you get is criticism without having actually taken the decision yourself. When I talk with Frank [Rijkaard] or Txiki [Begiristain, sports director] I give them my opinion and tell them what I'd do in their place. Usually, they are chats about hypothetical situations, but if it's something concrete and they don't agree with my view, they always return to their original decision. That's how it should be.

"Laporta, as my friend, can ask me as much advice as he cares to, but nothing could be further from the truth than saying that I'm behind all the sporting decisions of this regime."

However, during Laporta's presidency, his counsel would prove at least as valuable as if he were in charge and taking decisions. Perhaps even more so.

Above all, the thorn in the side of his critics is that he is Johan Cruyff. He's Dutch, not Catalan, and there are some in that part of the world who are utterly reactionary in their belief in Catalan superiority.

Moreover, some hate the fact that he's had so much power, or at least influence, without responsibility. Cruyff hasn't held a formal club post with salary and a contract since he was sacked in May 1996, but his vision, advice and criticism has steered the club for vast chunks of the intervening years.

Thirdly, his lifelong habit of telling it exactly as he sees it earns him enemies. His vision is not only brilliant, it is often diametrically opposed to everyone else's and if someone has earned his disfavour he can be mercilessly scathing, on television or in his enthralling newspaper columns.

However, the fundamental decisions he took when he returned to this club as coach remain his most important legacy – ahead of the solitary league title he won as a player in 1974, or even the great psychological liberation he gave FC Barcelona by leading them to the European Cup in 1992.

Of course, the crowning moment of Cruyff's playing career should have arrived at the 1974 World Cup. Holland were the neutrals' choice, the undisputed masters of Total Football. Famously, they blew it. Years later, in the spring of 2004, I asked Cruyff about that scarring experience. Whatever pain he feels at having lost a World

Cup final to Holland's most hated rivals, Germany, is now long hidden after decades of talk and, presumably, regret. Nonetheless, his answer was interesting: "I don't mind, in fact it might have been better what happened. We played beautiful football all the way to the final, we brought Holland and the Dutch style of football to the attention of the world and, because we lost, it generated huge amounts of sympathy and support for our brand of how to play. Perhaps there was more good than bad in losing that way."

His words might easily sound self-justifying, even delusional, but one thing must be understood: Cruyff has always stuck to the basic principle that there is a right and a wrong way to approach football. To him it's essential that the game must be played with intelligence, style, technical skill and vision. His bible preaches that if your first touch and your use of possession are top-class, then winning games or trophies will follow naturally.

His work at the Camp Nou between 1988 and 1996 can be broken into three basic sections. He won trophies, reshaped youth development but, above all, embedded beliefs which remain not only part of Barcelona's DNA but now part of the wider footballing culture in Spain, too.

The trophies? They live in history. Leagues often won on the last day of the season and usually at the cost of massive humiliation to Real Madrid, the Goliath to Cruyff's David. Four UEFA trophies, the most important of which came in defeating a good, but less clinical, Sampdoria side starring Luca Vialli and Roberto Mancini to win the 1992 European Cup.

The football philosophy is his most important work.

5 — The Theory of Evolution

The concepts that are fundamental to Barcelona's success were completely alien when he introduced them.

When he was signed from Ajax in 1988, Cruyff was coming to a club which had won the Spanish title only twice in 28 years. Real Madrid were in the midst of the Emilio Butragueño-Hugo Sánchez stranglehold on La Liga when *La Quinta del Buitre* won five straight titles. *La Quinta del Buitre* (The Vulture Gang, a play on Butragueño's name) was a fleeting and glorious moment when the youth team graduates, Butragueño, Manuel Sanchís, Martín Vázquez, Míchel and Miguel Pardeza, were the heartbeat (and heartthrobs) of Real Madrid – high-quality footballers, home-bred and adored by the fans. Sound remarkably like a modern club which you could name?

In the weeks prior to Cruyff's firm hand coming on the tiller, Barça had finished sixth, but only two points off 10th position, despite having been European Cup finalists under Terry Venables just two years previously.

Midway through that first season, the coach revealed what he had inherited. "The past was filled with hate and envy between almost everyone at the club. On the day I started, there were a number of players who wanted to have fights about the past. I had to tell them that the trainer is the boss in the dressing room, not the players. However strange this might sound, that was news to them.

"On both sides [board and players] there was a lack of discipline, so bad that the board had a sort of meeting room in the dressing room."

So, there was plenty of conflict for this remarkable man who seems to feed off confrontation, gaining energy and increasing in certainty that his point of view is right. However, away from the spitting and snarling which became a motif for his early months, Cruyff immediately began laying down some vital foundations for both the immediate and long-term future. To explain them, you need to know Charly Rexach.

Like Gerard Piqué, Rexach was born in the posh-boy neighbourhood of Pedralbes – it's a conclave of embassies, private colleges, a royal tennis club and, subsequently, the home of the king and queen's daughter.

Languid but highly-skilled, Rexach scored close to 200 goals from his position on the right wing in more than 600 matches for Barça, winning his only league title when Cruyff arrived in 1973-74. Both men enjoyed being coached by the brilliant, innovative Rinus Michels, who was Barcelona head coach between 1971 and '75. Each was a disciple of Total Football.

So, Rexach became Cruyff's right-hand man in 1988. Eventually, like Brian Clough and Peter Taylor or John Lennon and Paul McCartney, they would fall out bitterly. However, the Catalan's contribution to the club has also been immensely significant.

It was Rexach who fought to persuade the board that Leo Messi's diminutive size was a problem dwarfed by his talent. He, too, ensured that the youth system held true to Cruyff's values when the Dutchman had long been sacked.

When they first returned to Camp Nou in 1988, they illuminated darkness. Rexach explained: "When Cruyff and I arrived to take over at Barça, we decided to install the football which inspired us. The football of Rinus Michels. Make no mistake – it cost us to achieve.

"We inherited a culture at the Camp Nou where the

fans whistled and jeered at a defender if he passed the ball back to the keeper, or at a winger if he reached the byeline but didn't cross the ball – whether there was anybody there to take advantage of the chance or not.

"Our original task was to find and sign players who had the correct philosophy and skill set and to educate the ones we inherited, but a by-product was that we educated our fans. Everything flowed once we taught everyone that there was a baseline philosophy and we would not bend from it."

Nowadays, the Camp Nou is football-snooty. Barça players will often tell you they wish the crowd had a British or Irish football mentality – come to the ground, roar the team on tribally from start to finish and give the opposition a hard time. However, those who have been there long enough accept that what they have to do is both win and put on a show.

Back in 1988, not only did the Camp Nou crowd whistle its disapproval if the ball wasn't lumped forward quickly enough, there were many decision-makers around the club who "didn't think it was possible to play our way", according to Rexach.

With the youth system not yet productive, Cruyff and Rexach set about signing artfully. That season, they added some vital footballers, all of whom fitted the one/two-touch Ajax mould and who either pressed superbly or opened space well – Txiki Begiristain, Eusebio, Julio Salinas and José Mari Bakero, all in the plenitude of their career and all vital in winning two European trophies and two league titles in Cruyff's first four years. Others, such as Hristo Stoichkov, Ronald Koeman and Michael Laudrup would be added.

They built a team which, initially, had footballers

who knew the technical requirements of their position and how it related to those of their team-mates. Then, when the team contained multi-talented performers such as Laudrup, Begiristain, Stoichkov, Amor, and Guardiola, Cruyff began to ask them to switch positions mid-match, so that Stoichkov, principally a central striker, would play on the wing and Laudrup would become what is known as the 'false' centre forward. Full-backs became wingers, the *pivote*, in front of the back four, dropped in as an auxiliary centre-half – it was fluid, it made marking Barcelona's players very difficult and it brought success.

Neither Cruyff, nor Rexach ever claimed they were inventing anything. Both men were open about the fact that they were adapting and evolving concepts that they had been taught by Michels, and which many before that believe were introduced to Europe by the great Hungarian side of the early 1950s, but they were pioneering in their way. Cruyff fostered an atmosphere where experimentation, risks and lateral thinking were all encouraged, so long as the basic template of touch, technique, maintaining possession and stretching the pitch with quick circulation of the ball was maintained.

Most of the players who performed so well in that 'Dream Team' era are now inclined to admit that the present team is better in individual skills, more robust defensively, has a better mentality and also possesses, in Messi, a resource which is incomparably better than any of the players Cruyff had. However, Cruyff and Rexach were re-educating star footballers with a system of rules, particularly in regard to positional play, which was strict, innovative and which would outlast them all. Some understood the positional, one-touch, space-creating, overlapping, space-squeezing rules slightly better than others; Koeman, whose education in Holland had been first class, was one. Guardiola was another, partly because he had three years in what was now Cruyff's *cantera* before joining the first team.

However, compared to the teams coached by Guardiola, there wasn't a clutch of players who had come through the La Masia training school, where they had been schooled in these principles since the age of 11. The Cruyff-Rexach era must initially have felt like a handful of men against the world – in front of an initially hostile public, faced by a doubting media, at a club run by a president with an itchy trigger-finger and with footballers who sometimes thought they knew better.

The sporting infrastructure of La Masia had been functioning for only seven years when Cruyff arrived. That glorious, craggy old farmhouse where talented kids such as Guardiola were to find a footballing home had stood next to Camp Nou for centuries, but had been used for myriad other purposes.

It's a rather mournful place now. The farmhouse has been emptied of all its residents, who moved to the Ciudad Deportiva Joan Gamper , and the single pitch upon which generations of footballers have trained since the late 1950s has been ripped up for parking.

Barcelona inaugurated La Masia as a residence for young players who had been scouted from outside the metropolitan area and who couldn't be asked to travel to and from the Camp Nou for training every day. It was elitist and it was dreamed up before Cruyff's return to Barça in 1988, but when he came back, it was still evolving. The club was far more disposed to buying big-name footballers and in Josep Lluís Núñez they had a Basque, not a Catalan, as president.

When Cruyff arrived it took no time to discover that he disagreed, fundamentally, with the way in which the Barcelona youth system was run. He insisted it was nonsensical that all the age-category teams were being trained in a playing system which was particular to their specific coach. There was no FC Barcelona credo. What was then 13 youth levels under the first team could mean 13 different playing styles and kids having to re-learn every year.

Cruyff told his employers that a) every youth level must be trained based on the same concepts and in the same 3-4-3 formation b) the top kids needed to be pushed out of their comfort zone and played at an age group one, or even two years ahead, and c) that those *perlas de la cantera*, the jewels of the youth system, needed accelerated promotion into the first team.

They worked on positional play, one- or at most two-touch circulation of the ball, the concept of the sweeper-keeper, squeezing space – all principles which have thrived under Guardiola and Rijkaard. This strategy, plus an adherence to all his teams playing attacking, creative, rapid football based on pressing and accurate passing, is his most enduring legacy. However, Cruyff's reign was to end in acrimony.

The first time I went to work in Barcelona on a football story was in 1996. Scotland were playing in the semi-finals of the European Under-21 Championships.

It was a world-class field – France had Patrick Vieira, Claude Makélélé, Robert Pirès, Sylvain Wiltord; for Italy, Gigi Buffon, Fabio Cannavaro, Francesco Totti, Alessandro Nesta, Alessio Tacchinardi; Spain's team included Gaizka Mendieta, Raúl, Iván de la Peña, Jordi Lardín, Aitor Karanka, Fernando Morientes and Óscar García. Those players should have been enough to command attention, but there was another story in town. Ten days before Scotland's first match, up at the Olympic Stadium on Montjuïc, Cruyff had been sacked.

Prior to the appointment of Guardiola, the average tenure of a Barça coach was just over two years. Cruyff had reigned for eight.

There were many causes of his downfall: his relationship with the president, Núñez, had always been tainted by mutual disdain and resentment. The architect of youth development at the Camp Nou was being hammered by the home crowd and the Catalan media for what they thought was a quality gap between unsuccessful signings and more La Masia product. If the first team was struggling, and there hadn't been a trophy for coming up to two years, the locals wanted all the promising kids promoted instantly. Cruyff used youth players such as Albert Celades, brothers Roger and Óscar García plus De la Peña, but it wasn't enough, and so, on Saturday, May 18, vice president Joan Gaspart, the man who had been sent out by FC Barcelona to welcome Cruyff at El Prat airport as the world's first million dollar player back in 1973, was now sent down by Núñez into the dressing room and the Dutchman was sacked where he stood – as his players began to file in for training that morning.

"We haven't done anything abnormal, nothing which will go down in history as a bad decision," Gaspart told the media. He was wrong and, by 2001, he thought differently.

Reviewing what happened, Gaspart, who was to trade his status as an effective vice president for a woeful and brief presidency, confessed that: "I must admit that the way we sacked Cruyff lacked class.

"He remains a distinguished *socio* and he'll always be welcome at this club. You can only make peace if both parties want it, and I do."

For his part, Cruyff defended Gaspart two years later when some members were proposing legal action against him for the sale of some land near the new training ground. But being defended by Cruyff, if you are his enemy, can be less than comforting.

"After 22 years of him doing bad work, I don't see why he needs to be crucified now, so long as he's done nothing illegal. If the deal hasn't gone well, that's no reason to string him up," was the Dutchman's rather mixed message.

That fateful 1995-96 season was a strange one. Barça finished third, Real Madrid sixth and Cruyff bickered on and off with Núñez for a considerable amount of time. The net gain over the next three seasons was undoubtedly positive – seven trophies across the reigns of Bobby Robson and Louis van Gaal. However, Cruyff's last season saw the team reach the UEFA Cup semi-final, the Copa del Rey final and be beaten to the league title by a terrific Atlético Madrid side. The foundations were already in place.

Also, Cruyff claims that it was the fact that the board almost sacked him earlier that season, in January 1996, which torpedoed the signing of Zinédine Zidane from Bordeaux. "We try to sign in January for the following season and we contacted Zidane, who was available for $3.5m," he recalls. "I'm proud that giving my word was usually enough to get a player to commit, but in March I had to phone Zidane and Aron Winter to tell them that I couldn't ask them to hold on any longer when I didn't know whether they [Barça] would sack me or I would have to leave. I was the man at the club responsible for all the signings and I wasn't in a position go through with them."

Two years later, Zizou's brace of headers in the World Cup final made history and by 2002 he was clipping home a goal in the Champions League semi-final at the Camp Nou to help eliminate Barcelona – beginning the end of the Gaspart presidency – en route to that fabulous winning goal in the Hampden final. For Real Madrid.

One player, coincidentally, who played a straight bat on Cruyff's controversial sacking in May 1996 was Pep Guardiola. The club captain said: "Confrontation between the coach and board is hardly desirable and nor is it helpful that in the squad there are some who are pro-Cruyff and some who are anti," Guardiola told the Catalan media, very promptly after the drama broke.

"We have given the coach all our help since he's been here and if a new coach comes in now we'll do the same for him, because winning is the key thing we are here to achieve, but I'll remain indebted to Cruyff because he is the one who gave me the opportunity to play here and he has taught me a great many things."

In the spring of 2011, Guardiola gave an interview to his former club, Brescia, for a DVD to mark their centenary. He explained that after a certain time at a burn-out club like Barça, people can become irretrievably tired of each other and change can be vital to stay fresh and focused. You can hear echoes of what Guardiola learned way back during that crazy, volatile time in Barcelona's history.

The day after Cruyff's sacking, Barça beat Celta Vigo 3-2, Jordi Cruyff crossing for Óscar García's equalising goal, and the president received a monumental barracking, plus the traditional Spanish *pañolada* – the action of waving white hankies to show disapproval. Amid the confetti of white linen was a banner from one fan who seemed to believe Cruyff shared more than his initials with another miracle worker: "Forgive them Johan, for they know not what they do."

Almost as bad as his son, Jordi, being left in a poisonous situation on the playing staff was the fact that Rexach chose to stay as caretaker manager for the remaining couple of matches. Cruyff took that badly and their friendship ruptured.

He was gone, never to return in a formal post, but Cruyff's influence would redouble, simply because of the brutality of his sacking and the loss felt at his departure.

Cruyff's work in the 1970s, 1980s and 1990s had already begun to influence the team that would come later; that of Xavi, Iniesta and Messi.

Their ethos of how to play football had been planted at the Camp Nou by Cruyff. His promotion, coaching and education of Pep Guardiola contributed massively to the beliefs and behaviour of Guardiola the manager.

Cruyff explained in 2009: "When he was young, Guardiola didn't have the physique to make it at the top and without such intelligence as he possesses he'd not even have made it to our *Juvenil* [Under-18] side.

"Over his career this has been an advantage to him. We talked at great length about his vision and his organisational skills and, thanks to them, our team won many prizes. We also talked about how to mini-mise his deficiencies and he handled all that process just magnificently. After his Barça career he spread his wings, learned elsewhere and he's back with expe-rience, huge intelligence and that tendency of his to work obsessively. One day he'll have to take his foot off the pedal just a little or he'll end up ill, but for now he's the perfect model for Barcelona."

Cruyff reshaped the structure and content of FC Barcelona's youth development. He also made an enormous impact on a young, belligerent Catalan lawyer called Joan Laporta. And some alumni, who would go on to win Champions League medals under Rijkaard and Guardiola, were already in the *cantera*.

On the day Cruyff was sacked, 16-year-old Xavi Hernández was part of the Barça youth system and already had five years of La Masia training under his belt. Andrés Iniesta was being scouted. Víctor Valdés had already spent four years in the youth system at the Camp Nou, and a 17-year-old called Carles Puyol had just been scouted and signed – to play as a winger.

Cruyff's system was not only able to train players bril-liantly once the right ones were selected, but the criteria Barça used while scouting had changed. As a result, the club was now consistently choosing the best young players, or at least the correct ones for their system.

Cruyff's next important present to Barça arrived vicariously.

It was Laporta's outright indignation that his hero had been treated so shoddily that led him to fight elec-toral campaigns, eventually win the club presidency and kick-start the greatest era of the club's history.

When Laporta won his dramatic presidential victory in 2003, FC Barcelona were in a pitiful state. The last trophy had come in 1999, the debt was enormous, revenue generation was flaccid and qualification for the Champions League was becoming more and more difficult to achieve – Barça were in a tailspin.

The deal was sold to the electorate on three important tickets. Firstly, that Laporta, the president, Sandro Rosell, the sports vice president, Marc Ingla, the marketing vice president, and Ferran Soriano, the money maker, were components of a young, dynamic, Catalan A-Team. Secondly, that Cruyff was behind them. A vote for Laporta was effectively a vote for the Dutchman to come to Barça's rescue for the third time and in a third different role – consigliere. Finally, the third proposition was the Beckham sleight of hand, which we will slow down later so the trickery can be seen with the naked eye.

Having won, Laporta and his board found that Guus Hiddink's wages were too expensive and that Ajax's buy-out clause for Ronald Koeman was also too rich for Catalan tastes. New era, two failures to recruit a top-class coach. It was getting embarrassing. Cruyff was in the perfect position to recommend Rijkaard and Laporta trusted him, implicitly, but it didn't seem an obvious choice.

Rijkaard's work with Holland had been okay, but his single season with Sparta Rotterdam led in 2002 to the first relegation in the club's history and he had been fired. However, Cruyff not only knew the guy well, but used his intuition to detect that his former pupil possessed qualities which would invigorate Barcelona.

Speaking in 2011, he said that for 'inexperienced'

coaches such as Rijkaard and Guardiola there were particular criteria to take into account. "The coach of any world-class club needs to be aware of so many things, including what the club stands for and how to convey that to the public and the press. He also has to know his public, as well as managing the dressing room. In truth, the football really only accounts for 40 per cent of his work. All the decisions relating to who plays and how they will play are affected by all the other knowledge the coach already has. And what does experience consist of? Experience of the dressing room, of working under intense pressure, facing a big game. If you have dealt with all of that as a player, then you have a huge amount of experience."

The argument that Pep Guardiola's Barcelona would be less well equipped, less successful and might not even exist had there not been Frank Rijkaard's Barcelona, is both established and clear. Players such as Valdés, Iniesta and Messi were not only promoted, but given their first real experience of success and what it costs under Rijkaard. The Camp Nou fell in love with the 4-3-3, pressing and ice-hockey speed of passing – Cruyff-style football all over again. FC Barcelona, as an institution, rediscovered that winning was sweet. Rijkaard became a visionary appointment. He is so utterly different from Cruyff that it's hard to know where to begin, but despite some extremely volatile times between the pair, it was a sound move when the decision makers, Laporta, Rosell and Begiristain, sought and received counsel on signing the 40-year-old.

Back in 1991, Cruyff described the impact he'd had on Rijkaard the footballer. "One of the nicest developments has been Frank. You could say that I had a tough confrontation with him, but how he's now play-ing with AC Milan is beautiful. At one time, we had to use Wim Jansen to keep Rijkaard awake, to make sure he was always working. Some people need to be hit once to understand. Then, that little bit of extra quality they have will take them to the top."

Confirming to Laporta that Rijkaard was more than adequate for the job was not Cruyff's only vital input during those early 'fightback' months. His tenure needed to be underpinned.

In December 2003, Barça played Juande Ramos's Málaga at La Rosaleda and lost 5-1. Hysteria ensued. Papers, radio, fans, television, and almost certainly players too, all expected Rijkaard's sacking. In the newspapers you could read about a 'disaster', a 'foot-balling cancer'. Málaga's fans had chanted "*a Segunda, a Segunda* (going down, going down)" throughout the second half.

Next up, four days later, was the Camp Nou Clásico. Madrid, starring Ronaldo, Figo and Beckham, won 2-1 – *Los Blancos'* first victory at the Camp Nou on league duty for 20 years. An awful week for *culés*.

Cruyff told Laporta that Real Madrid looked frag-ile, not as good as their 13-point lead on Barcelona. And he said: "A coach, no matter how good, is con-demned to disaster if his team shows a poor attitude. At Málaga and in the first half against Madrid, that's what happened. If this team shows the attitude it did in the second half, then teams will find it hard to play against Barça."

Let me emphasise that last bit. Cruyff saw and com-municated something positive (and something which would almost instantly be proved 100% correct) in a humiliating 5-1 defeat. Not bluster, not bravado. X-ray vision.

However, by January, Barça were still 13th, Patrick Kluivert was their top scorer with a mere five goals, they had dropped 17 of 27 home points and along came an away match at Racing Santander.

Rüştü, Reiziger, Puyol, Márquez, Gio van Bronckhorst, Xavi, Cocu, Iniesta, Luis Enrique, Ronaldinho and Sergio García were utterly destroyed – 3-0 going on 6-0. Four of these players were or would become World Cup winners, another would play in the World Cup final and García would win Euro 2008, but they were soundly beaten that night.

Cruyff's public view was: "I'm far more optimistic now about the second half of the season and how it will go. Everyone is on the same page."

As usual, his was a lone voice. The easiest way for a new president to win favour with the fans and the media would have been to give them the head of a failing coach. Cruyff advised that Rijkaard was turning the corner. Laporta believed him. It was those two against the world, especially with vice president Sandro Rosell agitating for the Dutchman's immediate removal and the appointment of Felipe Scolari. Barcelona went on a stunning unbeaten run and finished second, very nearly winning the league, while Madrid fell away to fourth and sacked their coach, Carlos Quieroz.

It was remarkable – score points to Rijkaard, but more to Cruyff. Rijkaard's years remain, by far, a net gain for FC Barcelona, but they would have been cut off, long before their prime, if it hadn't been for Cruyff's consistent advice that the problems Rijkaard inherited were deeply ingrained and that patience would yield dividends. They also threw a spotlight on the difference between Cruyff the footballer and Cruyff the coach/analyst.

Ronaldinho was, without doubt, the most important signing of the Laporta era and the footballer who restored lustre to Barça's reputation by adding brilliance. However, even before his decline, his ear would be tugged by a comment from Cruyff in his weekly column in *La Vanguardia*. Usually, Cruyff would chastise the Brazilian for a little too much individuality, a lack of involvement in the team concept or a lack of pressing. But when I interviewed Cruyff about his own time as a player at the Camp Nou, which was a very moderate success in terms of trophies, he told me an anecdote which highlighted the disparity between how he thought and acted as a young, instinctive footballing genius and the more responsible, team-based utilitarian philosophy he now demands.

Part of his role in the team between 1973 and 1978 as he saw it was "to go out at the Camp Nou very aware of whether there had been a bad result or a bad performance the previous match. If that was the case, then usually what I would do would be to try something special, some tactic or some trick in the first 15 minutes to get the crowd back on our side, cheering and applauding, so that the pressure was off the team and then we could get on with winning the match".

You could imagine Ronaldinho thinking or doing precisely the same thing – and Cruyff the columnist/coach criticising him for it.

After two sterile, increasingly lumbering years at the end of Rijkaard's reign, at least one of which was a miscalculation by Laporta, it was time for change.

Rijkaard departed with Cruyff still defending his work, still attempting to point out that perhaps there were similarities with 1996.

Cruyff's final verdict was that "Rijkaard was true to himself throughout the five years. Unfortunately, the same cannot be said of some of his players. All you have to do is look at what they were doing during the three good years and then what happened after that.

"Every coach needs a squad which pulls together, in every sense. Rijkaard didn't change, but some of his players did and lost people's respect as a result."

Cruyff had one more chance to return to full-time work at the Camp Nou. Laporta wanted him either as coach or a hands-on technical director for Guardiola's first season. Cruyff refused and pointed out that Guardiola was ready. Was this his last great gift to Barcelona?

As Barcelona won the Champions League again in 2011, Cruyff remained far younger than his years. He and Guardiola still play golf during the summer holidays; his disciples still seek his counsel, although there is no doubt that the wisest of them sieve through it, keeping what they appreciate and showing their independence by disregarding the rest.

Cruyff's relationship with Sandro Rosell appears irreparable. You have to wonder, then, how, apart from constructive criticism in his media columns, Hendrik Johannes Cruijff can continue to channel his brilliance towards one of the two clubs he truly loves.

In the summer of 2011, not long after the most dramatic fulfilment of some of Cruyff's original ideas were played out at Wembley – the stadium where he won his first European Cup as a player then, 21 years

later, again as a coach – he moved back to direct matters at Ajax, where he sits on the club's supervisory
board.

His energy and vision will now be poured back into
the Amsterdam club where he was formed. Perhaps his
reconstruction of training, youth development, scouting and coaching will take time to show dividends.
However, if he's given that time, someone will be writing a book describing how Johan Cruyff's last great act
in his sport was to restore Ajax to its once formidable
power.

What about the prospects for FC Barcelona without
Johan Cruyff to keep it right? History reveals a pattern:
the club misses him, falters and craves his return. If
that happens then this time, he probably won't be there
for them.

MAKING-OF MATCH:
REAL MADRID 2 BARCELONA 6
LA LIGA, MAY 2 2009

On the night, the score and the performance were both scintillating. In retrospect, there are still more absolutely remarkable components of this historic thrashing.

First, this is supposed to be the daddy of all performances – neither team had ever scored six goals away to their deadliest rivals and this vicious win was less than a year after Barça had been forced to mount a parade of honour for Madrid, the new champions, as they trotted out to rip Barcelona apart 4-1. Xavi was sent off that night. To destroy Madrid, humiliate them in terms of skill, tactics, pace and effort was almost beyond description. However, the fact remains that the 5-0 performance at the Camp Nou in the 2010 Clásico may well have been still more thrilling, complete and audacious. The 3-1 win in Madrid, after a faltering start to the 2011-12 season, is also a pretty competitive contender, pound-for-pound.

Secondly, Barça go one down which, away to Madrid, is almost always a guarantee of defeat.

Thirdly, it needs to be noted that beyond scoring six goals at the Santiago Bernabéu, Barça have four one-on-one chances which Iker Casillas somehow saves against Messi, Thierry Henry and Samuel Eto'o. Casillas also makes four further saves on top of that extraordinary effort. If he'd had even an ordinary night, the scoreline could easily have been 2-10.

And while this was not the first time Messi has played the 'false No 9' role which has since become his trademark – and the key to him scoring so many more goals than previously – it is the night which defines the role as his. That position is most famous in Spain for Michael Laudrup's perfection of its subtlety within Johan Cruyff's Dream Team, but the Argentinian is so flawless that one paper, El Mundo Deportivo, describe him as "Maradona – plus Cruyff, Ronaldo and Georgie Best all put together". Perhaps hyperbolic, but...

One of the keys to the result is that Guardiola has made his players so robust in their confidence (there have been comeback victories and last-minute victories all season) that going 1-0 down to Higuaín's splendid header barely registers as a setback.

The next is that Xavi, with four goal assists, numerous possession-winning tackles and an 89.5% completion rate on his 107 passes, produces one of the defining nights of his career. There are more picturesque goals this night, but the one which symbolises the season has Xavi robbing Diarra and feeding Messi, who scores his first goal at the Santiago Bernabéu.

Guardiola has seen precisely how slow the central defensive partnership of Metzelder and Cannavaro is. Eto'o and Henry push wide, Messi plays in the space between Madrid's midfield and defence; with Iniesta and Xavi around him there is numerical superiority when Diarra tries to stem the tide and the two lumbering central defenders are forced to risk pushing up and leaving space behind, or wait and allow Messi to come bursting towards them at speed with the ball at his feet.

Henry, in both his finishing and his humiliation of Sergio Ramos, has his best game for Barça, who take a definitive grip of the title that night. They go seven points clear with four matches remaining and exceed 100 league goals for the season.

"We just needed a game of that quality to cap this spectacular season," Puyol says in the mixed zone afterwards. "Losing here last season and standing guard to them as new champions was one of the worst days of my football career and this, now, is one of the happiest."

Xavi adds: "We've done this with style, we were completely superior and we could easily have scored many more goals."

For months, the prelude to the symphony Guardiola is composing has been audible, but this is the trumpeted fanfare.

Real Madrid (4-2-3-1) Casillas; Ramos (Van der Vaart 71), Cannavaro, Metzelder, Heinze; Gago, Diarra; Robben (Javi García 79), Raúl, Marcelo (Huntelaar 59); Higuaín.
Barcelona (4-3-3) Valdés; Alves, Puyol, Piqué, Abidal; Touré (Busquets 85), Xavi, Iniesta (Bojan 85); Messi, Eto'o, Henry (Keita 62).
Goals Higuaín 13; Henry 17, Puyol 19, Messi 35; Ramos 56; Henry 58, Messi 75, Piqué 82
Bookings Abidal, Ramos, Puyol, Marcelo, Van der Vaart, Javi García
Referee Undiano Mallenco
Attendance 80,000, Santiago Bernabéu

6 – THE MAKING OF PEP

"It's not possible to please everyone and there is no point in trying to be what other people think you should be. For me, it's important to be who I am."
— Pep Guardiola

WHEN GOD MADE JOSEP 'Pep' Guardiola he used a mould marked 'Charmed Life – to be given all available gifts'. I forget for whom the description 'women want to be with him, men want to be him' was first coined, but it fits Guardiola as perfectly as those 30in-waist trousers which still, improbably, fit his snake hips at the age of 41.

Guardiola rules the club he loves, has a happy, long-term relationship with Cristina, is father to three young kids, has produced something so artistic, so thrilling in his working life that people all over the world are inspired by it – oh, and by the middle of his fifth season as a manager, he had won 14 major trophies. An impossibly perfect life.

However, everyone suffers for their art – even this phenomenal man. For all the talent, grace and intelligence, there have been some daunting hurdles in his path and some dark times. For instance: Guardiola was once told that his 'seven-stone weakling' build and his 'Charlie Chaplin gait' meant he wouldn't make it to the top level in football; he suffered a horrendous 14 months when a calf injury robbed him of serious playing time. His sister, Francesca, said of that period: "Pep was really down when I saw him. Although he's always been self-contained, the injury made him even more withdrawn." Worst of all, some people who should have valued his massive contribution to Catalan culture chose to hack away at his individuality with scurrilous behaviour which hurt him badly.

What is called the *entorno* around the Camp Nou, those within and outwith the club who pass titbits of information back and forth, began to speculate that, simply because Guardiola was fashionable, read poetry, went to the cinema and, once, trod the boards of a fashion show (for his friend Toni Miró), perhaps Barça's captain was gay. Neither Guardiola, nor any right thinker, would think of being gay as a stigma, but it was inaccurate and used maliciously against him.

At that time, I went to the Camp Nou to interview Bobby Robson, then manager of Barcelona, and I was already a huge admirer of Guardiola's play. I asked several Catalan journalists about the captain's injury, hoping for an understanding of the problem and a possible return date. Without exception, they muttered darkly about the player's lifestyle and what problems it might have caused him. They went further, but I'm not prepared to repeat their unfounded speculation.

This is a lad who, aged six, would take three-hour return bus journeys from the countryside for matches at the Camp Nou, often getting home in the small hours; who followed the path from ball boy to captain and champion.

When he conducts his final analysis of a life spent at the Camp Nou, nothing will strip away Guardiola's joyful memory of not only leading the club he loves to unprecedented glory as manager, but also winning 16 trophies as a player. However, there is no escaping the fact that he eventually left FC Barcelona an unhappy, disappointed player. His farewell statement in April 2001 was elegant and eloquent and it underlined his desire to gain experience by living and working abroad, but Guardiola deeply mistrusted the people who ran the club then and felt undervalued. He jumped before he was pushed.

Of all the gifts bestowed upon this passionate football man, the most important may be a relentless drive.

If there is one sure bet, it's that Pep will overcome. A mutual friend of his and mine dropped him an email to let Guardiola know that he'd had a promotion at work. The friend was amused, but not surprised, to receive the reply: "Congratulations! But don't relax!"

Guardiola proved all the scouts and senior players at the Camp Nou that they were wrong to doubt him because of his frail physique; he fought like a tiger to disprove and eventually be totally exonerated of the accusation of nandrolone use he faced while playing in Italy; and he walked away from the club he loves because he wasn't willing to be a pawn of people for whom he had lost respect.

It was a risk, but here he is, the most successful coach in Barça's history and proving that integrity and success are not mutually exclusive in the brutal world of football.

He's not an angel. He can be intense, quixotic and hard to please – *pesado* they say in Spain.

His history as a player at Barcelona has many highlights; what he achieved and how he achieved it tell us much about the man who leads the greatest club in the world, but I'm going to use his golden first couple of seasons as a microcosm of his early success. I want to highlight the similarity between what happened to him as a young footballer under Johan Cruyff and what he was then able to do himself, as a fledgling coach. The repeat pattern is uncanny and these were the years which formed the man we see now: gifted, fighting against the odds, mature before his time and already barking orders at people.

A genetic modification lab blending a bit of Sergio Busquets, Matthias Sammer, Cesc Fàbregas and a drop of Roy Keane, plus X-ray vision, would produce Guardiola. Today, in his prime, his transfer market value would be in the £40m-50m bracket.

He was a genius as a player. Maybe not a pure, 24-karat genius, because some of his skills were not on a par with others – his pace compared unfavourably to his speed of thought, his left foot compared unfavourably to his right – but some of what he did matched anyone who has ever passed a football.

Guardiola's best years probably came after being promoted by Cruyff and his assistant Charly Rexach into what became known as the Dream Team. Cruyff normally used a 3-4-3 formation where the *pivote*, in this case Guardiola, is in the middle of the midfield, protecting the back three, dropping into defence as an auxiliary when necessary but, above all, restarting the attack as quickly and efficiently as possible when possession is won back.

Two traits stood out about Guardiola the footballer. He could pass the ball onto the head of a pin from 40 metres, and regularly did so for Romario, Hristo Stoichkov, Michael Laudrup and Rivaldo to score for Barça. The second was his reading of situations. That included: understanding when the snapping, pressing players around him, Eusebio and José Mari Bakero, were going to cause an opponent to lose possession; being well positioned to receive or finally win the loose ball and then have a one-touch pass already worked out.

Those 16 trophies he won included six La Liga titles and Barcelona's inaugural European Cup victory at Wembley in 1992, but his very presence at Barça was his initial triumph.

He moved from Santpedor, over an hour away from

the Camp Nou, deep in the Catalan countryside, to live in the stone farmhouse which is situated just behind that Gol Nord of the Camp Nou where Teddy Sheringham and Ole Gunnar Solskjær scored those famous goals for Manchester United in the 1999 Champions League final.

Santpedor is a small, charming, largely agricultural town, part of whose name, quite aptly, given Guardiola's subsequent career, signifies 'the golden place'. Humility and the age-old order of things are important there, to the extent that, despite his stellar success, the town's website ranks him 11th out of 11 famous people to emanate from the little medieval settlement. I'd like to say that the other 10 are nuclear physicists, multi-millionaire philanthropists, Dean Martin and Sophia Loren, but they aren't. His description restricts itself to his playing exploits (which, at the Camp Nou, finished a decade ago) and the declaration that he was given the freedom of his home town in October 2009. Apparently, Guardiola will need to do a damn sight better than winning 14 trophies in just over four years, lifting the Champions League twice and becoming the most successful manager in Barcelona's history to be bumped up the list.

His mum, Dolores, recalls the day when Pep and his parents finally succumbed to the siren song from the Camp Nou. "It was very upsetting and I cried a lot. It was like they had stolen our child from us. We found it very hard and so did he.

"The day we dropped him off at La Masia we looked through the window of his room and he said, 'Mum, every day when I wake up the first thing I'll see will be the football pitch.' That's how he started at Barça."

However, Barcelona's scouts had initially doubted him. One of their most experienced, the late Oriol Tort, came back from a scouting trip to Manresa (the local club where Guardiola took his first footballing steps) with the verdict that "he moves like Charlie Chaplin". They weren't put off.

Carlos Naval, who still stands by the dugout at Barça matches, was probably a swaying voice and remembers: "He wasn't a big kid or very strong, but he played like an angel. He had such vision and a tremendous ability to anticipate everything.

"People at La Masia asked me how old he was and when I told them that Pep was only 11, they didn't believe he could be that good. 'Miracles like that don't happen,' they would say. I just told them to get out there and watch him."

Luis Milla would eventually move from Barça to Real Madrid, having occupied the prize *pivote* position, opening up the space into which the young Guardiola moved permanently. Milla remembers the kid from Santpedor's first steps at the club. "It was hard for him to come to La Masia aged 13 or 14. He had come from a small town and some of the kids like him couldn't stick it and went back home after a while, but Pep was very mature for his age."

The Dream Team full-back, Guillermo Amor, is now the head of Barça's youth development, but played alongside Guardiola for his entire Camp Nou career and admits: "Some people were worried that he was too skinny and wouldn't grow tall enough, but he was such a good footballer who could read the game better than any of his peers. They gave him the time to develop and grow a bit."

From this vantage point, such doubts over a young Catalan talent's stature and physique seem bizarre. Xavi, Pedro, Messi, Iniesta, Mata, Agüero and Alves are the toast of the world, and never in the history of football has the little big-man ruled quite this proudly. Perhaps the situation in 1990 needs some context.

Johan Cruyff was always going to be willing to promote those who could play the ball with confidence, vision and accuracy, but this was still a relatively early time in his reign and Barça were unrecognisable from today. When Cruyff joined in 1988, they had only won the league twice in the previous 28 years.

So, given that Cruyff took three years to lift the Spanish title, his job was already under threat when, in October 1990, Ronald Koeman tore his Achilles tendon in a defeat at Atlético Madrid.

Cruyff went to his president, Josep Núñez, and asked for Jan Molby of Liverpool as a replacement. The discussion went badly. Núñez wasn't happy with Molby's physical shape, his age or the fact that he played in a different position to Koeman.

For four or five days things went quiet. Cruyff came back and told his jumpy boss: "We've rethought. Give me and Charly [Rexach, his assistant] one extra year under contract and instead of buying we will use Alexanco [who eventually wore the captain's armband for Barça in their 1992 European Cup triumph, but who was more of a bench player at the time] a lot more at the back and promote this kid, Guardiola, from the *cantera*."

Today, such a decision would absolutely be the norm. Dani Alves has a saying that *"fútbol es para listos"* – football is for the smart guys. His theory goes that the short or skinny guys like him, Xavi, Iniesta and Messi need to be smarter than the 6ft 4in beasts who can run fast and jump high, but who would need a manual in order to control the ball or play one-touch football. It's why on the Brazilian's ankle there is a tattoo of the little cartoon canary, Tweety Pie, with a sword behind his back, about to slay the menacing Sylvester the Cat. Revenge of the little guys, he calls it.

However, in a different era, Cruyff's decision to promote Guardiola was the litmus test for the theory that quality, vision and intelligence, and not experience or size, would form the cornerstones of Barcelona's football philosophy.

An example of how the system still wasn't functioning, and many years later would fail in an identical way with Cesc Fàbregas and Gerard Piqué, was that Cruyff initially couldn't find Guardiola in the *cantera* – even though Rexach had told his boss that this kid was worth betting their futures on.

Rexach recalls: "Johan went to watch Barça B one Sunday [in late 1989] specifically to watch Pep, but he was told Pep didn't play in Barça B, but in the youth team [*Juvenil A*]. I explained that Pep was still in the youth team because he was so small and skinny. Johan had a look anyway and decided to promote the player to the B side and let him train regularly with the first team."

Eventually, in January 1990, Guardiola made the big step up, against Oviedo. He was in the first-team squad, not the starting XI, but it was a huge moment for the local kid who still looked like he was 15, but had just celebrated his 19th birthday. That weekend, Guardiola told the local Catalan station, TV3: "I play in midfield as a No 4 or a No 6. I am more of a technical player and I try to play a straightforward game. I pass the ball and don't go for too many complicated moves."

He didn't name the team position in traditional style – central midfield, right-back, inside-left – but in the Ajax style he named the position's number. What's more, if his current philosophy could be boiled down into a short phrase it would still be "play a straight-forward game, pass the ball and don't go for too many complicated moves". Keep that phrase in your mind if you truly want to understand Pep Guardiola.

Then came his debut. It is December 1990, week 15 of the La Liga season and the fluorescent yellow Cádiz are the visitors to the Camp Nou, bringing with them one of the few noisy, boozy travelling supports in Spain – all the way up from the furthest south-west tip of Andalucia.

Guardiola plays a serious, sober 90 minutes in a 2-0 win and then the drama starts. Between that debut and his next appearance there are 14 matches – and the shock of a cardiac arrest for his manager.

Cruyff reports chest pains after Barça beat Valladolid 1-5 on February 23, 1991 and by February 27 he is rushed to hospital. He does not return to the bench until a trip to Castellón on Jornada 30 when there is an awfully depleted first-team squad. No Alexanco, Stoichkov, Txiki Begiristain, Bakero or Nando. Still, this is Cruyff's first away game since his heart problems started and Rexach tells the players: "Win this one and it's pretty much game over for the chasing pack – the league is nearly ours." Again Pep plays 90 minutes, they win 1-0.

Two more games come and go, a 3-0 home win to

Sevilla plus a 1-1 draw at Mallorca and Pep keeps his place in midfield. But that's that for his first season, one that ends with Cruyff's first championship. With the youngster, the emblem of La Masia, protecting the back four in the *pivote* position, Barça have played four matches, won three and drawn one. Those appearances don't earn him a medal, but he's part of what is only Barça's fourth title win in three decades.

They cross the tape despite being whipped 4-0 at Cádiz, because the following night a goal from John Aldridge completes a glorious fightback for Sociedad against Atlético Madrid, handing the title to Barcelona.

Barça are defeated by Alex Ferguson's Manchester United in the European Cup Winners' Cup final but, at Rotterdam airport the next morning, president Josep Núñez promises: "Though it is a disappointment to lose a title like this, we won't react with knee-jerk signings. The kids from Barça B have already shown there's no need to go crazy – guys like Pinilla, Guardiola and Herrera are the future. They are phenomenal."

The Guardiola era had begun. Just like the astonishing success Sergio Busquets would have under Guardiola the manager – from third division football to the World Cup final within three years – Pep hit the accelerator.

Already he was a fundamental part of Cruyff's Dream Team. They were named in homage to the USA basketball squad as the superstars of the NBA – Charles Barkley, Michael Jordan, Magic Johnson et al – promised to bring the greatest collective in the history of that sport to the forthcoming Barcelona Olympics.

Just ahead of that Olympic summer of 1992, Guardiola, still only a kid, was preparing for the European

Cup final at Wembley. He said: "We have to show a lot of insolence and power. In cup finals it is fear, or holding something back in reserve, which can defeat you. The worst that can happen in a match like this is that nobody wants to have a shot, score the goals or assume responsibility for winning because nerves dominate their choices. We need to be brave. I've no doubt that a couple of hours before the match I'll have butterflies in my stomach, but we have to show what we are made of, how good we are."

Every word could have been lifted from his team talk before Wembley 2011. He was 21, it was his first major final and, already, he was talking like a battle-hardened general.

That's our Pep.

Barça won, famously, after Koeman's fizzing goal in the 111th minute. There was mayhem in Catalonia for days. Real Madrid had been rubbing Barça's nose in the fact that the European Cup was a private, Castilian, party since 1955 but, finally, the liggers were on the guest list. At that time trophies were formally presented by the club in Plaça de Sant Jaume, in the heart of Barça's ancient Gothic quarter. Everyone had their golden moment, but 21-year-old Josep Guardiola stole the show.

Fifteen years earlier, not long after Franco's death, the Catalan ideologist and politician Josep Tarradellas, who had been named 'President in absentia' by his people in 1954, returned as head of the newly recognised Catalan Parliament. On the same balcony as Barça's players would stand on May 21, 1992, Tarradellas roared: "*Ciutadans de Catalunya: ja sóc aquí!*" Citizens of Catalonia – I'm here!

Guardiola had not been allowed to attend, but he was inspired by Tarradellas and shouted out: "Citizens of Catalonia – now you have it here!" He instantly became both a saint and a humorist forever in Catalonia.

"I had the phrase prepared," he admitted afterwards. "I also set the video to tape the game and I'll watch it millions of times until I grow old."

However, domestically, Barça were still in a dogfight and had to face their bitter rivals, Espanyol.

The Dream Team is anything but fatigued, hitting six at Valladolid and four in Sarria against Javier Clemente's Espanyol, conceding not once.

Clemente refuses the newly crowned European champions the traditional *pasillo* or guard of honour and bitches afterwards: "Cruyff doesn't deserve a corridor, nor a step ladder, or a doormat. He's rude and uneducated as a person, that's my opinion."

Even with 10 men for over an hour, thanks to Nando's red card, Barça strip Espanyol to the bone. Before the match, Guardiola comments: "The great teams have always won a trophy one day, but been ready to fight for the next title 24 hours later. I want La Liga and if they bring back the Copa del Generalísimo I want to win it, then if they organise a friendly match, I want to win that, too. Then, if I'm in the Olympic squad, I want us to win that gold medal." The birth date on the passport says he was only 21. His words suggest otherwise.

With one game left Real Madrid are ahead of Barcelona by a point.

Barça ease to a 2-0 win against Athletic Bilbao, while Madrid lose 3-2 to Tenerife, despite being 2-0 up after half an hour. Tenerife score their third with 13 minutes left and, at the Camp Nou, 100,000 transistor radios are thrown in the air. The Dream Team have back-to-back La Liga titles and are champions of Europe.

On Wednesday, June 10, Guardiola is on the front cover of *El Mundo Deportivo* with the European Cup and the league trophy, accompanied by the words: *"Guardiola: el héroe más joven que jamás tuvo el club azulgrana"* – Guardiola: the youngest hero Barça have ever had.

By a quirk of fate Qatar, where Guardiola will later play league football and for whom he will controversially play ambassador as they ludicrously win the right to host the 2022 World Cup, are in Spain's Olympic football group. Spain beat Colombia, Egypt and the Qataris en route to a quarter-final against Italy, which is also won, 1-0, thanks to Guardiola's great friend, the Atlético Madrid striker Kiko.

La Furia Rojita then defeat Ghana in the semi-final at Valencia's Mestalla stadium (then named the Luis Casanovas stadium), in front of 15,000. Before the final, Spain move temporarily into the Rey Juan Carlos hotel, about 10 minutes' walk from the Camp Nou – five-star accommodation for the totally unexpected stars of the Spanish Olympic armada. The rest of the players were delighted to be isolated, but Guardiola, typically, admitted that having abandoned Valencia, their base for the rest of the Games, he'd far rather have "lived the experience" in the Olympic village down on the beach front.

On the eve of the final, Guardiola tells *El Mundo Deportivo*: "We are relaxed and confident of winning gold in the final, but we cannot underestimate the rival, there is nothing done yet. It's important we take them very seriously indeed."

He meant it then and it remains his mantra now.

Before the game, he reveals more of the drive and self-motivation that fuels his engine still. "Nobody believed in us, nobody backed us, but little by little people are beginning to realise that we play pretty well. Now I'm confident that at least 60,000 will turn up to support us at the Camp Nou because to fill it is going to be impossible.

"It's a super important moment to be involved in this world fiesta of sport. I just couldn't understand any sportsman or woman who didn't feel pride in competing here. To participate in an Olympics more than compensates for having lost your holidays. Being at the opening ceremony was a very intense moment for me and I reminded myself to enjoy the feelings and sensations because I wouldn't ever again wear the Spanish Olympic uniform. It's hard for me to put into words how strong that emotion was." Sixteen years later, Leo Messi would benefit from how strongly Guardiola believed in what he was saying.

As a proud Catalan, Pep had been streetwise enough to expect that the Barcelona public might not fully support Spain, even in an Olympic final at the Camp Nou. "It's impossible that there will be more than 60,000," he had predicted. A rare Guardiola error – in fact, he was wrong by a distance.

Spain beat Poland, having trailed 1-0 then been pegged back to 2-2 with 14 minutes left, and there were 95,000 people roaring them on – including the King and Queen, who hurried over from the Olympic Stadium up on Montjuïc on hearing that Poland were winning at half-time.

Approximately nine minutes after King Juan Carlos

takes his seat in the centre stand and the buzz dies down a little, Guardiola takes a left-wing free-kick and places the ball squarely in front of Abelardo's darting move at the back post for the headed equaliser. There is an exceptional television shot of the King and Queen, certainly delighted by the goal, but moved to wonderment at the Camp Nou roaring on Spain. Juan Carlos turns to Sofia and gestures to the vast high tribunes above and around him. 'Just look at all this!'

Since Franco seized power so bloodily in the late 1930s and maintained it so pitilessly, perhaps it's the first indication that parts of Catalonia can feel pride at Spain's achievements. At least so long as there are Catalans like Guardiola, Txapi Ferrer, goalkeeper Toni and striker Tony Pinilla in the squad. Kiko somehow scores a 91st-minute winner and the referee blows time almost as soon as the kick-off is taken.

In lauding the two Catalans, Guardiola and Ferrer, who have won league, European Cup and Olympic gold in a season, *Mundo Deportivo's* Francesc Perearnau writes, prophetically: "No Catalan footballer in the history of FC Barcelona has ever won more prizes in a season. Both of them have been the pillars of this team with seriousness and aplomb, plus a little dose of genius. But the most important thing is that they brought a winner's mentality to the team and one which seems to be contagious for their generation.

"Besides the courage and emotions of the team yesterday, Spain reached and won the final because their newly found champion mentality has allowed the side to approach each and every game with a special psychology. The best thing is that these two now have the rest of their lives to explore that and improve on it."

Pep himself said: "I don't give much worth to this golden-coloured metal, in general, but winning this final against Poland is an experience I'm never going to be able to repeat at an Olympics, so the exact worth of this medal, which is bending my neck, I'm certain won't really sink in to me for a few years."

He'd feel similarly at very regular moments during his Barça career. Four more Spanish league titles, two Spanish Cups, the Cup Winners' Cup, the European and Spanish Super Cups; even when the Cruyff magic wore off, there were important successes under Louis van Gaal and Bobby Robson.

Injuries cost him his place at the World Cup in France when Spain lost ignominiously to Nigeria, and the long enmity between Javier Clemente and anything to do with FC Barcelona was the main cause of him not being chosen for Euro 96. More fool Clemente.

His talent deserved more than his 47 caps and that partly explains Spain's glass jaw during Guardiola's era. He alone couldn't have made them world or European champions, but his absence was badly felt.

The spine of the Spain team looked like this: Guardiola's team-mate Andoni Zubizarreta in goal, the mighty Fernando Hierro at sweeper, Guardiola at the nerve centre in midfield and then one of Europe's all-time greats, Raúl, up front. The odd quarter-final was small reward.

Hierro, a Madrid legend, remains a Guardiola admirer. "Pep, with all his technical ability and force of character, was essential for the national team," he recalls.

Míchel, later Guardiola's opponent as manager of Getafe, has pointed out that "Pep was restless playing football. He used to talk non-stop and was always gesturing and trying to manage the whole team. It was like he was trying to direct traffic".

If those words explain some of the roots of Guardiola the manager, it is equally important to understand the dark end to his playing career at Camp Nou and the events which made him the tougher man on a mission that took control of Barcelona.

After Cruyff's dramatic and foolhardy sacking, the club were rebuilding under Robson and Van Gaal in a way in which marginalised Guardiola's importance and restricted his salary potential. Players were signed for huge money, rather than developed at La Masia. They legitimately demanded and were paid enormous wages, which meant that if the club was economising and if a hierarchy of importance was developing, Guardiola, and his ilk, were on the slide.

Guardiola holds firm principles, is sometimes reserved and is also a very 'black is black and white is white' kind of man. Perhaps he played a part in the decline in relations between himself and the board, then headed by the former vice president, Joan Gaspart. He was waiting for Gaspart to make a formal offer of renewal which reflected his status and achievement. It never came.

So, he grasped the nettle in a press conference, in April 2001, where he announced that he had taken a unilateral decision to leave Barcelona and to embark on a foreign adventure. That had a seismic impact. Not only was he the highest-achieving Catalan in the club's history, he was symbolic of La Masia. He was a darling of the fans, still a brilliant football mind.

Catalans often say "Catalonia has everything you could wish for". They cite the beach, the mountains, the skiing, the weather, the food, the football and the arts. It's a fair argument that life ain't bad there. But for some it means that there is no need, whatsoever, to expand horizons. *Tengo todo aquí* (I've got it all here) can be a stifling expression. Certainly it can stifle their need for expansion and experimentation.

Guardiola was different. This is what he said: "Last night at 11 o'clock I met with president Gaspart and we talked for two hours. I asked him to attend this gathering with me but it wasn't possible and he has had to be elsewhere today. He will talk to you on Tuesday, but I am here today to give you my interpretation on what we discussed.

"When I arrived at Barcelona I was a totally inexperienced lad of 13. Now I have kids of my own. This has been my home for 17 years and I am proud and happy to have grown up and matured here. But now I'm 30 years old and feel that I'm watching my career slip through my fingers. I don't have many playing years left and I have to weigh up my choices. Should I be content to finish my career here or take on the challenge of discovering other countries and their football leagues? Get to know different football clubs and new team-mates with whom I can play and compete? I have to be honest and say that I am more attracted by the idea of discovering new things.

"For these reasons I have to tell you exactly what I told the president yesterday, that I will finish my career abroad. I have no idea where, because up till now I have ignored any offers that have come my way. I needed to finish my business with Barça first. But from this moment on I'll be knocking on doors in England, Italy, France and Germany. Josep Maria Orobitg will represent me and he and he alone can speak on my behalf. Obviously, I will be looking for the best possible opportunity so that I can enjoy my last few years as a player. I am looking for a club where I can keep learning but where I can also share everything I have learned at this club.

"The president has also authorised me to tell you that if I don't find a club that I'm interested in, he will keep a place for me here. However, my mind is made up and I am going. This is not a decision I have taken on the spur of the moment, after a particularly good or bad match, it is something I have been thinking about for a long time. I am determined to give another club the benefit of the knowledge and experience I have developed here under the tutelage of many talented people.

"I would like to take this opportunity to thank presidents Núñez and Gaspart, all the directors and all my coaches who have guided me from the age of 13. I want to thank Serra Ferrer, all the back-room staff and my team-mates who have helped make me a great footballer. I consider myself fortunate to have played with them. I would also like to thank you too, those with whom I've got on well and those with whom I've had my ups and downs. We've come a long way together. I would also like to thank those fans who have supported me as a player and those who haven't been so impressed, because at the end of the day, we are all driven by our love for this club. Thank you to everyone who has helped me become what I am today."

I reproduce the statement because it is so telling. A symbol of the club leaves and the president can't be bothered to be with him on the occasion. They go on to give two separate verdicts on what has happened.

6 – The Making of Pep

Also, consider Guardiola's formal, articulate tone. It's how he tries to comport himself to this day – particularly in public. His adoration for the club and his time there is patent.

But his statement that he feels his "career is slipping away through his fingers" and his unashamed admission that he'll be knocking on doors (rather than waiting for the queue to form) is typical of Guardiola's perfect willingness to wear his heart on his sleeve. No false dignity, nor false modesty.

Sleeves up, work hard, don't be afraid to admit how much you want something.

He also spoke of his "passion for the English teams".

"They are honest, aggressive, and normally they don't play for a draw like Liverpool recently tried to do when they played at the Camp Nou. In the stadiums of England you breathe football in its pure, natural state. I still remember the first time I played at Old Trafford. It was unbelievable."

It was the start of immensely turbulent times. Luciano Moggi, president of Juventus, offered, and then reneged on, a chance to play in Turin which Guardiola wanted to accept.

His time in Italy included playing for Carlo Mazzone at Brescia, and ended with what turned out to be a false accusation of nandrolone use. Between two short stints at Brescia, Guardiola joined Fabio Capello's Roma with the intention of learning from one of the great modern managers. By the time he left he'd had more than enough of Capello the man, but he'd learned things which would feature in his future coaching life.

His years in Qatar were bittersweet. Without real pressure, there was time to muck about with mates like Hierro and the De Boer twins, playing golf, going to the movies and learning English, while also devoting more time to family life. Hierro recalled: "After Pep's career at Barça and his experiences in Italy, all we wanted to do was enjoy playing football again, just like we did when we were 17 and just starting out. We wanted to recapture that joy."

A Spanish television interview from the time reveals that he was feeling at least as Catalan as ever, after a total of four years away. Having admitted that only the fact he could get home every few months made life away from Catalonia "more bearable," he restated his wish that the Catalan 'national' team were recognised by FIFA.

"Unfortunately the football law states that Catalonia can't play as a national team in all the big competitions. When I played in the Spanish league I was called to play for the national team and I was happy to do so, but you can't change what you feel and I love my country with all my head and all my heart. My country has had its own language for hundreds of years, unique to Catalonia."

And having touched on identity, he spoke from the heart about the myriad misinterpretations which his character had inspired about him.

"Loads of people my age read and enjoy going to the cinema, it's just that when I talk about that stuff in interviews I come across as a bit different. The truth is that a lot of footballers love books and the cinema. There are those who are quite happy with a McDonald's and others who prefer good restaurants.

"I strive to live with passion and not to be desensitised to life. Things matter to me. You've got to live like that. Otherwise what's the point? It's not possible to please everyone and there is no point in trying to be what other people think you should be. For me, it's important to be who I am, not just to be different but to be as authentic as I can be."

His friendship with the fashion designer Toni Miró had led to the two of them talking about a new clothes line in spring 1993 and then Guardiola volunteering to model part of the new range in July that year. It was off-season and his time was his own but, as Miró recalls, Cruyff wasn't happy.

"Pep and I were chatting, he liked the idea of going on the catwalk for me, but Cruyff was so displeased that he punished him by dropping him."

When my friend Gabriele Marcotti, *The Times*' excellent European football correspondent, visited Guardiola in Doha, he found him lamenting the rapid changes in the game since his debut 14 years earlier. He told Gabriele: "I think players like me have become extinct because the game has become more tactical and physical. At most clubs, players are given specific roles and creativity can only exist within those parameters. I haven't changed, my skills haven't declined. It's just that football has changed; it's a lot more physical. To play in front of the back four right now, you have to be a ball-winner. If I were a 20-year-old at Barcelona I'd never make it as a professional. At best, I'd be playing in the third division somewhere."

What dismal, depressing words they were. But he has gone on to prove himself wrong.

The young Pep Guardiola would fit right in to the current Barça side, even if his tackling was slightly less powerful than that of Sergio Busquets.

One man who felt differently about the Catalan passing machine was Paul Jewell, which accounts for one of Guardiola's unsuccessful flirtations with English football. At the end of 2005, he was tired of life and football in Qatar, but had decided to follow his pal, Hierro, who had joined Bolton Wanderers for a season. Hierro loved his short time in England.

Jewell wasn't forearmed with that knowledge, but he did know that Guardiola might still have that vision and professionalism to offer his Wigan team as they strived to establish themselves in the Premier League. The Wigan manager phoned Guardiola, left a message but, as he told me, "never really expected to get a reply. But just over two minutes later, Pep phoned back.

"He was very interested in my proposal and stopped me when I tried to explain a little bit about Wigan by saying, 'I've been watching you, I know exactly how the team plays and I'm not at all surprised Wigan have been successful.'"

Terms were discussed and, despite Wigan's maximum wage then being just over £10,000-per-week, Guardiola was keen to sign up. Jewell says now: "I'd always loved the way Pep played; he was ahead of his time. Of my era, he was the best passing midfielder and he made football look like a stroll."

What happened, to Jewell's great misfortune, is that Guardiola's close friend and fellow football romantic, Juanma Lillo, took over at Mexico's Dorados de Sinaloa and put the squeeze on the Catalan to come and help him in midfield. Loyalty being as important as it is to Pep, he said 'yes' and shelved the Wigan idea. It remains a regret for Jewell.

"Simplicity is one of the most effective, but most

difficult to achieve, components of football at its best," the Ipswich manager told me. "He had that as a player and just look at how his team plays now. Too many players and coaches complicate the game unnecessarily, but Barça under Guardiola never do.

"I remember he always knew where the ball was going to come free because of Barcelona's pressing in midfield and then he used the fewest touches necessary to move the ball to the right place for an attack. Now his team replicate that; of the hundreds and hundreds of passes they completed against Arsenal and Manchester United this season [2010-11] so many of them were one or at most two-touch. And if they don't need to touch the ball they don't. If the pass is good, his players just let the ball roll across their body position and keep moving it forward. I wish I'd had the chance to work with him."

What Guardiola discovered in the desert, and then in Mexico during that very short, unfulfilling spell with Lillo, was that he utterly needed to remain involved in football. Typically, he wanted to do things the right way, not grab the first opportunity.

In 2003 there were epoch-defining presidential elections at the Camp Nou. Joan Laporta would win, and the good times would roll, but his closest rival was Luis Bassat.

Bassat had been smart enough to identify Guardiola, then still with Roma, as a brilliant asset for the club. The candidate for the presidency of FC Barcelona wanted him to become coach, aged only 32.

He remembers: "When I ran for the presidency in 2003 I went to Rome to sign Pep. I knew he was a clever guy who loved Barça and would work hard for the club. We talked for six hours and he convinced me that he wasn't coach material yet. He hadn't sat the coaching licence by then.

"So I changed my mind and decided that he would be better as my future director of football. He would have been brilliant, just as he is a brilliant coach now."

Bassat finished second in the polls and Guardiola went back to playing and preparing for his future. Via the Spanish federation, Guardiola achieved his coaching badges and, almost immediately, was appointed coach of Barça B.

It was June 2007 and although just over a year had passed since Barça won their second league and European Cup double, rust had set in to Frank Rijkaard's team. Just after winning the Champions League in Paris, defeating Arsenal 2-1, two important figures had left. Henk ten Cate, who had been the bad cop to Rijkaard's community policeman, left to take over at Ajax. Though Rijkaard had been a tough footballer and a remorseless winner (he once told me that the street football in which he learned his skills was 'kill or be killed') he didn't have it in him to crack the whip.

Rijkaard's personal life was also pretty messy. He lost focus, he lost his sergeant major and he lost his cutting edge. He wasn't working as hard or as hungrily and so, naturally, some of his players stopped doing so too.

And Henrik Larsson departed the squad. His impact had been enormous. Relentlessly hard-working, smart, utterly professional and with a cold attitude to anyone who didn't match his standards, it wasn't hard to understand why the Camp Nou crowd absolutely adored him.

The responsibility to keep a squad on the right lines

doesn't rest solely on the players, certainly not on a single individual inside the dressing room. But if Larsson had still been at the Camp Nou when things began to unravel, there would have been harsh words about standards, fitness and behaviour.

A year after Guardiola's low-key return to Barça, in May 2008, Rijkaard's team reached the Champions League semi-final but were turgid and ready to be punctured by Paul Scholes' fizzing winner at Old Trafford.

The weather check had been there for anyone paying attention – the Camp Nou crowd had actually jeered their team into the semis because the quarter-final display, against Schalke 04, was so tentative and patchy. The players simply didn't look as physically fit, as determined or as happy in their work. It was like watching a ferocious hunting dog transform, pretty rapidly, into the podgy Labrador who could fetch your slippers but would cower in the face of a yappy poodle.

Rijkaard had given Barça some exceptional, exciting years and his rebuilding was complemented by intelligent support from Joan Laporta and Txiki Begiristain. Behind the scenes, Ferran Soriano and Marc Ingla had utterly transformed the club's finances and stiffened its marketing punch. They are two under-rated brains in the resuscitation of the modern FC Barcelona.

But it was only Laporta's fierce loyalty to Rijkaard and the quality of work which the Dutchman had originally brought to an ailing giant which earned him the chance to continue as coach during that 2007-08 season. It proved a mistake.

What of our hero and his 12-month stint with the kids in the meantime?

When a brains trust of Laporta, Cruyff, Begiristain and Evarist Murtra (a board member) decided that Guardiola needed to be repatriated, there had been a bit of a debate, even then, as to whether he was the right man for the Barça B job.

Below the first team there are around 12 youth levels from the age of seven years upwards. There is no reserve football as such in Spain; if a first-team regular has been out injured and needs to play his way back to fitness, he can't drop in for a few 'B' games. The B team is a proving ground for the young bucks, a selling forum for those who, at 22-25 years of age, haven't made it into the first squad, and a thermometer for the overall health of the FC Barcelona gene pool. It's a professionally paid squad; in 2011 it had 27 players and in the past such as Juande Ramos have cut their managerial teeth there.

There was a trace of sadness in the move for Guardiola in that it had been Quique Costas, a man who, in a previous life as Barça B coach, had given the young midfielder much advice and impetus ahead of his playing debut under Cruyff, who was being replaced after a bleak season.

There was a horrible atmosphere around the club because the decline, in one year, had been so steep. The day that Guardiola was ushered in, relatively unheralded by even the Catalan media, Begiristain was fiercely criticising the first squad. "Training has to be more rigorous, more professional. We are losing games from winning positions, we are losing goals in the last minutes of games and not until we train better will we play better."

Laporta, that same day, added: "Some players I take

my hat off to. Others I have no reproach for, at all. But there is a third group, talented, whose behaviour hasn't been what it should be."

Most telling of all was Rijkaard who, history shows, should have been removed then and not 12 months later: "From this past season I'll choose the memory of Carles Puyol – my captain. He's felt alone in the desert, yelling his lungs out to try and maintain team spirit. He's suffered a lot this year."

He also revealed that: "It would be too easy to blame the players, they behave as you let them. I'd rather turn the blame on myself."

Guardiola, though unproven, already had the air of a fresh, urgent, hungry leader. At his presentation as Barça B coach, he said: "What I was as a player is gone. As a coach I'm nobody and I'm starting from zero. Only winning will bring me credibility, that's my only way to grow as a coach.

"The priority here is to continue producing first-class footballers, but if I don't win, if we don't achieve promotion, then I won't be allowed to continue here. That's the way things are.

"I didn't have any other offer and for that I must thank Barça, because if they hadn't come looking for me, I'd be sitting at home. The first thing I want to do is transmit the pride and honour that I feel at being involved with this club again. I don't view this as working in the third division, but working for Barça B. The players shouldn't think they are playing in the third division, but pushing at the doors of the first team."

Laporta, never short of a bon mot, later recalled: "From what we could sense, Pep would probably have accepted coaching Barça B without a salary."

The year went well. The B team had just suffered the humiliation of relegation to the third division and Pep was arriving without the benefit of a stable, established squad. There was a telling moment before the first home game, in the 15,000-capacity Mini Estadi about 100 metres from the Camp Nou. His enthusiastic, raw players were trying to over-impress in training and Guardiola could be heard shouting words which were utterly evocative of his first Catalan television interview, nearly 20 years earlier.

"I don't want you all trying to dribble like Leo Messi, pass it, pass it and pass it again. Pass precisely, move well, pass again, pass, pass, and pass.

"I want every move to be smart, every pass accurate – that's how we make the difference from the rest of the teams, that's all I want to see."

The game stood as a marker for most of the season. Balaguer hit it long, lumped into Guardiola's young players, had two sent off and lost 4-2. For the record, his first home XI as coach of Barça B was: Oier; Córcoles, Xavi Torres, Botía, Víctor Sánchez, Espasandín, Crosas, Dimas, Abraham, Jeffrén, Víctor Vázquez, Guerra. Both Pedro and Eneko came on with Pedro, now a World Cup-winning superstar, scoring the third goal on the hour.

Far from the elegant lounge lizard we now see on match days, the new coach ran his first home match in a pair of jeans and a pink Italian t-shirt.

At home, Guardiola made Barça B near to unbeatable. Much of what we see now was available at a cheaper ticket price then. Along with the passing mentality, which was still harder to enforce amidst the long ball, hustle and hassle which was the norm in the third division, Guardiola made them work. Training was rigorous. Anyone, no matter how important, who didn't cut it in their daily work simply didn't get picked at the weekend.

There were fines, rules, and a cute little bonus system. Guardiola met with his captains at the start of the pre-season and promised that every time the team won three in a row he would take the squad out to lunch after training and pay for it personally. It only took his lads a month to hurt his wallet and it wouldn't be the last time that season – they were seen a number of times in restaurants El Gorría and El Asador de Aranda. But he offset his own expenditure with fines for anyone late, anyone caught not training well enough, anyone out past midnight on a working day and for red cards. I can't swear that he fined himself, but Guardiola felt the tension that season and was sent off. They won the third division by a point.

Full-backs became wing-backs, wingers cut inside to make five forwards when the wing-backs overlapped, Sergio Busquets cut his teeth at *pivote* and often dropped back to help at the back when the original 4-3-3 went to a 3-4-3. The *pivote* ordered the play, used the ball most frequently and dropped back as an auxiliary central defender alongside either Botía, Chico or Valiente. The central striker and the two *interiores* (right and left midfield) combined to press if the opposition tried to play the ball from the back.

Barça B went 21 games unbeaten at home. There was also the emergence of what would become most famous in the pre-match build up to the Rome Champions League final in 2009 – the motivational video. For example, before Barça B's first play-off tie, against

Castillo, he showed them the movie 'Zidane – A 21st Century Portrait'; it's an inspirational piece and the kids won 6-0.

Guardiola has a quite understandable obsession with his teams starting like hungry animals in the first five minutes, which is where the idea of sending his players out behind a massive adrenaline buzz from a film like that stems from. Before the final game of the season, the decisive second leg of the play-off against Barbastro, he showed a video of a 60-year-old father and his son, who suffers from cerebral palsy, competing together in an Ironman contest. He chose to show the film 15 minutes before kick-off. In many of the events, the father has to carry his son. Some players later admitted that they went out to play with tears nipping at their eyes.

It was all a template for his first three seasons in charge of the first team.

Ten thousand fans in the Mini Estadi saw a Víctor Vázquez goal seal promotion back to the Segunda B division. For the record, his final B team was: Oier, Córcoles, Chico, Xavi Torres, Espasandín, Sergio Busquets, Dimas, Víctor Vázquez, Abraham, Pedro, Emilio, Guerra, Gai.

By then, Guardiola had known for a few months that he was likely to succeed Rijkaard the following season. It was one hell of a way to sign off from his first coaching job.

SERGIO BUSQUETS: THE ENFORCER

I N MY TIME IN SPAIN I can't recall a player who has divided opinion like Sergio Busquets did when he emerged into the first team as part of the Pep Guardiola revolution.

As it transpired, every member of the first-team squad understood from the start what his talents were, but very few in the outside world appeared to share that knowledge – fans or media. Busquets changed all that, of course, but those early days were strange.

He seemed unusual. Maybe it was because this lanky organiser appeared to be so different to the small, deft improvisers to his left and right. However, what became clear to us all – and what was underlined every time we spoke to any one of his team-mates – was that Busquets added three vital things to the transition out of the poisonous end of the previous manager's reign.

First, he is a ferocious competitor and there are many people who believe he uses those instincts to nefarious ends. Nevertheless, I believe he is the member of Guardiola's team who, in percentage terms, most resembles his manager as a player.

At Gol Television in Barcelona, I worked with a guy who played some exceptional stuff in his day, Jordi Lardín. A Catalan contemporary of Guardiola's, but an Espanyol star, Jordi emphasised that while Pep was a towering footballer, he would also employ the dark arts to put an opponent off his game if it helped gain a yard of space. Insults, studs on the foot – let's not sully his image unnecessarily, but you get the picture. Now think about how Busquets plays.

Next, there is an extremely keen football brain in there. In Guardiola's idea of a utopian Camp Nou, he would have at his disposal 20 fantastic footballers, but their brains would also be expected to function at top speed all the time. The impact Busquets has had on where the pressing takes place – an aspect which has become a signature part of the Guardiola era – and how regularly effective it is, makes an eloquent case for his importance to this team.

This is what Javier Mascherano told me about 'Busi'. "He has the talent to play for any team anywhere in the world, but he's made to play for this team, literally the perfect guy. He robs the ball, has superb technical skills and brings tactical order. I watch him and try to learn."

Víctor Valdés allows the back line to push high, Busquets shoves the midfield up a few metres, so as to support the strikers when they press. It's all a process.

Finally, I'm happy to hand over 'plaudit duty' to Xavi, who knows a little bit more about this than I do. It was the elder Catalan who pointed out a lack of *mala leche*, or 'nastiness', in the squad. He revealed that Busquets learned his football on the mean streets of Badia del Vallès, and was willing to take this 'enforcer' personality into situations where Barcelona's artists were being bullied. The wee guys like that. A lot.

He's been winning over doubters ever since, all the way to the World Cup final in Soccer City (Busquets became the natural successor to Marcos Senna between Euro 2008 and South Africa 2010), but whether you like him or not, do not doubt that Sergio Busquets has been a vital component of Barcelona's success.

7 – THE EMPERORS OF BARCELONA

"It was both conscious and well-discussed in our campaign sessions that we had to depict freshness and change. I think we won because of that ... it was all a different story."
— Marc Ingla

B Y CONTRAST WITH the preceding Friday, Sunday March 8, 1998 was a very pleasing day for Louis van Gaal. Forty-eight hours earlier, the Dutchman had slipped on the dressing-room floor at the Camp Nou after training and twisted his ankle so badly that he needed one of those Frankenstein-style protective boots ahead of a decisive Clásico that Sunday night. However, by the time he clumped into the dugout in front of 115,000 fans to watch his Barça side thrash Real Madrid 3-0, the Dutchman already knew that the man who wanted to oust Barça president Josep Lluís Núñez and replace Van Gaal with his implacable enemy, Johan Cruyff, had been defeated.

Immediately prior to that defeat of Madrid, the Barça *socios* (members) had been called to a vote of no confidence which, if lost, would have made Núñez's position untenable. Of the 91,815 eligible to vote, 40,412 did so, with 24,863 against the *moción de censura* (vote of no confidence) – there were 1191 spoiled or blank papers. This meant that the reigning president knew he was quite safe when, 45 minutes after the result was made public, he took his seat in the luxury Palco Presidencial to watch the Clásico. Núñez must have felt untouchable. Van Gaal evidently did, given the nature of his post-match press conference.

"This has been one of my best days ever, first because of the victory over Madrid and secondly because the president won at the ballot box – although I think we did an even better job than he did," Van Gaal barked with his mix of humour and swagger.

"Tomorrow morning I think I'll wear a blue tie with white elephants on it because elephants have always brought me luck, which has been proven tonight."

He was referring to the *Elefant Blau* (Blue Elephant) opposition group which had been defeated in their attempt to force Núñez out.

What none of them knew was the 14,358 votes gained by the *Elefant Blau* and their charismatic 35-year-old general, Joan Laporta, was the voice of the future. He would become the most successful, most effective president in the history of FC Barcelona. His board inherited the weak man of Spanish football and transformed them into the world's dominant team. During his mandates (2003-2010), Barça won 12 trophies, including two Champions Leagues and four Spanish titles. Context? Barça had won 16 Spanish titles in the 75 years prior to Laporta taking over.

While Real Madrid had famously dominated the European Cup, winning the trophy nine times to Barcelona's single triumph (Wembley 1992), Laporta's reign produced two more Champions League victories and left the incoming president a squad and coach able to add a third just one year after Laporta left (again at Wembley).

He didn't do it alone. Men such as Ferran Soriano and Marc Ingla were vital motors of the institutional success which took root at the Camp Nou. However, it was all Laporta's idea and, yet again, everything started with Johan Cruyff.

When Núñez sent his vice-presidential sidekick, Joan Gaspart, to sack Cruyff in May 1996, Laporta was amongst the many thousands of *culés* who not only disagreed with the decision but deplored the manner of the Dutchman's dismissal. Allied to other criticisms of the Núñez era, notably his dictatorial style and the club's debt, that brutal treatment of the only coach to have brought Barça a European Cup win was sufficient to catalyse a rebel movement which Laporta would eventually lead.

In 2006, Laporta explained to me the powerful reasons he'd first become a lifelong fan of Cruyff. "The summer of 1973 was hugely exciting, because all the *socios* were hanging on every twist and turn of Barça's move to sign Johan," he explained. "I was 11 years old and I followed every moment. At the time, it was the signing of the century. His competitive debut was against Granada and Johan scored twice. Then, we went on a 30-game run unbeaten, including the 5-0 win at Madrid, and we won the league five matches before the end of the championship. It was wonderful.

"It was a kind of revolution in our city and in our culture – as if the fifth Beatle had come to Barcelona. He brought an air of modernity, blowing away cobwebs, and he put us at the vanguard of sport in the world.

"As a player, he created love. He was imitated in everything – how he walked out to the pitch, how he directed everyone around him when he had his foot on the ball, how he combed his hair! Every kid wanted to be him, or be like him – myself in particular.

"There was a totalitarian government, so Barcelona had the sympathy of the progressive people, the democrats. He won support here and also across large parts of the country. Cruyff supported Barça's identity, but he lit up Spain, too.

"Every time Barça travelled then, it was like now: hundreds of fans, a clamour. What was very important was that with Johan arrived an idea of modernity. He unleashed progressive, democratic sentiments that widened the gap between Barça and the Francoists."

7 – The Emperors of Barcelona

Laporta grew up a committed Barça fan and as an articulate, ambitious young lawyer he knew how to organise and promote an opposition group when, in 1996, Núñez kicked Cruyff the coach out the door.

In hindsight, his adolescence houses signposts to some of his more eccentric moments from late in the presidential era.

Educated in a priests' college, Laporta had originally intended to become a missionary. An interesting thought. He was expelled because he rebelled against a physics teacher who had suspended the entire class during the first part of an academic year. Consequently, Laporta pinched some test answers and shared them with the class. When students who could barely sign their own name suddenly got top marks, the teacher sensed that something was up, locked them all in a classroom and demanded that the culprit own up. Letter home, no more school.

Nor did his mandatory military service bring out the conformist in Barça's future president. Army maladministration sent him to Tenerife instead of a posting one hour from Barcelona, as had been agreed. There, he rebelled because the army were serving expired camel meat at meals and received two weeks' solitary confinement.

Another incident, sneaking home when he thought that the administrative chaos of the army meant he wouldn't be missed, brought him a further two weeks in an army cell. Then, when he still had a month-and-a-half of his military service remaining, in the fortress in Pedralbes (overlooking the Camp Nou) where the dregs were sent, he decided to go with a girlfriend to Egypt on holiday. Without permission. Only when he returned, expecting to see the inside of another military jail cell, did he discover that, at roll call, his friends had shuffled about and called 'Present!' whenever the name Laporta was called out.

By the time his hero, Cruyff, was brutally dethroned, this was a man who knew how to rebel.

He was joined in those early stages by Albert Vicens, Jordi Moix, Albert Perrín and his old school friend, Alfons Godall, all of whom would go on to become directors on his board while Barça president.

Laporta first stood on the presidential ticket of Ángel Fernández in 1998, but their campaign was swept aside by Núñez. Two years later, when the residing president decided to retire, Laporta allied himself to the candidacy of the public relations and marketing magnate Lluís Bassat in the extraordinarily heated presidential elections of 2000.

Luis Figo was in the process of deserting for Real Madrid but Joan Gaspart, Núñez's long-time vice president and the man who told Cruyff he was sacked, defeated Bassat comfortably, 25,181 to 19,791.

However, themes emerged during that campaign. Bassat spoke out loudly against the "violent and drug-selling parts" of the club's most boisterous fans – the Boixos Nois. As president, Laporta would attempt to eradicate the worst elements from the Camp Nou and for years would be the subject of a campaign of intimidation that included threats on his life.

Bassat also appointed Txiki Begiristain as his proposed director of football, had the implicit support of Cruyff and spoke often of how much Pep Guardiola's values, playing style and background meant to him. All three men would be cornerstones of the new Barça.

7 — The Emperors of Barcelona

Worryingly for Laporta, an election inquest in one of the local papers found a majority of those questioned believed that Bassat's incorporation of members of *Elefant Blau* was hindering his cause – at the time the media regarded Laporta's protest group with, at best, scepticism.

However, Gaspart's reign was ruinous and a horrendous 4-2 home defeat by Rafa Benitez's Valencia in January 2003 not only brought a monumental *pañolada* (the white-handkerchief protest) but was the beginning of the end for the president, opening a path to new elections.

After the experience of being relegated to the sidelines during Bassat's campaign and in view of the atrocious state of his club, on and off the pitch, Laporta decided that he would head his own presidential campaign the next time the opportunity presented itself.

He contacted Sandro Rosell, a Barça blue blood; they persuaded Marc Ingla to join and he then inveigled his corporate partner, Ferran Soriano, to throw his considerable intellect behind the project.

Soriano was then a wealthy businessman, still only 36, with experience in international marketing and telecommunications. He would become vice president from that summer onwards. A born *culé*, passionate about Barça, Soriano was nonetheless an ingénue to football politics and the perfect brain to be headhunted by a group which was passionate, but lacked this kind of nous.

He told me: "I met this group of people, Laporta and so on, and they were keen to go for the presidency but they had no idea how to organise a winning campaign."

Soriano at once began to shake off the normal football

rules and to apply some of the common sense he'd learned in business. "An important point is that when you are approaching something you don't know about, it's both fair and advisable to go and look for expert help, right? So I phoned an expert in Washington, DC, a Catalan woman who was a campaign consultant there. I asked her, 'How do you organise a winning campaign?'

"She gave me a one-hour tutorial on the phone and I jotted it all down on paper then adapted those rules to the local issues. When I put it all to the group they commissioned me to get on with it."

Not quite the Dirty Dozen, the Laporta group was nevertheless a patchwork of people who seemed to believe in the same idealistic goals, who were young, energetic and heartily sick of how their club was limping from embarrassment to ridicule and back, via incompetence.

In the excellent Storyville documentary, 'Barcelona: The Inside Story', Rosell admits: "Being a Barcelona fan had started to make you feel ashamed."

While another vice president in the making, Rosell, started pulling in contacts and favours to improve the popular perception of a group that was still an underdog in the election race, it emerged that Laporta was a natural 'Golden Boy'. When programmed properly his articulacy, charm and self-confidence began to elevate his chances of electoral success.

"Joan was the perfect candidate for two reasons: First he has a natural charisma, particularly so at that time. He is brave and he expresses himself well," adds Soriano. "But the second thing, which was very important, was that he would just believe what we were saying, absorb it and repeat it, without deviating one millimetre.

"Eventually that became quite different when we faced the no-confidence vote in 2008, because he would not allow his people around him to tell him what to do. He would go off message. He'd get emotional.

"Back in 2003, we would start in the morning and tell him, 'Today the message is, virtuous cycle, plus new players.'

"We would warn him, 'You are going to repeat these messages over and over. You are going to feel very tired and dizzy due to saying the same things over and again, but don't worry about it – these are the two things for today.' And he would say those two or three things impeccably, time after time. Always convincingly. Zero deviation."

Ingla, despite not feeling supported by the president later in Laporta's mandate, shares this view of the president-in-the-making. "Jan [Laporta] was and is very idealistic, energetic, charismatic," he says. "The right chairman for the right moment.

"There was very little doubt over who would be the lead figure. Maybe, right at the beginning, Sandro said he wanted it, but it was clear it was Jan.

"It wasn't just opportunism. He had good values and proposed those values in a charismatic manner. People follow him. Also, when he is against something he does it with the same energy. It creates sparks."

As is often the case with great men and women, the same seeds were sewn for both glory and defeat. Ingla describes Laporta well. When he was right, his overwhelming self-belief overcame doubters and good things followed. When he was wrong, his overwhelming self-belief led him to ignore good counsel and disaster followed.

The campaign was already going well when Rosell engineered a colossal public relations coup that moved Laporta to the brink of power.

June 10, 2003. Those of us covering the election filed into Laporta's Passeig de Gràcia campaign offices ready for what we had been told would be a major announcement.

For months, I had been reporting that the deal between Real Madrid, Manchester United and David Beckham was complete. The price between the clubs had been agreed during a meeting between José Ángel Sánchez of Real Madrid and United's David Gill and Peter Kenyon on the island of Minorca. Beckham's people, free to negotiate with Madrid, had done so to their satisfaction but, because the deal had not yet been announced, the player was, theoretically, still on the market.

"I can announce that we have agreed a price with Manchester United to buy David Beckham," Laporta told us that day. Behind him was a screen onto which was being projected an official Manchester United statement confirming just that. From United's perspective, they simply wanted a fee for Beckham – regardless of who from – and were happy to confirm the fact that Laporta and his team, pending his election, had met their asking price.

The president in waiting wouldn't answer questions about the price, but handed the floor over to Sandro

7 — The Emperors of Barcelona

Rosell, his vice president of football, so that the man who had negotiated the deal could take the credit for it.

Disbelieving questions flooded in.

"How will you persuade him not to go to Madrid?"

"Is he the right type of player for your technical project?"

"Does the coach you have approached actually want him?"

"Is he just a marketing signing?"

Rosell batted all of these away with calm, slick answers.

This was a side show. Beckham was going to Madrid, but given that there was a formal Manchester United statement confirming the agreement over a transfer fee, the Catalan press went into frenzied overdrive.

From the outset it was a sleight-of-hand trick. Beckham was set on going to Madrid, Barcelona were struggling in the league and offered no guarantee of Champions League football – yet it worked perfectly.

Laporta had sold the voters what they wanted to believe – that this young, vibrant team of businessmen would make Barcelona big hitters on the European stage once more.

Marc Ingla was there that day and would become vice president of marketing after a landslide election win. Soriano and Ingla had founded a telecommunications firm that had offices from Boston to Dusseldorf, London and Paris to São Paulo.

Ingla told me: "When we announced the Beckham deal we were overtaking our opponents in the polls. The momentum had been built, but the Beckham deal fostered our majority because it gave us credibility: 'These guys can go to Manchester and sign the rock-star player.'

"Sandro Rosell was very involved in those dealings and I believe his very good relationship with Florentino Pérez helped this situation to go forward. It was 'half' a deal. Sandro made his game behind the scenes with all parties."

Sandro Rosell and Florentino Pérez had – and to an extent still have – a long-standing relationship of mutual respect, even friendship.

Beckham to Madrid was a done deal. Real Madrid were in the driving seat, yet here were their historic rivals announcing an agreement over a transfer fee for Beckham if Laporta won the presidential race. However, there were no angry rebuttals or attempts from the Bernabéu to discredit the Laporta deal for Beckham. The waters were pacific, a spirit of brotherly love existed for that brief moment between announcement and election.

If Pérez's friendly relations with Rosell were enough to persuade him not to attack the announcement, to allow the quickness of hand to deceive the voters' eyes, then it was an error. The incendiary effect of this announcement catapulted Laporta to victory and Barça back on the path to greatness.

"It was both conscious and well-discussed in our campaign sessions that we had to depict freshness and change," recalls Ingla. "I think we won because of that – or that's how it appears with perspective. The age of our board members, our CVs – it was all a different story."

Laporta and company defeated his former associate, Bassat, by nearly 9000 votes; it was the mandate for radical change which Ingla yearned for.

Laporta's manifesto had included the idea that his

board would be willing to discard one of the fundamental ideas of *Més Que Un Club* and accept shirt
sponsorship. Barça had been proud of the fact that
they were one of extremely few teams in the world
to keep their jersey 'pure'. This move by Laporta pre-
election, ratified by a special assembly early in the first
year of his presidency, was an enormous step away
from tradition.

Beckham went to Madrid, of course. Pini Zahavi, the
agent who had been instrumental in helping Rosell
and Laporta in the background, helped to bring to
Barcelona the Turkish international keeper Rüştü
Reçber (who failed outright), while Luis García, Rafa
Márquez, Gio van Bronckhorst, Ricardo Quaresma
and Ronaldinho also signed up.

It was interesting, not to say strange, that United,
who had been helpful in adding the Beckham allure
to Laporta's campaign, dropped the ball on signing
Ronaldinho from Paris Saint-Germain. The president
of the French club, Francis Graille, became so irritated with Peter Kenyon, then United chief executive,
flip-flopping between one price verbally and another
by fax, that the player was offered to Barcelona. Real
Madrid, too, wanted Ronaldinho, but not for another
year, something he would not accept. Rosell's excellent
relationship with Ronaldinho, stemming from their
past with Nike, where Rosell was an executive, and the
Brazil national team, that firm's stellar clients, did the
rest. An extraordinary footballer and a joyful personality was added to the rebuilding project – it was one of
the most significant moments in the modern history
of FC Barcelona.

Then another: Frank Rijkaard was signed as coach.

"He was young and without that much experience, so probably we were building another layer of risk into a new project," recalls Ingla. "We believed that if we had a very senior coach he might not help us achieve the right turnaround with the energy and momentum we needed. Frank's age and outlook were probably more aligned with our interests. It was a partnership. The mandate we got from the elections was that the club needed to be re-engineered and we would not do that with someone who had already a booklet on how to do things.

"We had to be true to the membership and what they had asked of us: A young coach who believes in grassroots football, offensive play, style and who has football intelligence – Rijkaard met that description."

The backstage team and the front-of-house talent were assembled.

At the same time, Laporta's group were learning the extent of the mess they had walked into. The new board inherited a debt of €150m and discovered that the previous regime had, in its final year, spent €196m, but only earned €120m. Soriano was stunned at what he found.

"The most striking thing was that the management style was based on what you might have done in 1970," he says.

"Our simple concept was that if we were to manage this club, which is so relevant for so many people, we had to have somebody in the marketing department who knew about marketing. Not just somebody who had been there for years from the 'football family' and had ended up in that job. Get someone from Proctor and Gamble who knows about marketing. That person can then learn about football. It was the same with finance people, and so on."

However, there was far more to achieve than had initially been anticipated and, on the pitch, results went from average to appalling. A crisis was looming.

At this time, Soriano recalls receiving support from an unexpected source. "I remember how instrumental Luis Enrique was to the changes," he told me. "He was the captain and sort of looked at us with big question marks.

"After a while he relaxed because he saw Ronaldinho and Rafa Márquez and players like that arriving. His view was 'We have been here so many years and the club has been buying players who did not have the quality year after year'. That's exactly what he said to us.

"It is a fact that expensive players who didn't have the quality were regulars. Geovanni Deiberson and Fabio Rochemback are two good examples. Luis Enrique waited, saw the players we signed and then came back to us to say, 'Okay, this is much better. These players are at the top level.'

"Another factor was important. At the beginning of the first season, Frank put Luis in the team every game. We would say, 'Why are you doing this?' Luis Enrique was getting close to his retirement and technically he probably wasn't the right guy.

"Frank said, 'I have to give the first opportunity to the old guys, to the owners of the dressing room, so that they are treated fairly. Then, if I have to change them and give space to the new guys, they have been given that opportunity.'

"Eventually, Luis started playing less, but because of how he'd been treated he was instrumental in creating unity. There was a sense that he would help pass things on to the new group and only then he would go. This one decision by Frank Rijkaard was extremely important."

Gradually the board began to convince people and institutions around the world that, despite slow returns on the pitch, Barça were back.

Revenue streams had been poor, the club's identity was shrouded, marketing was either old-fashioned or non-existent, debt was huge. Ingla, as vice president of marketing, was a key strategist.

"[Barcelona were] trying to sell a friendly game for between €120,000 and €200,000, which is the appearance fee for an average team in the league today. After three years, we were selling that game for €2m, 10 times the fee from when we took over.

"This is a very sexy media property with people dying to have a part of it, anywhere in the world. There had been a lack of vision on what the club really meant."

Laporta, Soriano, Rosell and Ingla, the four musketeers of the original era, had no shame in looking left and right and copying what was already being done well. They found that in 1996, Barcelona and Manchester United earned roughly the same from marketing, but by 2003 Barça made €120m to United's €260m.

"Madrid was a model for us because they had some amazing iconic players," says Ingla. "Everyone could see the way their club was achieving this amazing projection. We thought that Barça was managed too locally. We also looked at Manchester for how to manage the process of change and what to aim at.

"However, above all we needed to go back to our traditional attacking playing style."

However, cracks began to appear in Laporta's young board. Rosell, the current president of Barcelona, was uncomfortable within a very short space of time after taking office in 2003. Early in the new era, the Storyville cameras caught him with his guard down. "When a team is unified and pulls in the right direction success follows, but the team is fundamental," he said. Rosell was talking not about Frank Rijkaard's Barça, but the group which won the election.

Before long, he referred to his fellow board members as 'flower children'. It was a rebuke of what Rosell saw as the naïveté of the initial Camelot ethos, where everyone was to be considered equal and Laporta a figurehead president. There was a spell when Laporta made use of the collegiate vibe and the big brains around him. Perhaps those were the golden years of his reign. They didn't last.

"In the first year Joan was delegating a lot," remembers Ingla. "To Ferran, to me and, on the football side, to Sandro and Txiki. But the following year he started to do more things on his own as an executive chairman. He was the 24/7 president of the club in a fully executive role and I don't think that the president needs to be taking those kind of managerial/technical decisions. The president needs a more social role – involved in decisions, but leaving some of the work to the experts around him. In retrospect, Jan had to be less executive and we did too. We needed to let the professionals run the club."

I asked Soriano if he was aware that in feeding Laporta political tactics, advice and then gifting him power, they were unleashing a different kind of beast? "Not in the first months. It went well and this was a successful process, but along the way there were some bombs. After three or four months we had the guy who is now president [Rosell] suddenly totally against some of us on the board and creating lots of troubles.

"As for the problems in 2008 [when Laporta faced a vote of no confidence], I think that being president, you can survive if you are mature enough and you don't believe totally in the character you are playing. If you become that 'character' totally then there is a problem. In those two years, from 2006 to 2008, he was attacked every single day in the papers from the opposition. It's difficult to cope with, particularly if you are an emotional, combative person.

"At some point in time he developed this idea that 'I am the one who is receiving all this pressure so I have to be taking all the decisions. Everything is on me'. That's where he went wrong because he stopped listening to all the very bright, very honest people he had all around him. That's why he was possessive, I think, but the wrong decision for him was, 'I have pressure so I have to have more power'. Distributing the pressure and making the most from the team would have been the answer."

"I've always been an executive president," Laporta said in 2008. "FC Barcelona travels at a very high speed and it's important to have the desire to innovate. It needs a firm hand on the tiller to take the club where we want it to be without deviating from our objectives. Things which made sense a few months ago, now do not."

Not the voice of a long-term strategist.

7 — The Emperors of Barcelona

As the Storyville cameras rolled, back in the infancy of Laporta's reign, he was already on the way to losing the man who would succeed him as president and move from being an influential ally to a sworn enemy.

Rosell was the most vocal of those who believed that Frank Rijkaard needed to be dismissed during the winter of season 2003-04. The team was playing with lead in their boots and two defeats, 5-1 at Málaga and 3-0 at Racing, seemed to indicate an irreversible slump.

Rosell is a bright, talented, go-ahead man whose background as a Nike executive and a footballer of some talent make him an ideal football club administrator, but he quickly felt thwarted by the board – Laporta particularly, after Rijkaard was maintained and Rosell's idea of hiring Phil Scolari ignored. Tensions grew, as Ingla recalls.

"We believed in Frank. Also, we were very reluctant to trust Sandro's proposals. Sandro would have sacked him. It felt like Sandro's agendas were anti-Cruyff, anti-Txiki [Begiristain], pro-Scolari, pro his 'book' of players. Conceptually, Sandro was providing players and that wasn't the job of the vice president. That had to be the job of the football director and the coach in tandem.

"From the beginning, Sandro almost had a paranoid manner about Cruyff. He remembered his father being general manager of the club and Cruyff being there as a player and the money dealings of that time. So, he was totally obsessive about Cruyff."

Soriano is still blunter. "Sandro Rosell was on our board for two years but he was against everybody else.

He didn't say much and didn't even bother to explain to us why he left.

"At the time of Rijkaard struggling there were board discussions, amongst the same people who are now in charge of the club. After six months of Frank they wanted to hire Felipe Scolari. Their idea was that this kind of football [the Barça style] was outdated. At the time, we played against Chelsea and we lost and so those voices would say, 'You see. We should hire a Scolari-type of manager and start hiring bigger, stronger players.'

"The magic we achieved was to say, 'No that's not what we are. We play spectacular football and we can't deviate from that.'"

Rosell, wisely, bottled up his frustration until the team had won a trophy while he was on the board – La Liga in 2005 – and then walked away.

In the meantime, despite the tension between the Cruyff-loyal Begiristain and Rosell, the club achieved in the summer of 2004 one of the most impressive transfer turnovers football has seen. They sold or released 16 players, including Phillip Cocu, Patrick Kluivert, Luis Garcia, Marc Overmars and Rüştü. In came Samuel Eto'o, Deco, Edmilson, Ludovic Giuly, Juliano Belletti, Sylvinho and Henrik Larsson. Even if he felt outmanoeuvred by the Cruyff sympathisers, Rijkaard and Begiristain, Rosell was directly implicated in this work, which laid the foundations for two titles and a Champions League victory.

Laporta still claims Rosell was completely opposed to the purchase of Eto'o and, according to Laporta, was 'boycotting' every decision. The reason, alleged by Laporta, is that Rosell was considering the potential damage which might be done to his and Barça's harmonious relationship with Florentino Pérez as Real Madrid were still part owners of the Cameroon striker. The move for Eto'o was a massive success for Barcelona, but a contributory factor in the fracture of the relationship between Rosell and Laporta.

When Rosell left, in June 2005, it was with an open letter to the *socios* that attacked the board at the time and painted the picture of a disheartened man.

Dear Barcelonistas,

I must tell you that today I've communicated to the president that I am resigning my position as vice president of the FC Barcelona board.

I wanted to keep this decision under wraps until now for two reasons. Firstly I didn't want any action of mine to destabilise the sporting performance of any of our players. Now we have finished and won the league there is no such risk. The second was until June 1 the club had not renewed the contracts of those who have been so fundamental to our success in fútbol base. For the good of the club I wanted them to have their futures, with regard to next season, assured before leaving. Waiting this long has come at a cost.

I know it must seem impossible to walk away from a responsibility like mine without it causing a stir.

I've always put the club's benefit ahead of mine and if that's not the case this time then I ask your forgiveness. I'm leaving and I want it to be without doing damage to anyone.

I'm a loyal club socio *and someone who takes responsibility for his actions but, friends and* culés, *there are problems which do not have simple solutions. For months my situation has been very uncomfortable and has saddened me. The project which that group of proud, ambitious young men explained during the last election campaign has been consistently diminished during the management of the last two years at Barcelona. Either I didn't originally understand the idea with which Joan Laporta sought the presidency or things have been changing towards a style of management which lacks independence, transparency or democracy in its direction. For these reasons I must step down and for those reasons I must also avoid giving more details of our differences in public.*

In fact these divergences are not between me and him. They are between the management of Joan Laporta and the original electoral manifesto he presented. We have been accused of being a media-oriented board. It didn't have to be that way. The attention should always be on and for the players who defend the Barça shirt with their efforts. A Barça director should be sound and of high standing, plus be proud of and loyal to the club.

And, of course, he should be loyal to the board's decisions and actions – so long as they are democratic. He should work with discretion, honesty,

*efficacy, humility and transparency. With hand
on heart I can say that I've tried to act that way
but the circumstances have dragged us into
indiscretions which have quickly been made public.*

*I'd also like to say that the divergence of views I
have with this president should not be used as a
means to criticise this generation of people. Our
hard work and belief in the idea 'Barça First' made
us winners. If that spirit was still our prime guide
then I wouldn't be stepping down.*

*I know that I'm the loser, but if I go the president
will feel more relaxed. Nor do I wish to force him
to fire me. I know how he works and I know that
leaving like this will help him. But I'm not losing
'to him'. I'm losing with myself for having made
the mistake of investing so much time, so many
contacts and so much sacrifice in a project which
he has diminished. However I must say that I don't
mind because all the benefits of that work and
effort have gone not to the president, nor the coach,
nor me personally – but to the club.*

*That compensates for everything, including that
which is said about me from now on because I'm
a born culé. In my family, from grandparents to
parents, brothers, sisters, kids and grandkids, we
are all socios. Because of that I'll leave without
rancour against anyone despite the disagreement I
have with the president.*

I'll finish with a message for the president. "Jan,

don't forget the socios *more than you have already.
They are the bosses of the club, they elected you and
you'll be accountable to them. Barça must always
be a democratic club."*

*I hope that this league we have won is the beginning
of a series of successes. To achieve that we already
have a good squad base built over the last two
years. I just hope those who are responsible don't
spoil that which they are inheriting. I'll end with the
cry which unites all of us who are Barcelonistas.*

¡Visca Barça!

In the press conference to announce his departure,
Rosell put the spotlight on one of the issues which
divided him and Laporta. Asked about the influence
of Johan Cruyff on the club, Rosell answered: "For the
good of all, Johan, step back, leave Jan [Laporta] to
work without pressure – relaxed. Without this influence maybe he will reconsider and return to the original project. For his sake, let Jan work."

For a long time after leaving he kept his counsel,
but by the time Laporta faced a vote of no confidence
in 2008, Rosell announced that he would stand for
president at the next possible occasion.

He said then: "The crisis we face isn't simply sporting, it's institutional. There is an absolute lack of proper
governance and that's not what I say, it's what the 9,500
socios who have signed the vote of no confidence say."

Laporta narrowly survived the vote of no confidence,
although eight directors, including Ingla and Soriano,
resigned in the face of such substantial opposition. It

was but one controversy in a presidency that collected them as regularly as the team won trophies.

THE FRANCOIST BROTHER-IN-LAW
No Barcelona director receives a wage or any direct remuneration from the club, other than expenses, and what's more each of them has to lay down a financial guarantee (which was €1.5m when Laporta took office) before their election can be formalised. Laporta's initial inauguration had to be delayed while he and some of his board raised this money and he received some financial backing from his in-laws.

Alejandro Echevarría is his brother-in-law and was co-opted onto the board. A man of influence, he made it his job to be a friend to the players, to sweeten their life at FC Barcelona. As such, he was popular and useful. But a determined journalist found out that Echevarría was a Francoist. Initially both he and Laporta denied it, but the deceit was unsustainable and the combination of a Francoist at the new 'super-Catalan' Barcelona, plus the fact that Laporta had lied about it led to Echevarría's resignation, in October 2005.

CAUGHT WITH HIS TROUSERS DOWN
On Saturday, July 9, 2005 at about quarter past three, Joan Laporta was passing through security at Terminal C of Barcelona airport. Over and again the machine bleeped when the Barcelona president walked through, despite having removed phone, belt, keys and money. His fellow passengers watched in astonishment as Laporta lost his temper, raised his voice and shouted, "Right, if you want to see me naked, then that's what you'll get". He stripped off his trousers and threw them

on the conveyor belt for the scanner, at which point the Guardia Civil intervened. Laporta was taken away, lectured and, fortunately for him, not arrested.

LAPORTA'S WATERGATE

In late 2008 Laporta hired a man called Joan Oliver to be the club's general director. A year later, he pushed through a salary hike for Oliver: €600,000 plus variables which could rise by an extra €300,000 depending on objectives achieved. Questioned about this salary by an incredulous media, the president replied: "I think he actually deserves more."

Oliver, apparently without informing the president, engaged a firm of private detectives to spy on four of Laporta's vice presidents – Joan Boix, Joan Franquesa, Rafael Yuste and Jaume Ferrer. With Laporta's mandate expiring that summer, the campaigning to form the opposition to the declared frontrunner, Rosell, had begun; allegiances were being drawn, clandestine pacts formed. Was Laporta seeking information with a view to handpicking his successor?

When the news broke, Laporta claimed: "This risk management information was legal and was to protect these guys and the club. Things are being exaggerated. The director general [Oliver] and the head of security took this decision without informing me because it was within their ambit. When they had the results, Oliver shared them with me and I decided it was important to tell the vice presidents. They understood and accepted the matter."

THE AUDITS

When Laporta and his board handed over the

outgoing accounts when their final term came to an end in summer 2010, their audit claimed that they were handing over a final year profit of €11m. Within a few months the audit commissioned by the incoming board, from KPMG, stated that there was a €79m loss in that final year. A stark difference in figures in part down to some outlandish expenses: private jets, seven-figure expenditure on tickets for a U2 concert, trips to the Champions League final in Rome and a Final Four basketball tournament.

SHIRT SPONSORSHIP

The issue that straddles the two presidencies. A principle held so dear before Laporta's board was remarkably straightforward to discard. Getting the right sponsor, and then changing it when the Rosell presidency began, was another matter.

After a beauty parade of lucrative sponsors, including the Beijing Olympics, Laporta's board sprung a shock. Not only were the first ever sponsors in that prime position on the front of the Barça shirt to be UNICEF, but Barça were going to pay at least €1.5m per year for five years for the privilege, money designated for work fighting AIDS in Swaziland.

Soriano was the main author of the idea. "*Més Que Un Club* [More than a club] has great political significance in Catalonia but not anywhere else in the world," he told me. "We faced a challenge and there were still voices who would say 'This is not more than a club. It's a football club. Let's go and sell shirts in China'.

"The beauty of this idea was that we integrated who we were with selling a lot of shirts in China. We wanted to find something that would help us communicate our *Més Que un Club* message that everyone in the world could understand.

"We also wanted a deal which was universal and global. And it had to be self-explanatory. UNICEF was perfect for this. That's why putting the Qatar Foundation on the shirt [as Barcelona have done under Rosell] instead has been so controversial. It doesn't achieve the same things as UNICEF."

The man who made the call to switch from UNICEF to the Qatar Foundation, and who now governs Barcelona, is Rosell, whose journey from ball boy to president is reminiscent of that made by Pep Guardiola, his coach.

This early after his return to the Camp Nou, on the back of the biggest landslide election win in the club's history, in 2010, it is not simple to compare his work with that of Laporta, the man he did so much to get elected in 2003.

However, the bitterness between the former allies makes the absolute priority given by the new board to reviewing the honorary president position given to Johan Cruyff by the outgoing board just before the 2010 elections appear vindictive.

Of far greater significance is the decision by Rosell's board to invest heavily in the club's new training facility and the way it is staffed. Making the key coaches at every youth level full-time employees is a giant leap forward and provides administrative support to Pep Guardiola's ambitions to produce *canteranos* for the first team.

Possibly Rosell's biggest decision yet has been to take what he and his board claim was indispensable investment from the Qatar Foundation, which replaced the altruistic funding of the UNICEF brand on the front of the Barça shirt with a commercial deal.

In summer 2011, FC Barcelona announced that global debt had fallen from €532m to €431m and the net debt from €431m to €364m. Take all of that in good faith and the guaranteed revenue of €165m (plus a potential add-on of €5.5m) across five years from the Qatar Foundation deal seems like a no-brainer. In his electoral campaign, Rosell described the club he was inheriting as "an ocean liner powered by a superb team but with a hull full of holes". Remedies were needed.

The board insisted on a deal with Qatar Sports Investment (whose brand, Qatar Foundation, appears on the shirt) which "a future Barça board will have the option of changing or quitting". Javier Faus has explained that "We wanted to solve our economic problems, but make a deal which wasn't irreversible".

Those who made the UNICEF deal lament that it has been diminished, but Ingla and Soriano, two key figures in that landmark partnership, are far from condemnatory about the arrival of a commercial sponsor.

"I believe it's a bad idea to remove UNICEF from the chest of the shirt," says Ingla. "This does not make us a vulgar club, but it prevents the world viewing us as a very special club."

The task which most challenges Sandro Rosell as president of Barcelona is how to retain both the key stars of this era: Lionel Messi and Pep Guardiola. Injury, in the case of Messi, and burnout, in the case of Guardiola, are two unpredictable factors. They can be prepared for, staved off, but they remain anarchic elements.

However, recent years have clearly shown that the strategies adopted to keep Messi fit and happy have paid dividends. Changes to his diet and training regimes have had positive results. A mutual trust has been carefully developed between Barcelona, Messi and his father, which has strengthened that relationship. It all stemmed from a strategic realisation that Messi was about to become a phenomenon.

The arrival of Neymar is patently on Barcelona's agenda. The president of Santos, the Brazilian prodigy's current club, has revealed that Rosell asked for and was granted permission to speak to the player and his father in the summer of 2010 – an indication that this is an interventionist president.

That may have an influence on Guardiola, who has already stayed in charge at Barça for longer than he expected to and, by his own admission, expects to reach a point when his appetite for the job diminishes. Rosell's task here is to create an atmosphere of trust and openness between the board and the coach in order to put off that moment for as long as possible.

Rosell is not tied to the Cruyff philosophy and would have exchanged what proved to be an important era, that of Rijkaard, for one with Felipe Scolari and bigger, stronger players at the Camp Nou. His conversion to the current style of football comes from the success it has generated rather than through the cult of Cruyff which has been such an influence on Rijkaard, Guardiola and Laporta.

Rosell is planning for a future which will not necessarily include Carles Puyol, Xavi and Pep Guardiola; one in which Barça may be economically more powerful. If he can harness the current and next generations of footballers, if he can maximise the work of the coaches and *fútbol base* brains he has empowered, if he can maintain this level of excellence then, like Laporta, he will leave a legacy of which to be proud.

MAKING-OF MATCH:
BARCELONA 2 REAL MADRID 0
LA LIGA, DECEMBER 14 2008

Juande Ramos won his first game as a visiting coach to the Camp Nou 2-0 with Rayo Vallecano in 2000. The defeat brought pain to a team containing Carles Puyol and Pep Guardiola, but still more for Louis van Gaal, who was soon to be removed from his post as coach. Despite his seven subsequent defeats with a variety of teams at the Camp Nou, Ramos had also inflicted spectacular damage on Barça with Málaga (5-0 at the Rosaleda in 2003) and with Sevilla (a 3-0 thumping of the new European champions with his terrific Sevilla side in August 2006).

So even with Ruud van Nistelrooy, Arjen Robben, Lassana Diarra and Pepe absent from his Real Madrid team, the combination of the fact that it was only seven months since Madrid had humiliated Barça 4-1 at the Bernabéu, and Ramos's evident knowledge of how to beat *La Blaugrana*, meant that this game was one of high risk for Barça.

Guardiola had given good press conference all week. "This could be my last Clásico," he said of his first meeting with Madrid as coach. "They are on the throne, they are the champions and no matter what I hear about people asking us to hammer them, you simply don't take apart a top team like them. I respect them and will treat them as a threat – even more so if they are missing some players. But it's our job to get after them, to hound them and to win."

On a night when the elements make the battle for football superiority seem like something out of Apocalypse Now, either Ramos or his players appear to have settled on a tactic of trying to hack Leo Messi out of the game. Between the second and 41st minute five different players commit six nasty fouls on the Argentinian, each rotating the damage they try to do to his ankles, shins and knees. Sadly, referee Medina Cantalejo does too little to enforce the laws and Madrid are in the match.

Víctor Valdés makes vital saves from Royston Drenthe and Rafael Van der Vaart while Miguel Palenca, a youth team winger drafted in to cover for the injuries, hits the post. Barça dominate as the Camp Nou bays for revenge, a goal, a red card … relief from the mounting tension.

Then, Iker Casillas saves a penalty from his ex-team-mate, Samuel Eto'o, and Madrid think they have won the lottery: dominated but not defeated and the Guardiola bandwagon derailed.

There are 20 minutes left. Then only eight. Xavi's corner is met by a massive Puyol leap and Eto'o flicks in the half chance. He goes absolutely mad, racing away, whirling his top in the air, soaking in the cold November rain.

Then, Thierry Henry's neat assist sends Messi through in injury time and he conjures a little chip over Casillas which has the kind of spin on it which would please Shane Warne.

"I was kicked a little harder and more often in this match than usual," he points out mildly after the win, "but let's not make too big a deal out of it."

Guardiola is almost as happy with the raw, gritty determination he has witnessed as with the two goals and the three points. "Winning like that, feeling that emotion was better than winning 5-0," he reasons. "We battled to the end, we believed, we got our reward."

Epic.

Barcelona (4-3-3) Valdés; Alves, Puyol, Márquez, Abidal; Xavi (Keita 90), Touré, Gudjohnsen (Busquets 63); Messi, Eto'o (Hleb 88) Henry.
Real Madrid (4-4-2) Casillas; Salgado, Metzelder, Cannavaro, Ramos; Sneijder (Palanca 36), Gago, Guti (Javi García 72), Drenthe; Higuaín (Van der Vaart 76) Raúl.
Goals Eto'o 82, Messi 91
Booked Metzelder, Ramos, Márquez, Drenthe, Salgado, Eto'o, Casillas, Messi
Referee Luis Medina Cantalejo
Attendance 96,059, Camp Nou

8 – THE ODD COUPLE

"We've reached the stage now that we don't
need to talk, it's sufficient for a little glance at
each other to agree what needs to be done in
any given situation"
— Gerard Piqué

I T IS JANUARY 5, 2011 AND Barcelona, playing at *El Catedral* of San Mamés against Athletic Bilbao in the Copa del Rey, are clinging on. Éric Abidal has made it 1-0 and Barça will go through to the next round if they don't concede twice in the last 16 minutes, but Athletic have their tails further up than a peacock in heat.

Fernando Llorente, muscles bursting out of his XXL shirt, is close to unplayable and the ball is being launched to him by player after player in red-and-white stripes. High above them in the coliseum, the eager Basque mob bays for Barça's blood.

On Pep Guardiola's bench sits his captain, Carles Puyol. Tarzan. The man for a crisis. However, he's not fully fit. He has missed the previous couple of games due to a knee problem which is about to cripple his season.

The plan was to take him to the game but mop up a win without using the 32-year-old. Now there is no choice and so the talismanic defender, whose absences that season coincided with all six of his team's defeats, strips off and waits for the referee, César Muñiz Fernández, to wave him on. There are 13 minutes left.

Puyol trots out and takes up his position next to Gerard Piqué. The younger man turns to his captain and says: "Bloody hell, Puyi, I've really missed you – it's good to have you back."

Instead of a quick high five or a little wink to confirm that Butch and Sundance are back in the saddle, Puyol explodes: "Stop fooling around Geri and concentrate on the bloody game!" Although Llorente scores, Barça see out the match and power onwards to a final against Real Madrid.

8 — The Odd Couple

It's a constant theme between them. Piqué admits that his concentration powers aren't on full beam all the time; Puyol might admit that his playing partner's youthful zest has taught him not to be on guard, tense and serious 24 hours a day, 365 days per year.

Off the pitch, Piqué calms Puyol down. On the pitch, the older man gives his playing partner hell if his intensity drops for a split second.

Ladies and gentlemen, I give you Gerard Piqué and Carles Puyol – football's Odd Couple. You should have the theme tune to Neil Simon's Academy Award-winning film of that name, about Felix and Oscar – the sport-obsessed, testosterone-fuelled Walter Matthau foolishly offering niggly, neurotic Jack Lemmon a place to stay in his apartment – playing in your head as you read this.

Honestly, the World Cup-winning partnership shouldn't even like each other, never mind have a bountiful playing relationship and a friendship which has changed each man profoundly.

There is nearly a decade in age between them, a world of difference in their upbringings, a six-inch gap in height, radical differences in their style, haircuts, personalities and life experience – and yet they have forged a remarkable bond.

By the time he was 23, Carles Puyol had not won World Cup and Champions League medals, dated a pop superstar, been chosen as the face of Spanish clothes store Mango, or published an autobiography.

No prizes for guessing that Piqué had.

At 23, Puyol had not won a single trophy and had spent his early years dodging Louis van Gaal's demands that he get a haircut. Far from being compared to the game's most elegant sweeper (Piquénbauer is a nickname which even Franz Beckenbauer has endorsed) Puyol was a winger, converted to a full-back, who was about to become a centre-half.

When Piqué was signed back from Manchester United for £5m in 2008, he was a rarity. Other exiles from La Masia had been bought back – Luis García, who went on to win the Champions League with Liverpool, was one; Gerard López, a Champions League finalist with Valencia, another. Each returned for sizeable fees, but encountered relatively little success. They certainly didn't represent value for money. The return of Piqué was not universally popular – and he knew it.

Think about the other defenders in the dressing room. Puyol had just won Euro 2008 with Spain; the proud Mexican World Cup star Rafa Márquez was his regular partner at centre-half; Gabi Milito (who at least Piqué knew from his loan spell at Zaragoza) was there; Éric Abidal wanted to play at centre-half more often and Martín Cáceres had been bought that summer for a remarkable €16m.

Piqué was born to a well-to-do family in posh Pedralbes. He was confident, a practical joker and he had been repatriated at a cost. Nothing would have been easier than for the other central defenders to take against him. Instead, Piqué quickly matured into a vital component in the revitalisation of team spirit and quality of football at Barcelona.

In his debut year, season 2008-09, he ranked sixth for minutes played in all competitions as Barcelona won the treble (he was the third most-used in the Champions League). At the end of that first season, Piqué produced a world-class tackle to prevent Manchester

United scoring first in the Rome final. Barça owe that triumph almost as much to Piqué's remarkable block on Park Ji-Sung as they do to their goalscorers, Samuel Eto'o and Leo Messi.

"One of the problems in football is that defenders ... they don't value us that much, because there isn't as much spectacle and prestige in our work as for a forward," explains Piqué.

"The most beautiful thing in football is scoring a goal, and then you have the assist. Personally, I think moments like that one in Rome are key, because if United had got the advantage it would have been much tougher to turn it around. Park could definitely have scored after Ronaldo's free-kick. I stayed aware and was able to produce the block."

That Piqué inspired Puyol to form a three-man Rat Pack with Cesc Fàbregas and radically change his entire character is an extraordinary achievement. To appreciate it, we have to get to know Puyol.

Though history will mark him down as one of Spanish football's all-time greats, his achievements can appear to be triumphs of effort, rather than talent. That's a false impression partly driven by the fact that Puyol was the most emblematic player at the Camp Nou during the great trophy drought of 1999-2005.

This raw, 17-year-old country boy arrived at the Barcelona youth system just a few months before Johan Cruyff was ousted. He was the ultimate utility player: not tall, but possessing a great leap; not supremely talented, but driven to work on every aspect of his game. Eventually, he would become a World Cup-winning centre-half, but in his youth he'd played almost everywhere, from goalkeeper to striker, and in his first couple of years in the first-team squad at the Camp Nou he was a winger and then a right-back.

Born in deepest Catalonia, in the small village of La Pobla de Segur, his parents, Josep and Rosa, had land and a herd of cows. Their two sons, Carles and Josep Xavier, attended the local Sagrada Familia School. Josep Xavier, known as Putxi to his younger brother's Puyi, was perhaps the more talented – a striker – but Puyol the younger was fired by a raw determination. His sentiments haven't changed and one of his tattoos reads: "Power is inside the mind. The strong can endure."

A devoted Barça fan, he would stomp upstairs and slam his bedroom door for the night without eating his dinner if his team lost.

They played on a hard-packed sand and gravel pitch, life-threatening for a guy with Puyol's never-say-die playing style. Any contact between skin and playing surface meant horrible lacerations, and sliding tackles were for those completely oblivious to their own well-being.

Puyi had the great good fortune to chance upon a local coach, Jordi Mauri, who was as driven as he was. Mauri and Puyol were tough enough to agree on extra training in the freezing cold of the dark mornings.

Mauri recalls two incidents that taught him that this was a kid of extremely rare determination. "In the training we used to get old socks, fill them with 10 kilos of sand and tie a knot so that they were linked," he remembers. "Carles would put one on each shoulder and do sit-ups with them like that. It was freezing cold, a home-made training solution and his mates faded away, but he was completely driven. Perhaps I could have got away with that with the younger kids, but the other guys of Puyol's age just wouldn't have come back to the next session. He did, though.

"Once, when we were playing foot-tennis, Carles threw himself full length to try to rescue a point with a diving header. When he got up he had mashed his face and it was all covered in blood – but he was just pissed off that he'd lost the point and wanted to get going to win it back.

"Most kids of 14 would have been lying there moaning and feeling sorry for themselves. He was ultra-competitive then, a thoroughbred who had the capacity to learn things very quickly."

Puyol would have a football with him at all times, whether he was playing a match, practising, or just at home. His progression from that bloody game of football-tennis to lifting the World Cup was never fuelled by a desire for fame and fortune, always by a 10,000-volt will to win.

"As a youngster, I used to completely lose it if we were beaten," he recalls. "I'd find it very hard to think about losing a match and not being pissed off – I get pissed off even if it's just a match during a training session. I don't think I'll ever change. You need to be very competitive to make it to the elite."

There was only one senior team in the local area and Puyol therefore played street football, seven-a-side or *fútbol sala* until midway through his teens. This emblematic warrior of Spain and Barça's golden eras didn't start at 11-a-side football on a full-sized pitch until he was 14-years-old.

When the call from Barça came there were around 30 kids at the big test to decide who would sign. Puyol seized the gauntlet. "Throughout it all I had no idea if I was doing well or not," he remembers. "There was very little feedback, but I loved every minute of it. What a dream, just to be wearing the Barça shirt!"

It would be a decade before 'Puyi' would win his first senior trophy with the club, but the golden era was forming. Xavi and Víctor Valdés were already in the system, Iniesta had been selected and, two years later a pair of 10-year-old kids, Francesc Fàbregas from Arenys de Mar and Piqué, signed up too.

When he was a kid and playing as a fearless goalkeeper, Puyol's mother Rosa was sufficiently worried about her younger son throwing himself about the hard pitches that she took him to the local doctor. The wise medic laid a stone in the foundations of Spain's World Cup win by advising her that her son risked developing spinal problems and should throw away his goalkeeping gloves. Puyol had only become a keeper because he played with his older brother and his friends and the smallest kid was ordered to play in goal.

Piqué started out in the *Torneo Social* for six and seven-year-olds, where the disparity between ability levels can be jaw-dropping. Barça began charging for kids who had no proven talent but wanted to play social football. Very few would get invited to La Masia for trials, but Piqué was one.

"I remember I had to pass a test to be a striker," says Piqué. "I scored a couple of goals and we won 3-1. My whole life at the time was schoolwork, playing football and having fun. I didn't want or need anything else.

"I tried not to indulge in dreaming about playing for Barça, because I'd seen other guys who didn't make it and I didn't want to end up living with frustrated dreams and feeling like a failure."

Piqué's upbringing could barely have been more different than that of Puyol in rural Catalonia with his cows and his socks full of sand. To begin with, Piqué's grandfather, Amador Bernabéu, is a genuine Barça blue-blood. Under three different club presidents – Josep Lluís Núñez, Joan Gaspart and Enric Reyna, across 23 years – he was a director who represented the club with the Spanish Federation, UEFA and FIFA. Under Sandro Rosell, he has been invited back to do the same job.

He was on the board when his grandson was tempted away to United. Amador Bernabéu made Piqué a *socio* (club member) the day he was born and the boy with the silver spoon in his boots grew up with the Camp Nou as a second home. Pedralbes, his neighbourhood, is a 10-minute walk from the Camp Nou.

So the young Piqué could spend as much time as he wanted down there, playing junior football, watching the B team, attending basketball matches. Living the Barça life.

However, there was an incident which nearly cost this elegant world champion not only his career but his mobility, perhaps even his life. As a toddler, back in 1988, he was at his grandparents' holiday home in Blanes, on the Costa Brava. The house was being renovated and the first-floor balcony had only a temporary barrier, rather than a wall. Piqué was chasing a football and ploughed right over the edge of the balcony, plummeting a few metres to the ground. Pandemonium ensued. The local medical facilities were insufficient for a child with head injuries; the trip down to Barcelona initially took the petrified grandparents to the wrong hospital and only when Piqué was hurtled to where his mother was working was he properly treated. Even so, he remained in a coma for a few hours before recovering fully. He's made of tough stuff, this kid.

Piqué's dad, Joan, a more than decent amateur footballer, qualified as a lawyer and is a director of a construction company. Montse, his mother, is a director of the Institut Guttmann, which was inaugurated in Barcelona in 1965 as the first hospital in Spain caring for people with acquired spinal injury and brain damage.

Piqué's mother sometimes took her sons to her work as a reminder that there were people in the world far less fortunate than them and they should make full use of the gifts they had been given – more academic than footballing in Gerard's case, if you asked Montse Piqué.

Ultimately, the difference in the backgrounds of the two men reached its starkest point in November 2006, a few months after the best day of Puyol's life, when he lifted the European Cup in Paris. His father Josep was constructing a road on the family land. He was using an earth-mover, approaching the end of a hard week's labour, around five o'clock that winter night, when it tipped over, killing him. He was 56.

His son was en route to a Barça match in La Coruña, but flew back, then drove the three hours to his small, heartbroken community for a funeral which brought together the ordinary humble people of Pobla de Segur, plus those great and good of the football world who hurried to be there for the immensely popular Puyi. The months that followed must have seemed catastrophic to Puyol.

Frank Rijkaard's rebuilding of Barça had been fun and stimulating. The Camp Nou was vibrant and the football breathtaking. However, the physical, psychological and sporting decline after the 2006 Champions League final was almost instant.

One minute Barça were lions, the next lemmings. Their form fell off a cliff, standards were ripped up and if there was a responsibility that fell on Puyol, as captain, to assume the role of Rijkaard's 'bad cop' it coincided with one of the low points of his life.

Meanwhile Piqué, who would eventually be part of the remedy to this slump, was living it up. In Sale, Lancashire.

One of Piqué's great virtues is his directness. He has often talked about the fact that his life was *mimado*, which can mean spoiled or indulged, while growing up. In Manchester he discovered what it was like to be alone, to have to grow up fast and fight for what you need.

However, the reasons he is sometimes viewed as a lucky, silver-spooned *pijo*, or posh-boy, are clear. He is tall, handsome, smart, and talented. He was born into a well-educated, successful family and pushed to do well at school; selected for excellence by the club he loves and, by fluke, born to that 1987 generation which includes Cesc Fàbregas, Leo Messi and Víctor Vázquez.

Fàbregas and Piqué were partners in crime and they admitted in a television documentary to running into trouble while stealing petrol caps from parked cars.

Patrolling the Barceloneta beach front, they spotted one target and were in the middle of effecting their robbery when the car owner clocked them, roared out of the restaurant he'd been eating in and set off in furious pursuit.

Charmed lives that they lived, they got away with it.

The football philosophy at Barcelona has not always been as clear-cut and well-executed as it is now. Cruyff's philosophy of pushing talented players through the system quickly has flitted in and out of fashion. Much more important than the idea that 'if you are good enough you are old enough' has been the concept that the best players must be pushed out of a 'comfort zone' and into a level where their team-mates are more experienced and their opponents bigger and more brutal.

When Piqué, Fàbregas and Messi were youngsters, things could seem moribund. They got tired of winning by double-figure margins.

Around this time, the then Barcelona coach, Louis van Gaal, came to Casa Piqué for dinner. On being told that Amador's grandson, Gerard, was in the *fútbol base* system designed to feed the first team, the Dutchman roared about how skinny the kid was and gave him a firm shove, which sent the bewildered young Piqué sprawling to the floor of the living room.

Whatever embarrassment he felt at the time has since been repaid handsomely via defeats of Van Gaal's Bayern in the Champions League and Holland in the World Cup. Don't even imagine for a second that Piqué wouldn't think like that. He would.

By 2012, Pep Guardiola had promoted Sergio Busquets, Pedro, Thiago, Andreu Fontàs, Jeffrén, Marc

8 — The Odd Couple

Bartra, Jonathan dos Santos, Martín Montoya, Rafinha and Isaac Cuenca. This hasn't just been highly successful, it has also become deeply fashionable as far as the media, fans and other clubs are concerned. Barça's youth coaches know that they are expected to find, train and promote the best talents.

Both Piqué and Cesc, since returning for a combined total of about €46m, have hinted that, had there been proper promotion, then they probably wouldn't have left. However, it's hard to fault Fàbregas' decision. Practically upon his departure from Barcelona in the summer of 2003, he became Arsenal's youngest first-team player.

The Camp Nou then was a chaotic place. Arsenal nipped in and pinched Cesc. Six months later, Laporta discovered to his fury that something similar was about to happen again. This time it was Piqué and there was no way that another gem was going to be allowed to go without a fight.

Both Arsenal and United came looking for Piqué. It was, and remains, simple to scout such talents, given that they often play on what amounts to municipal pitches in the *Juvenil* leagues around Spain. Mick Brown or Martin Ferguson at United, or Steve Rowley and Francesc Cagigao for Arsenal (those clubs' elite scouts then) could discreetly turn up and pay a couple of pounds in Sabadell, Girona or Tarragona to watch one of Barça's youth teams play a league match and get a good look at their best young players.

Barcelona's treatment of Piqué contributed greatly to his departure. He was dropped from the *Juvenil A* side, in which he was a dominant figure, and which was the stepping stone team to Barça B. Before being relegated to *Juvenil B*, he was prevented from playing for nearly two months. That decision would cost Barça £5m.

In December 2003, Barça were first alerted to Premier League interest in their tall, elegant, but still pin-thin centre-half. By spring, Piqué chose United and by July, he was presented at Old Trafford with the United manager, before defending himself ably on Catalan radio.

"Barça didn't want to negotiate with us over a contract and just told me that I was 'theirs' as if I was a slave," he said. "And if they won't negotiate with me, my agents or United, there is a FIFA process for agreeing compensation. That means I am free to move to Manchester.

"When you are a young footballer and your club shows that it doesn't want you, then you must seek out your living. It can also be useful to seek fresh pastures in order that, one day, you can be better valued and return."

Piqué's grandfather, Amador Bernabéu, went a good deal further. "Gerard has been with the club since he was nine, but since Barça found out, in December, that United and Arsenal were very interested in him, they have made his life impossible," he said.

"The people in charge of youth development at this club knew they were dealing with the feelings of a 16-year-old kid, but they punished him by relegating him down a level and then stopping him from playing."

Laporta swallowed his indignation four years later, not only repatriating Piqué but paying good money for him. In retrospect, Barcelona inadvertently gained by losing Piqué. He matured in England, learned what a man like Sir Alex Ferguson demands from his footballers, tested himself in training against Paul Scholes,

8 — The Odd Couple

Ryan Giggs, Cristiano Ronaldo and Roy Keane and he became stronger – adding nine kilos in pure muscle. However, he also experienced some of what the new recruits at La Masia go through, the experience which finishes so many of them off.

From being the 17-year-old golden boy, at home and in his junior teams, to living alone in an apartment, working in a foreign language, is quite a challenge. Unlike Cesc, it was pretty clear that instant access to the first team would be very limited. It became an occasionally tearful experience.

I met Piqué in early 2004, just before his move to England. What struck me back then was that he was extremely slender for a top quality centre-half and that he was unusually articulate. One thing changed in England, the other didn't.

On his return, he said: "It was a completely new experience for a boy who was used to being picked for every match, to have to suddenly compete in a team of outstanding players. I had to live in a little house there and at times I used to say to myself, 'Nothing is worth this misery!' But I learned so much at Manchester United during the training sessions. It was no longer enough for me to be tall and kick the ball well. I had to learn to use my whole body, to defend without the ball – and I learned to overcome the moments of loneliness.

"I used to call my mum and tell her that everything was fine, but I was always holding back the tears. She really missed me and I couldn't tell her, 'Mum, I'd give anything to come home tomorrow. I'm sick of this and I miss you.'"

Piqué has often referred to Ferguson as a 'second

father' and, had it not been Barça calling him, Piqué would have stayed with his Scottish manager and pushed to displace either Nemanja Vidic or, more likely, the injury-plagued Rio Ferdinand at Old Trafford.

However, training against the great players of United was an education for Piqué. He hated being out-jumped by players more street-smart about when to leap, or when to use a well-timed nudge. He realised that while the Barça classroom had made him a fine footballer, there were other schools of thought on how to defend. The Carrington training ground is where Piqué's unbounded competitive spirit was unleashed (pick any leisure pursuit from table tennis to Play-Station and he'll tell you he'll beat you).

Once back in Barcelona, he explained to me: "English players have the reputation of partying and drinking a lot of alcohol, but they are very professional in their everyday work, in training, following the coaches – they are all very much there. They stay together after training, stay out longer. They all go together to the gym. They have the culture to spend a lot of time with sports and that's what I brought back with me from there. It's the professionalism with which they do things.

"It was a difficult time, and there were hard moments when you don't understand why you're not playing, but they just had two great central defenders, Rio and Vidic. It was tough for me to get a chance to play, but it was still a great experience to play there with the likes of Cristiano Ronaldo, Rooney, Van Nistelrooy. They always have great players there and it was a nice experience. I went there when I was 17 and came back to Barcelona when I was 21. The Gerard who went there was very different to the one who left."

8 – The Odd Couple

The year United sent him on loan to Zaragoza (2006-07) was also hugely valuable. He featured regularly in cup and league, sometimes deployed at centre-back, sometimes in the midfield *pivote* role – and when on the road, he roomed with his defensive team-mate, Gaby Milito.

They decided that facing them should be a roughhouse experience for any striker and used to jump up and down howling and roaring on their hotel beds to get 'into the zone' before a match. Then the two central defenders would lump into each other, dealing out slaps and punches to get into warrior mode.

Zaragoza, with the gruesome twosome at the back, beat Barcelona, Sevilla and Villarreal at La Romareda, drew with Real Madrid and finished sixth, six points off Champions League qualification. The following season, Milito went to Barcelona and Piqué went back to Old Trafford. Zaragoza were relegated. Draw your own conclusions.

Piqué admits that it was during this time that "I proved to myself that I was ready to play consistently in a top league". However, his final season at United was to prove bittersweet. His three Champions League appearances yielded two wins and a draw plus a pair of goals for the Catalan – at home to Dinamo Kiev and away to Roma. At the same time, his excellence while at Zaragoza had been well noted at the Camp Nou.

Barça contacted Piqué, his agents IMG, and finally Manchester United in February 2008. Ferguson was a believer in his developing sweeper, but the Vidic-Ferdinand partnership was excellent, and he had back-up in Jonny Evans, John O'Shea and Wes Brown. Nonetheless, he initially fought for Piqué to stay, but eventually, negotiations advanced – at a cost to the player.

The two clubs were drawn in the Champions League semi-final in April 2008. On the eve of the first leg, at the Camp Nou, Piqué was in form and, he felt, in contention. Then, on match day, Vidic was declared unfit and Piqué was sure he would play. However, following United's afternoon siesta, Ferguson came to the defender and told him he was not, because within a couple of weeks he was almost certainly going to sign for the opposition. Apparently it wouldn't be proper. "It was a monumental disappointment," Piqué admits.

"With regards to Sir Alex Ferguson, I have to say that although I didn't play a lot, I had a good relationship with him," explained Piqué, the last time we spoke about it. "He was always very direct with me. There are other coaches that kind of hide from you and just don't let you play, but we talked openly, and I never had a problem. We had a good relationship. Then I got the offer from Barcelona, and I went to tell him that I wanted to go back home to the club of my life, and he understood. He still tried to convince me, but in the end I decided to come back. It was just the best thing to do."

So, what of the defender he was returning to partner at the Camp Nou? Like Piqué, Carles Puyol once appeared to be unloved at the club he would come to symbolise.

The summer of 1999 had been pivotal for Puyi. Both Málaga and Sevilla enquired about him and football director Lorenzo Serra Ferrer told them that he would consider offers for the Barça B winger/full-back. In training with the B squad, Puyol was larking about in goal and injured a shoulder – lightly, but enough to slow the moves down. During the down time, he made a decision to stay and fight for his place. Reward promptly followed.

Puyol's first game for Barça, under Louis van Gaal, who trusted him more than Serra Ferrer, came in October 1999. The timing was symbolic. Barça's centenary coincided with a monumental crisis on and off the pitch, which would need new footballers with a different mentality and different priorities. Puyol would prove to be one of them.

There were relatively few La Masia alumni making it into the first team – only Xavi and, much more intermittently, Gabri and Pepe Reina – because of a policy of high-price international signings.

Van Gaal gave a brief summation of the hairy kid he was promoting which stands examination today. "He's got a great mentality, impressive strength and his technique isn't too bad," said the Dutchman. "He is quick, he can get up and down the pitch and his attitude is perfect."

Guardiola captained the side that day. Nine years later the Barça coach paid his defender a huge compliment in the press conference before hammering Madrid 6-2 in the Bernabéu during Guardiola's first, devastating season in charge. "He's a shining example. I can put him at right-back, left-back, on the right or left of the central defensive pairing and not only does he never moan about it, he also never puts a foot wrong," said Guardiola.

Puyol's father would tell him, 'Give everything you

have got to fulfil your dream, because if, eventually, you don't manage it then you won't be left with the feeling that it's your own fault.' That sentiment drove Puyol, as did his competitive edge.

He told Albert Puig, a *fútbol base* coach, in Puig's book, *La Fuerza de un Sueño*: "I've shared a dressing room with many players more talented than me but who didn't go as far as I did simply because I had a better attitude. Until the *Juvenil* level [from 16-19] you can look as if you will fly through your career, but without the correct discipline, hunger and predisposition to hard work you won't make a career, especially at Barça."

Puyol began his Barça career as a rampaging wingback, less devastating in attack than Dani Alves, but just as fond of lung-bursting runs up the pitch.

His home debut was the frantic Camp Nou Clásico of late 1999 – Barça's last enormous match of the century. While he didn't start against John Toshack's side (who would become European champions under the Welshman's mid-season replacement, Vicente del Bosque), he came on for Sergi after half an hour in a team which then lined up: Hesp; Reiziger, Abelardo, Cocu, Puyol; Luis Enrique, Guardiola, Zenden; Figo, Kluivert, Rivaldo.

Toshack's side was Illgner; Salgado, Campo, Julio César, Karanka (José Mourinho's assistant at the Bernabéu); Geremi, Redondo; Anelka, Raúl, Sávio and Morientes.

Rivaldo and Luis Figo wiped out an early Raúl header for a 2-1 lead, but after Kluivert was sent off, Real Madrid's legendary No 7 scored a famous late goal to tie the match 2-2 and put his finger to his lips to silence a furious Camp Nou. Typically, Puyol made straight for Raúl on the final whistle to swap shirts: 'Never mind what anyone else thinks. I'm doing it my way'.

Perhaps his boldness was fuelled by relief. "I wasn't as nervous as I thought I was going to be," he revealed to reporters afterwards. In fact, this game was going to have a major impact on Puyol's immediate prospects.

Figo was brilliant that night, five-star, but he accepted an outlandish offer by a new powerbroker called Florentino Pérez: If this construction magnate won the 2000 Real Madrid presidential elections and paid the buy-out clause in Figo's contract, then the winger would jump ship.

It is history now, but at the time it was a move of seismic proportions. Figo didn't deserve the bicycle chains, mobile phones, cans, bottles and a solitary suckling pig's head which were subsequently thrown at him when he played at the Camp Nou, but he did leave a gaping wound.

Madrid, now European champions, coached by Del Bosque, with young Iker Casillas in goal and featuring Figo, were back in the Ciudad Condal nearly a year after Puyol's first Clásico. Lorenzo Serra Ferrer had succeeded Van Gaal and the Mallorquín came up with the idea that asphyxiating Figo's creativity, especially in a coliseum-like atmosphere with the fans constantly baying their outrage at him, might pay dividends. Puyol was the shadow stalking Figo.

"The boss just told me to man-mark Figo and follow him everywhere on the pitch, which I was delighted to do," he recalls. "It was tiring, but it worked because I concentrated really hard and I don't think Figo contributed to the game. However, he showed what a great player he is, irrespective of the result. The atmosphere was boiling, but he never hid, he was up for the ball all the time and he made me work hard."

In the interim, between his debut Clásico and this 2-0 win almost a year later, Puyol had emulated Guardiola and Albert Ferrer, gold medallist in 1992, as Camp Nou Olympians of note, when he won a silver at the 2000 Games in Sydney. He and Xavi were part of a cracking squad, including Carlos Marchena, Joan Capdevila, David Albelda, Raúl Tamudo, Gabri and Albert Luque. In a thrilling final, Cameroon beat nine-man Spain on penalties thanks to Samuel Eto'o making it 2-2 after Xavi and Gabri had put Spain 2-0 up in the first half.

A gentle easing back into Barça B football when they returned might have been more logical, but while they had been away Barça had hit the rocks and sent out an SOS call to the returning young heroes.

Thumped 3-0 away to Beşiktaş, defeated 2-0 in the Camp Nou by Milan and humbled 2-0 in La Coruña, things were pretty desperate (Barça would fail to qualify from a Champions League group of Leeds, Milan and Beşiktaş).

Puyol's 'seek and destroy' mission on Figo's return to the Camp Nou earned him a run of matches which helped Barça to the semi-finals of both the Copa del Rey and the UEFA Cup (including Guardiola's last European match as a Barça player, a 1-0 defeat by Liverpool at Anfield).

His marking of Figo and his Olympic heroics made Puyol a folk hero among Camp Nou fans, enduring a woeful Barça side that season. At last! Here was another *canterano* – full of the Migueli spirit (Migueli

was Barça's original 'Tarzan', playing nearly 700 matches as a 'no-prisoners' central defender). After a breakthrough second season, the fans voted Puyol the club's
outstanding defender.

Then came the decisions which sealed Puyol's status with the fans forever – long before he began lifting
trophies.

Madrid's buy-out of Figo's contract (a world record
£37m deal) had devastated FC Barcelona. A truly great
player had been ripped away, Barcelona's board had
been made to look penny-pinching and dopey while,
suddenly, Real Madrid looked immensely powerful –
football-wise and institutionally.

Florentino Pérez fancied a repeat smash and grab:
buying out the rescission clauses (the mutually agreed
buy-out fees written into each player's contract in
Spain post-Bosman) of any or all of Cocu, Kluivert and
Puyol. Each of them, in turn, received golden hand-
cuff contracts to stay at the Camp Nou, despite the fact
that Puyol would have been an extremely unlikely Real
Madrid signing. So he stayed and became a lynchpin,
enduring four changes of president and four changes
of coach before lifting his first trophy with Barça, La
Liga in 2005. These were chaotic times.

"I can't pretend I've never thought about leaving," he
recalled, much later. "There was a time when not only
were we not winning any trophies, but it didn't feel like
we were even trying to. I got really annoyed and was
thinking about leaving, but eventually decided to stay
and fight.

"There was a lot of talk at the time in the press about
me signing for Madrid, but I've never met with anyone
in Madrid to talk about going there. I can tell you that

it will never happen. Winning is the most important thing of all. You can play brilliantly, but if you don't end up with any trophies, it's totally unsatisfying. It's like in 2004 in the knock-out match against Chelsea. We played lovely football, but were knocked out all the same. That's no use to me. We've got to win."

While all around him was crumbling, Puyol's standards never slipped. The match that embodies what was going on came on October 23, 2002. Lokomotiv Moscow came to town in the Champions League. With the score at 0-0, Barça's Argentinian keeper, Roberto Bonano, foolishly came racing out to try to intercept a run from the Lokomotiv striker James Obiorah. The Nigerian stepped round him and had an open goal from about 30 metres out, but Puyol was sprinting across to cover. As Obiorah jogged forward, Puyol arrived at breakneck speed. The entire goal remained at the striker's mercy, with 'Puyi' standing on the penalty spot, arms wrapped behind his back to avoid handling the ball, eyes looking intently down at Obiorah's feet, waiting to guess the next move.

All of this happens in a split second: Obiorah shoots and Puyol flings himself to his left with the speed of a cobra, saves the shot with the club badge on his chest and the Camp Nou erupts at this little footballing miracle.

Nine years later, Puyol is in Monte Carlo for the draw for the 2011-12 Champions League and the UEFA Super Cup match, the next night. It's a gala, so everyone else is in formal dress, but Puyol pitches up on stage in his club polo shirt and Barça's official, plaid, knee-length summer-shorts. Inevitably, Piqué ridicules his partner on Twitter. Back comes the answer, quick as a shot: "I was at home looking through all these nice suits I've got and I decided that I couldn't be more comfortable or happy than in my club gear with the Barça badge right next to my heart."

That message sent me right back to that night when Puyol saved his team's bacon with the club crest, just above that raging-bull heart of his.

At the time of the Lokomotiv match, he explained: "I thought about my old goalkeeping skills and just tried not to save with my hands out of sheer instinct."

That victory put Barcelona top of their group. By the time they played in Bruges, Barça were already through to the knockout stages and Louis van Gaal could throw in a handful of *canterano* debutants ... including one named Andrés Iniesta.

Puyol enjoyed the Rijkaard years – winning in Madrid, taking the title, beating Arsenal in Paris and becoming the first Barça captain to lift The Cup with the Big Ears since Alexanco (who had first called Puyol for a trial at La Masia) in 1992.

Not that he found it easy. At the time, he admitted that Thierry Henry had been "easily the hardest player I have ever had to mark. They only had 10 men, but I still needed help from Rafa Márquez to contain him and even then it took some fantastic saves from Valdés to stop him scoring".

Immediately prior to that Champions League win, I interviewed Puyol, and asked him who the most under-rated guy in the squad was. He instantly named Valdés and then, as now, it is hard not to agree.

More than one Barça player didn't hit peak that day and, while Puyol admits there were nerves, it is an important comparison with the Guardiola era that there was no Messi and Rijkaard's team was about to begin its descent into mediocrity.

Puyol has kept his shirt, boots and both captain's armbands (the club one in Catalan colours and the official UEFA one), but I would wager that the 2009 triumph means more to him than that victory in Paris.

His father's death in the winter of 2006 changed Puyol radically. Struggling to cope with the impact of his loss, he found some solace in *The Tibetan Book of Living and Dying*. It so intrigued him that he took steps to make contact with the Honourable Thubten Wangchen, the Dalai Lama's representative in Catalonia, and also spent some time at Tibet House.

Puyol also met the Dalai Lama when he visited Barcelona in 2007 and is supportive of Tibet's push for autonomy from China. "I really identify with the Tibetan people," he has said. "I like their philosophy and way of seeing the world."

Puyol went from his most anguished moment to a radical change in lifestyle. Exposure to a culture of meditation, forgiveness, tranquillity and dignity coincided with him taking up pilates and yoga, which have greatly extended his peak years. What's more, just as he was lightening up, along came Piqué, this 6ft 4in lump of vital energy, full of noise, pranks, a lust for life and immense footballing potential.

The surprise, I think, was that Puyol was up for the larking about on and around the training pitch. Not in the matches. He's not changed that much.

The on-pitch symbiosis between Puyol and Piqué is easier to explain. Puyol once looked happiest when it was chaotic on the pitch. He would be running around with his superman pants over his shorts, putting out fires, saving small children from pile-driver opposition shots, leaping in and out of danger; certainly not happy if his night didn't contain some high-octane heroics.

However, over the years Puyol has adapted. It started under Rijkaard, who as a player switched between centre-half and *pivote* for Holland, Ajax and Milan, teams where imposing control of the ball and dictating the pattern of play meant much more composed, decisive and dominant defending. Rijkaard helped change his captain.

Puyol still relied on pace, anticipation and tackling power, but now he wanted to be a controlling, rather than a reactive, influence on a match. He used his judgement differently, was happiest when a clean sheet also included clean shorts – not a night of diving in and making the type of skin-ripping tackles which once failed to save him a point at football-tennis back in Pobla de Segur.

The decline during the latter years under Rijkaard was something that Puyol could neither understand nor reverse, no matter how much work he put in. He expresses the horror of it all with one, bitter memory. "There were lots of bad matches … Losing to Sevilla in the UEFA Super Cup in Monaco was the beginning of the end – but we didn't know it then," he recalls. "Then you remember losing the World Club final in Tokyo, but easily the worst of all was the defeat at the Bernabéu [a 4-1 loss in May 2008]. No question that was the pits. Forming a guard of honour for them, the pasting we took in the match – everything we had built was coming crashing down. It was the worst game of my life and it seemed to go on forever, like it would never finish. Them lapping it up, us suffering – it was the end of an era."

Losing is part of the sporting life, but humiliation, desolation and frustration were not what Puyol had earned. So, as a present, the sporting gods sent him not only Guardiola, but Piqué.

Their very first game in the saddle had a nicely appropriate venue. Puyol had missed the 6-0 and 5-1 wins over Hibernian and Dundee United during the Scottish pre-season camp in the summer of 2008, but was ready for the next friendly. The football renaissance began at the Artemio Franchi stadium in Florence, the city of the artistic and cultural Renascimento, when Barça beat Fiorentina 3-1 with a stunning performance.

There is no question that Piqué's arrival had beneficial effects on and off the pitch. Xavi said: "Since Gerard's arrival, everyone is much more laid-back. He's young and his character has fitted brilliantly into this group because he's full of the joys of life. When he first arrived it was obvious that he wanted to have a good time, but that's not what football's all about.

"You can have a laugh, but at the end of the day it's a job of work, we are under tremendous pressure and Piqué had to adapt to that. To a certain extent it was the captains, Valdés, Puyol and I, who taught him about that – but he learned quickly and he learned a lot.

"However, Piqué and Puyol are really close friends who work brilliantly together on the pitch. Off the pitch, Puyol has changed completely. He's so much more relaxed now. Piqué is the chief joker in the squad. He is behind every prank, whether it involves mobile phones, team-mates' shoes or clothes."

8 — The Odd Couple

The degree to which Barça's Odd Couple like to fool about has become famous. It was Puyol and Piqué who planned to surprise Fàbregas during the World Cup celebrations in Madrid, by hauling a Barça shirt over his head while Pepe Reina was introducing him to the adoring throng. It wasn't a universally popular jape at the time.

When Piqué and Puyol were sitting together in the Camp Nou main stand watching a cup match against Ceuta, for which they hadn't been squad-listed, Piqué was filmed throwing sunflower seeds at Juanjo Brau, the club's senior fitness trainer. The more cheesed-off Brau got, the more Piqué blamed Puyol, sitting next to him.

Twitter is where a lot of the Odd Couple's nonsense is played out.

They and Fàbregas pepper their Twitter exchanges with the phrase "Ooooooohh. Moc moc!" That started when Piqué saw a YouTube video of a Spanish pensioner being shown an image of how a mirror could distort her face and making weird 'Ooooooooh' noises. Piqué showed his mates the video, added 'moc moc' as a kind of air-kissing noise and a new language was born. It doesn't make much sense written down.

Or take this Twitter exchange. Piqué: "Right! That's my warm-down session finished. I'm off to eat with some kid called Carles Puyol who I'm helping find his feet in the team."

Puyol: "And many thanks for that, I hope that we can both retire at the same time. How many years have you got left? 3? 4?"

At training, there are bursts of abuse and laughter, perpetual ear-pinging and horse-play. However, when the daily work is being accomplished to such high standards, all of this becomes a stress release and the antidote to boredom.

Before the Champions League final at Wembley I asked Piqué to tell me a bit more about his playing partner. "We've reached the stage now that we don't need to talk, it's sufficient for a little glance at each other to agree what needs to be done in any given situation," he told me.

At least that's the situation when they are in the midst of the action and the game is in full flow. Piqué also admits that there are still moments when he gets a massive row from his friend and playing partner.

"There was one match where we were winning by four or five and there were only a few minutes left," Piqué told me, laughing at the memory. "One of the opposition was injured and the stretcher was coming on and I just went up to see how he was. The next thing I knew Puyi was roaring at me to concentrate. He was on me like a hawk, telling me to leave them to it, get back in position and concentrate. He never stops."

But it's more than just their Odd Couple banter. Piqué accepts that, particularly when the team in front of you is playing fantasy football, and your crucial interventions in the match are usually few and far between, concentration can be a test. He knows his mind wanders and, also, he expects not to play to a grand old age, doing the same things over and over again. Games when you know you will win handsomely, return legs when the first match was 5-1 in your favour, matches like Spain played in Lithuania on a criminally poor pitch during qualifying for Euro 2012 – sometimes it's hard to get up for the test.

8 — The Odd Couple

"Good concentration is a fundamental part of the game and I have to admit I struggle with it sometimes," he said. "I look at Ryan Giggs, who's still playing at 37, and wonder what planet he's from. Or Puyol, who approaches every game as though it is a Champions League final. I always look at him and think, 'Relax buddy, relax.'"

Puyol and Piqué are united by more qualities than separate them. Each is a born athlete, with exceptional footballing qualities. Each of them cares passionately about winning and doing so with a certain degree of style.

However, the work that they have invested in their careers, and continue to invest, is probably the single element which has brought them such success.

At Guardiola's Barça, talent isn't sufficient. The effort put in to every single training session marks which players will, or will not, earn the coach's approval, and on top of all that, Piqué and Puyol represent something else that is crucial to the spirit of this remarkable era. Between Piqué's remarkable zest for life and Puyol's serious-minded quest to push himself to the limit every single day lies a zone where they can laugh, joke and cut through the boredom and tension – carpe diem, seize the day

During the 2010 World Cup I was exposed to Barça's Odd Couple at first hand. One of our jobs was to film the Spain squad, one by one, in front of a green screen so that their images could be projected individually on the giant stadium screen at each match, while the announcer named the line-ups. Spain were one of the last squads to arrive in South Africa and they did so with a mix of travel-tiredness and nervous energy.

The only gap in the schedule for our filming was immediately after an hour-long briefing by the referee supervisor Horacio Elizondo. I was left by the FIFA delegate to the job of breaking the bad news to the players. There was a collective bear-growl when I made it clear that this was an obligatory task and we would be ready to start in five or six minutes. They were told that every single player and coach had to be dressed in Spain's first-choice playing kit and that no jewellery or watches of any kind could be worn.

The cameraman and technician were working furiously to clear chairs at the back of the room, set up the lights and use tape on the floor for the 'marks' (each player had to step forward and turn, arms folded to stare at the camera) while I placated the growlers.

Puyol was first and he was restless.

"Ready yet?"

"Can we start now?"

"Let's just do this now."

Impatience began to overcome politeness. However, having told them all, repeatedly, that there were to be no watches or jewellery, I noticed that Puyol was wearing one of his own range of timepieces. So we started, got him in position and just as the cameras were rolling I gently pointed out that he had been warned about not wearing any accessories.

For a second I thought I'd be killed on the spot, then the group took over, Puyol's team-mates pounced on the defender's slip-up like hungry wolves and he gave a sheepish smile. Everyone relaxed and the rest of the session was terrific fun because the atmosphere changed completely. I doubt he would have been quite so easy-going before teaming up with Piqué.

8 — The Odd Couple

Later in the tournament, we were asked to get the Spain players to do short films which would be used for mobile-phone subscribers to watch. Spain's training camp was located right in the heart of rugby country – Afrikaner farming land. We had the idea to fool about with a rugby ball and Puyol was our guest that day in our improvised studio on the North Western University campus. Once it was explained to him, he was happy to start in a close-up shot, with a rugby ball held up towards his chin and say, "They tell me this is rugby country. Well [dramatic pause and bemused face] I know nothing about rugby".

He throws the rugby ball out of shot to his right and almost simultaneously catches a football thrown to him from off camera, to his left.

"But I do know how to play football". He follows his pay-off line with a steely look down the barrel of the camera.

Okay, it's not Battleship Potemkin, but it's a nice promo and he did it with a sense of fun. Some of my Spanish colleagues were amazed that he'd been happy to fool around, but it was another example of the new Puyol.

One of the famous images from Wembley in May 2011 is Piqué, plus his army of helpers, cutting down the entire goal-net and then wandering off with it as a souvenir. It wasn't a new caper, simply a technique improved on since the night of the World Cup final.

Having beaten Holland in extra time, Vicente del Bosque's players lifted the trophy and paraded around the pitch in triumph. The dressing room was mayhem, but my cameraman and I were allowed in to make an exclusive film as the Queen of Spain, Rafa Nadal, and

Placido Domingo danced and sang with the Spain players (watched by a dignified if disappointed former Barça player, the Dutchman Phillip Cocu).

Not long after we completed our work and edged out to the reception area between the dressing room and the start of the tunnel, Piqué burst out of the door carrying tiny bandage scissors and a bottle of lager, then trotted off down towards to the playing surface.

Instants later he was back again, agitated and urgently asking where the nets had gone. None of the tournament officials looked particularly interested in his enquiry, nor did the stadium staff, so he asked me for help. Off we headed with one of the tournament volunteers, who could envisage the prize of a signed strip at the end of the mission.

Having promised that he knew where the nets were, the volunteer led us all over the stadium, with Piqué's metal studs threatening to spill him all over the concrete stairs. But the entrepreneurial kid had lied. He'd simply led us to a different pitch entrance – Piqué had already been down to the pitch, knew the nets had been gathered and was now volcanically unhappy.

Piqué swallowed his rage and we started banging on the doors of equipment stores, where goal-nets might be housed, only to burst in on the take for the stadium's food concessions being counted in high stacks of bundled South African rand.

It all degenerated into a farce, with Piqué increasingly and justifiably irritated. Every official wanted an autograph or picture with him, but not one of them would lead him to the souvenir he so desperately wanted.

We finally found the stadium manager's office. There we met a South African who lied about where the nets were and snuck away to hide them from us. Piqué had been containing his growing fury, attempting to smile and accepting dozens of requests for attention, but he was near the edge now.

He'd been operating in English, but turned to me and suggested, in Spanish, "I'll punch him, you take the nets and we'll make a run for it."

Now, I think it was the famous Piqué sense of humour in action (although at the time I was pretty sure he meant it), but with redoubled negotiating skills, the intervention of FIFA, the name-dropping of a few sponsors and the arrival of the Spain-supporting South African stadium manager, a deal was finally reached. Watching this World Cup winning centre-half snipping a 2ft by 1ft portion of the goal-net with tiny little scissors was both comical and a massive relief.

Now comes the sad part. At the start of season 2011-12, Carles Puyol was working towards his comeback, having played only a handful of games in eight months, including a few minutes on the Wembley pitch in the Champions League final of 2011. It led to a knee operation that summer and made the level of his participation in the new season, and the European Championships that would follow it, a matter of debate.

Perhaps Puyol's incredible levels of fitness and dedication mean that he has another two or three seasons at the top of his profession. Despite his injuries, it was still Captain 'Tarzan' who lifted the Club World Cup in December 2011. Nevertheless, I think the shrewd bet is that we are beyond autumn and well into the winter months of the Piqué-Puyol Odd Couple partnership.

In due course, I expect we will see Puyol become part

of the Barça coaching set up, although my bet is that he will not beat Xavi to the job of first-team coach.

Piqué? Well, history is his to write. Barcelona is his club, he is immensely happy there and it would surprise me if, in due course, he wasn't captain of club and country. Only time will tell whether or not he remains at the Camp Nou for the rest of his career, but I think the balance of probabilities is slightly against it. His taste of English football was tantalising, not satisfying. There will come a time when Pep Guardiola is no longer the coach of Barça and that may bring change to the playing staff, too.

It's a stated aim of Piqué's that, in due course, he wants to become Barça president and if he wants it badly enough then it is something I expect him to achieve – and excel in. Perhaps another spell abroad towards the end of his playing career would do him and his career aspirations no harm at all.

So, the credits roll on the story of Barcelona's Odd Couple, Puyol and Piqué, with a montage of their defining moments: Puyol hectoring Piqué to 'pay attention'; Puyol practically using his partner as a step ladder to soar high above the German defence and score a World Cup semi-final winning header; Piqué laughing, always laughing; Piqué scoring that goal in the 6-2 win at the Bernabéu while Puyol minds the shop.

Thanks for the memories, guys.

VÍCTOR VALDÉS:
THE HEARTBREAKER

A NDRÉS INIESTA'S BEST friend in football is also the most consistent Barcelona player of the last six years. Every top-class goalkeeper will tell you that the less to do, the greater the test on your concentration.

The goal he conceded against Arsenal at the Emirates in February 2011 – when he let the ball slither past him at the near post – and the mental aberration in the 3-1 Clásico win at the Bernabéu in 2011, where his misplaced pass led to Madrid's first-minute goal – stand out because of how rarely he makes mistakes.

His team-mates repeatedly underline the security Valdés' footballing skills and one-on-one prowess gives them. This is essential to their ability to play high up the pitch and regularly to use a three-man defence.

Since Pep Guardiola took over, Barcelona's results against Real Madrid speak of total domination. Anyone who has been at all those games would also mention how often a Real Madrid breakaway ended with Valdés making an unlikely block in that nerveless way of his – particularly in the first two Camp Nou Clásicos of Guardiola's reign, which ended 2-0 and 1-0, but were utterly nerve-racking.

The Barcelona *fútbol base*-trained goalkeeper must be part sweeper. Valdés fits this profile perfectly. His willingness to spend much of the game patrolling the high edge of his penalty box stems from him being unfazed by opposition breakaways and the eyeball-to-eyeball, winner-takes-all contests.

He is a tough man, somebody who demands high standards from everybody around him – even the media – but is also very funny. It was his clever idea to prepare and show a DVD of his impersonations the night before the first leg of the Champions League semi-final against Real Madrid, which helped reduce tension and catalyse a winning atmosphere.

He has eliminated the impetuosity of his early years. I remember him being infuriated when Louis van Gaal would regularly return what looked like a budding first-team footballer to the B squad – as he did with Xavi. Valdés once stormed out, missed training and jeopardised his future at the Camp Nou. Now, his ability to harness that ferocious competitive instinct is at the heart of his game.

This Catalan dispelled the myths that he did not value the Spanish national team and might be a disruptive influence by fitting in perfectly with Iker Casillas and Pepe Reina en route to World Cup victory. I watched him train every day and support his team-mates with intensity, despite knowing that he would not play.

I've found him a gem, as likely to face up and speak about issues when his team loses as when they win. A real man. He loves music and the birth of his son Dylan has helped him find happiness, something which will be augmented when he finishes playing and is allowed to kite-surf and ride a Harley whenever he wants.

Wembley 2011 did not provide him with the toughest medal he has won, but Barcelona fans will never forget his defiance on a different occasion, the Champions League final in Paris five years earlier. He broke Thierry Henry's heart that night, but he won those of Barcelona supporters forever.

9 – THE BREEDING GROUND

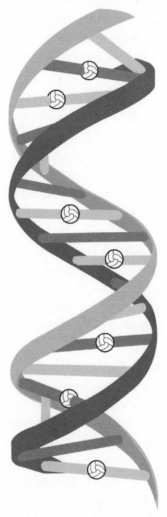

"The one thing which can never stop at this club is the cantera."
— Pep Guardiola

T HE BARCELONA STORY is about a team that wins trophies in breathtaking style, playing some of the best football we have seen, with stars whose talents will live forever in the memory. However, there is an irresistible sub-plot that adds to the intrigue: they do it with a squad full of either Catalan-born or Barcelona-educated players.

Víctor Valdés, Carles Puyol, Gerard Piqué, Sergio Busquets and Xavi Hernández are all Catalans and have been in the Barcelona youth system, called either *fútbol base*, (basic football education) or the *cantera* (the quarry, from which diamonds are mined) from a young age. Pedro, Lionel Messi, Andrés Iniesta and Thiago Alcántara were scouted and brought to the *cantera* as kids. The coach, Pep Guardiola, and his assistant, Tito Vilanova, are also Catalans who came through the same system as the players. Practically the entire Guardiola staff are Camp Nou alumni.

Albert Benaiges coached Piqué, Messi and Cesc Fàbregas before joining the Al Wasl youth academy in Dubai in the summer of 2011. "In one of the photo montages in the New Masia you'll see, as youth players, Pep Guardiola, now the coach, alongside Tito Vilanova, assistant coach, Aureli Altimira, physical preparation coach and Jordi Roura, the scout and video analyst," Benaiges points out. "They were all together as young kids in La Masia and now they're all working for the first team. What better tribute to La Masia that nearly the whole technical team has come through its ranks? It's hard to imagine anything going wrong in these circumstances."

Seven of the Spain squad that won the 2008 European Championships were alumni of the FC Barcelona youth system. Four of them started the final. Seven of the Barcelona team which started the 2009 Champions League final against Manchester United came through the Camp Nou system; the number was the same two years later at Wembley.

Now the headline statistic: Spain's starting XI in the World Cup final of 2010 contained six players who were taught how to play at FC Barcelona.

When football can appear sterile or robotic, played by 6ft 4in athletes who earn six-figure weekly wages, distancing them further than ever from the supporters, the concept of 'homegrown lads' winning trophies with superb football is deeply seductive. If we need a simple way to explain the object of that affection, then the term 'La Masia' has been hijacked for that end. It now stands for everything people think is good and pure and proper about FC Barcelona – a footballing Camelot, where dragons are slain and the table is round, so the players can practise passing exercises on it.

Here I will try to explain what La Masia is; how the *fútbol base* system at Barcelona functions; how the football language these young players are educated in is translated to the tactics applied by Guardiola on match day.

Masia (n): an old-fashioned Iberian farmhouse, usually made of stone

Barça's youth academy is nicknamed 'La Masia' because the old stone farmhouse building next to the Camp Nou is where talented kids who needed a residence in order to train with Barcelona have stayed since 1979. The building itself is over 300 years old and was subsumed into the FC Barcelona campus when the club moved to its present site in the late 1950s. One of the first graduates from La Masia, Guillermo Amor, is now director of youth development at Barça.

Barcelona have 12 age-group squads under the first team, from age seven or eight right up to the 'B' side – an eclectic mix of footballers aged up to 25, who are now not going to make it with the top squad, plus kids of 16 and 17 who are on a fast track to the first team.

Anyone who is part of this massive system is a *canterano*: part of the *cantera* or La Masia. However, these are just descriptive terms – *fútbol base* or *fútbol formativo* is the actual system which sustains Barça and everything else is simply a component in that overall strategy.

La Masia ended its life as Barça's principal residence for junior footballers in June 2011. Precisely what happens to the old building now has yet to emerge, but the importance this club places on youth development can be seen in its successor.

Half way between the Camp Nou and the airport is Barça's Ciudad Deportiva Joan Gamper training ground, where the first team has been training since shortly after Guardiola became coach. Built at a cost of just under €70m, it took six years to complete because, rather shockingly, the club ran out of money during the construction process. The youth sections also train there and in October 2011 the building to replace La Masia, the Centro de Formación Oriol Tort, opened its doors in a glitzy ceremony attended by dozens of graduates from *fútbol base*.

Most of them are in debt to Johan Cruyff. When the Dutchman returned to Barcelona as coach in 1988, he transformed the youth development system, aligning all age-group teams in the 3-4-3 system his first team would play and fast-tracking Catalan *canteranos* including Toni Pinilla, Albert Ferrer, Guardiola and Óscar García.

Charly Rexach was Cruyff's assistant and had been at the Camp Nou during altogether different times. "This club has always loved talented footballers and the Barcelona I remember from my childhood played really well," he said. "Then fate took a bad turn.

"Our football became dark and sad – overly physical. There was no imagination. It was all about running. If you didn't run you didn't play. I ended up totally sick of hearing how the players had to sweat. 'You have to be prepared to die for the jersey,' they used to tell us. And I would think, 'I'm 20 years old and I want to play football and enjoy myself. I'm too young to die.' 'Get that shirt dirty!' The bastards! Good football is played with the feet. If you haven't sweated much it's because you've played more."

Little wonder that the return of Johan Cruyff, his former Barcelona team-mate, was an epiphany for Rexach.

Cruyff and Rexach were involved in missionary work. Initially, the possession game they introduced was met with jeers inside the Camp Nou, but they educated their public and the trophies that followed made a convincing argument. They also gave weight to his demands that the young players at the club be instructed in the same way. His plans were not only implemented, they formed a footballing identity for FC Barcelona: successful, attractive, football, meshed with the broader *Més Que Un Club* idea – and it was all being executed by Catalans.

Alexanco, Cruyff's centre-half and the man who lifted the European Cup for him at Wembley in 1992, was the first of the Dream Team to graduate into Barça's youth programme. "Cruyff created a great model which began when he arrived to coach in Spanish football and which endures today," he says. "He developed well-structured training sessions, timetables, the style of working, efficient scouting and an entire footballing ethos. From that point, there has been a steady drive to improve the model but continue with its basic aims. Everything we have today flows from that original Cruyff impetus."

When Cruyff was sacked in 1996 many of his concepts were abandoned. Barcelona moved from a model where *canteranos* were expected to ensure the continuity of that Barça DNA in the first team, to one where vast sums of money were spent on foreign 'guns for hire'. The *fútbol base* was both less trusted and less well used. Yet throughout these years when Bobby Robson, Louis van Gaal, Lorenzo Serra Ferrer, Charly Rexach and Raddy Antic were in charge, the *fútbol base* just kept on going, like a metronome in the background.

Alex García – who guided the careers of many of today's first-team stars before taking up a similar youth role at Dinamo Tbilisi in the summer of 2011 – reveals how this system survived the turmoil between the eras of Cruyff and Frank Rijkaard. "Without patience, calm and hard work everything would have come apart, but the great thing now is that there has been continuity of a philosophy, at least in *fútbol base*, since Cruyff implemented the system," he says.

"Quite independently of the ebb and flow of first-team coaches after Cruyff or what style of play was fashionable for the first team, the youth system was set apart and kept to the same rules and ideals. That is the specific reason why now, when Pep Guardiola has taken over, well over half his first team can be home-produced *canteranos*."

Txiki Begiristain believes that one of the greatest prizes of the Guardiola years is that it has made this model now impossible to erode, even after Barcelona's coach moves on.

Here is how it begins. Recruitment can start at the age of seven, or certainly the process of assessment does. From that stage, right through to the multi-million Euro pursuit of a superstar, it falls into three categories.

The club will constantly be seeking players ready to go straight into the first team, such as David Villa or Dani Alves.

Secondly, they will recruit footballers who are in the *Juvenil* category (16-19 years old) and are mid- to short-term prospects for the first team. An ideal example would be Carles Puyol (aged 17 in 1995 under the Cruyff system) or Pedro Rodríguez (recruited under Frank Rijkaard but promoted by Guardiola when some *fútbol base* coaches were ready to loan the winger out). This type of player can come from a range of sources – a youth club, a local amateur club, a school team or, increasingly, from the junior ranks of another professional football club, within or outwith Spain.

Finally, there is what some would call the most important category: kids of seven or eight years old and upwards, the raw talents that Barça's voracious system can nurture, educate and polish, as they have done with Xavi, Iniesta and Messi.

There is an emphasis on Catalan players, a determination to beat other clubs to the cream of Spanish talent and a priority drive to find the best young players from across the world.

The integration of Leo Messi and his subsequent success was obviously a catalyst for this part of the strategy, but so, too, was a joint initiative between FC Barcelona and Samuel Eto'o's football foundation in Cameroon while the striker was still at the club. Barça helped invest in the scheme, loaned coaching talent and promoted the Eto'o brand, with the agreement that they would receive the cream of the crop. As a result, Jean Marie Dongou, Frank Bagnack, Vivaldi Leonid Bakoyock and Wilfried Jaures Kaptoum have all been at Barcelona for the last three years.

Previously, the different demands of these three recruitment groups meant that they ran concurrently but separately. However, since 2010, the work of those who seek out talent for Barça has been unified – information is shared throughout all the tiers, the selection criteria are uniform and whatever lessons learned while, for example, scouting and recruiting a player like Ibrahim Afellay, might be codified and passed down to those who select the youngest players entering the system.

What do the scouts within the *fútbol base* system look for?

There are myriad clues to potential talent – some as old as the hills. For example, they will try to find kids who just love having a football with them at all times and who are addicted to playing or practising with it.

Pep Guardiola played constantly in the town square of Santpedor when he was growing up, using garage doors of shops in the plaza when there wasn't a full-scale match going on. Neighbours would sometimes chase him and his pals away. As Barça coach, he said: "Part of a player's technical ability is innate, but obviously if you've spent five, six or seven hours a day playing football since you were a young kid, then that helps a lot. The problem with young lads today and particularly those who live in big cities is that they only play football at training. That's likely to be an hour and a half at most."

Carles Puyol was identical in Pobla de Segur. Even though he didn't play organised 11-a-side football until he was 14, Puyol would always have a ball near him, would practise his skills relentlessly and dribble the thing around the house.

Xavi Hernández spent hours and hours developing what he admits is his 'obsession' with keeping the ball.

Laureano Ruiz is something of a legendary name around Barcelona. He was a visionary in the field of youth development before Cruyff and left behind an anecdote that illustrates the value placed on this love of the football.

Ruiz was at a trial for young Catalan footballers as

the crowd of kids thinned out. It hadn't seemed like a productive day's work, but he spotted one kid who stayed behind, kicking the ball against the wall of one of the changing rooms. Ruiz asked him what he was still doing there. "Waiting for my dad," said the kid.

The Barça *cantera* director followed his twitching nose and asked the local coaches and scouts who had organised the trial who the kid was and what he was like. He was told that this was just another junior who hadn't done well enough and was to be passed over.

Ruiz informed them that his instinct told him differently. Any youngster who was so dedicated to the football was not to be discarded without further examination. They persevered, and when that same kid, Albert 'Txapi' Ferrer, climbed the Wembley stairs in 1992 as part of the first Barça team to win the European Cup it proved that long day had included a piece of vintage work by Ruiz.

Everything Barcelona looks for in a young player reflects the skills required to play in Guardiola's first team. How is his first touch? Can he retain possession? How quickly can he read situations and how is his decision-making under pressure? Can a winger play off either foot? Does he press when his team does not have the ball? Does a centre-back have the technical ability to start attacks?

"The most basic but most important task in *fútbol base* is to get the right kids into the system," says Alexanco. "You can't afford to get it wrong. They must be players who are compatible with our system. Pretty much from when they are little kids you are adapting everything about them so that they excel at the Barça style of play. That's the key – capture the right lads, as early as possible, so that they spend years learning everything which must be second nature before, finally, they get to the first team."

Barcelona often find themselves at a tournament or match with many scouts from across Europe. However, they will regularly select players that scouts for the other teams have discarded. Despite the fact that Barcelona, and Spain, have proved that talent and intelligence are more important than height and athleticism, their scouts still find that the type of young player who carries the Barça DNA will be rejected by others because he is small, frail or doesn't stand out in the traditional categories such as tackling, heading or goalscoring.

Albert Benaiges, the venerated youth coach, admits that this model of *fútbol base* was not always as popular with the Camp Nou hierarchy as it is now. "It all depends on who is in charge at the top," he says. "For many years it has all been about selecting technical players – our model is based on the calibre of the footballer, not whether he is tall, blue-eyed and handsome, but there were stages in our history when great importance was placed on physique.

"We weren't playing the kind of football we are now. It's a good model, but you have to be aware of the small important details. It's a bit like cooking – if you don't know how much salt and spices to use, you'll never make a good stew."

At the senior level, there have recently been two examples of why the search for this 'Barça DNA' should be applied to recruitment for players from the age of seven right through to multi-million Euro transfers. This is what happens when you don't follow the rules.

By nobody's standards is Zlatan Ibrahimovic a poor player. He has skill, an excellent goalscoring record, a winning mentality and a physique perfect for the modern game. His record at the Camp Nou was 21 goals, nine assists and four trophies in one season, but his understanding of and integration into the playing system of Pep Guardiola did not fit the template.

Had he been selected at 14 or 16 the same thing would have happened – his talent, his goals and his physique would probably have opened the door to *fútbol base*, but his inability or unwillingness to adapt would have seen him released or sold. In which case the operation wouldn't have been as ruinously expensive as it actually became.

Similarly, Barcelona found Dmytro Chygrynskiy hugely difficult to play against – the Ukrainian central defender was big, strong, technically able and a good organiser for Shakhtar Donetsk and his national team. His purchase looked sound given his age, his pace and his aerial ability. However, he could not cope with the pressure of having to bring the ball out from defence.

Barça players and staff talk a lot about *automatismos* – habits which become so ingrained that they are second nature. Chygrynskiy just couldn't learn these; his natural instincts were to get rid of the ball to someone else, to freeze in the spotlight if he was advancing with the ball.

Pep Guardiola was extremely keen to keep him, because the Ukrainian had a good attitude and was a willing pupil. The coach believed his defender could adjust and improve, but was encouraged by incoming president Sandro Rosell to sell the player back to his original club to balance the budget.

The two big men, part of whose attraction was to add physicality to the squad, showed that for all the multitude of skills they possessed, the ability to adapt to the Barça way wasn't one.

"Xavi warned me that the *culés* expect a lot and lose patience quickly," reflected Chygrynskiy. "That's when the whistling starts. Even he had been on the receiving end of it a few years previously.

"At Shakhtar [the club he rejoined after leaving Barcelona], when I get the ball I feel like a king. At Barça, when I got the ball I had to look for Xavi or Iniesta. At Shakhtar we look for the long, deep pass. At the Camp Nou it's totally different. It was my fault. I never really stopped feeling under pressure. Coming from another league, like Mascherano, Abidal and Ibrahimovic, it's very, very difficult to adapt to Barça."

For both categories, the ones who do grow up together in the *cantera* and those signed at the peak of their careers, Barcelona try to assess the personality and background of their player as much as their ability. Development on all fronts has become one of the goals of the *fútbol base*.

"When we look at a kid, Barça doesn't just see a footballer, but a young lad with a family and a community behind him," explains Benaiges. "We believe it is really important our boys develop personally and academically because if they don't make it, they have to find a different career route. We try to instil values like self-sacrifice and team spirit. We work hard with them and as a result we currently have seven or eight youngsters in Barça B who also attend university. They need to work on their all-round development, as well as their technical ability."

Carles Folguera is in charge of La Masia, a task he took on in 2002. He believes this attention to the non-football aspects of a young player's life is central to decreasing the 'fail rate' and getting more outstanding prospects to graduate into the first team. As Barcelona increase scouting in Africa and Asia, this becomes even more important.

The kids from the Eto'o Foundation are almost unique in arriving at *fútbol base* without parents or guardians accompanying them. If a youngster is changing language, country and culture, then not only must he be able to withstand the terrible pressures of immaturity and loneliness, but his football qualities must be utterly beyond doubt. If the players in his position who come from Catalonia merit a B– mark, then the kid from Japan or Nigeria must be an A+.

Case study: Cesc Fàbregas

Rodolfo Borrell is the guy who found the young Cesc Fàbregas and brokered what was, even then, a complicated deal.

"I first saw him play in Mataró and spoke to Oriol Tort about him, and he ended up joining the *Alevín A*," recalls Borrell. "It was the 1997-98 season and in those days coaches would go round Catalonia checking out our opponents. During my first visit to Mataró during the pre-season, I didn't see anyone special but then, once the season had started, I went back and there was this brilliant young player I hadn't noticed before.

"At half-time, Mataró's coordinator told me that the

coaches had been instructed to take the lad off the pitch the minute a visiting coach appeared. They knew that we would all want to sign him.

"In those days, once a player had played five league games with a team, they couldn't join another club. When I asked for his details, the extra joy was that Cesc absolutely stood out against them all yet they were all at least a year older and bigger than him – it was the best possible indication.

"Cesc was an important player for Mataró, but they agreed that he could train with us every Wednesday until he reached the age for *Alevín A*. One year later he joined us full-time alongside Piqué, Víctor Vázquez and, eventually, Messi."

If a kid gets into the *fútbol base* system at Barcelona around the age of 10 and makes his debut for the first team aged 20, he should have amassed something upwards of 2300 training sessions. Vast chunks of those 3070 hours will be spent on routines which train possession retention.

At many clubs the youth training will start with the physical, the development of power and stamina, followed by the tactical and then the technical. At Barcelona it is quite the reverse. Almost everything will focus on technique to start with, tactics follow soon after. Only at 15 or 16 will there be increased emphasis on physique, stamina and power.

In the early years there will be emphasis on the core skills – first touch, protecting the ball, exercises to teach positional play (movement with and without the ball, attacking and defensive pressing) and so on. Seven-a-side games will be played, usually using an outfield lineup shaped as 3-2-1, where the wide defenders will play as wing-backs, the two behind the striker will use movements similar to Iniesta and Xavi, while the central player in the back three will either be a *pivote* like Sergio Busquets or a centre-half like Gerard Piqué.

It is called *fútbol base* because it's basic football education. If you have released the ball as the centre-half to the right midfielder, what do you do next? Where do you move to? What are your responsibilities?

If you are the striker who has dropped deep to receive the ball from the 'Xavi' player in midfield, do you play a wall pass? Do you turn and dribble?

If possession is lost on the opposite side of the pitch to where you are, how should you react?

This detailed programming of young players is consistent across the age groups. It is like ballroom dancing: the moves are set, but what separates those who are best of all is the ability to express themselves within set movements and rules. Deviate or fail to practise and you'll stand on your partner's toes, the judges will notice and you will dance no more.

Over and over and over again the Barça *canteranos* will practise these movements which become ingrained, second nature, and which begin to separate them from the ordinary footballers of their age at other clubs.

Fran Sánchez, another *fútbol base* coach, explains how this process integrates those recruited later in their development. "We teach them general concepts initially and then add more detail later. We like to increase the level of difficulty gradually. We work with the whole group, so that the boys who have come from outside catch up with the others in terms of their understanding of our system."

Case study: The possession game

It is part of the Barça ethos that the possession they hope to dominate by having better first touches, quicker and more accurate passing and constant, intelligent movement should not be sterile possession. It has nothing to do with beating the other team into submission, everything to do with seeking superiority of numbers, establishing a key player in space with time to see a killer pass and then taking advantage of the anarchy caused in the opposition defence.

Xavi explains it like this: "We are always looking to out-number our opponents, two against one, so if Puyol is on his own with the ball, I'll say, 'Bring it up, bring it up!' He'll bring it up to the point where the guy marking me is forced to break away and press him, so now we have two of us against one and I'll shout, 'Puyi! Puyi! Puyi!'

"You see, if I stay behind the guy marking me, I'm no use. I have to keep moving, so that we can attack. Once I have the ball, I'll tell [Dani] Alves to get into position and I move towards his full-back. We just keep passing and passing and passing. We keep attacking."

Of paramount importance in the development of a Barcelona footballer is a simple possession drill called the *rondo*. You've seen it. Perhaps you have tried it.

There will be a circle of players, often seven or eight,

with two defenders in the middle. The ball is to be passed between those on the outside of the circle without the two in the middle, who are intent on blocking, deflecting or seizing control of the ball, breaking the flow. Barça legend has it that this is a technique first invented, or at least applied in training, by Laureano Ruiz, the discoverer of Txapi Ferrer and a founding father of La Masia.

The first, most obvious, purpose of the exercise is to better the circle players' ability to receive and distribute the ball under pressure with one touch or 'half touch' movements.

The second is to teach the defenders how to press intelligently. The two need to work in co-ordination to be successful.

The third is that, as eventually each player takes his turn in the middle, fitness is built which is tailor-made to the Barça playing style.

The fourth is team spirit. The circle players work together to keep the ball from the defenders.

If you watch the *rondo* done well at Barça you will find that they are at least as competitive as any five-a-side game at Manchester United, Arsenal, Milan, or Bayern Munich. Perhaps you have seen them do it before a match and thought 'I could do that', but that warm-up version is 10 times slower and less intense than the real deal in training.

The circle players want to break records – how many consecutive passes, how long in possession; there are endless variations on the number of touches allowed, the number of defenders, banning passes between adjacent circle players and so on.

When you see it, you understand an anecdote which

Xavi often tells about his own youth training days. Charly Rexach was taking the session and roaring at them, "Not one-touch football! Half-touch football!"

That half-touch is in the Barça DNA. Look at Barcelona v Arsenal, the Champions League knockout tie from March 2011 and the goal scored by Xavi.

It is 1-1 when Iniesta scampers away from Tomáš Rosický, Abou Diaby and Johan Djourou. His pass is aimed into Xavi's run but it gets just the faintest flick-pass from David Villa, which prevents Laurent Koscielny's intervention and Xavi scores. Villa's is the 'half-touch' which Rexach was roaring about 10 years earlier. It is not unique to Barça, but they often use it better than everyone else because it is an intrinsic part of their development as players, as Xavi explains. "They taught us to know who was around us before the ball arrived and to be prepared to use a flick or a cushion or a volley in tenths of a second to keep the circulation of the ball flowing."

For all the brilliant ball control which Iniesta, Xavi, Messi and Pedro possess, the moments when Barça open teams up with lightning passing, the ball moving at the speed of an ice hockey puck, stem from the *rondos*. Throughout their career they will do tens of thousands of them.

For a coach, it's like a doctor putting a thermometer in a kid's mouth. Pay attention to the result and he'll know whether all's well or not. If these guys are suffering in the *rondo* then something's wrong – mentally, physically, confidence, concentration. Something's up.

Arnau Riera was Messi's captain during his relatively short spell with Barça B. Arnau was talent spotted at a relatively advanced age – a compliment to him in that few are good enough to fit in if they haven't been nurtured there, but also a drawback as it is an intimidating culture to walk into.

"When I began the first *rondos* in training I couldn't keep up," he says. "I saw players like Thiago Motta effortlessly better than me at it and I phoned my father to tell him, 'I don't think I can make it, these guys are so far ahead of me.'

"One thing which stands out about the *fútbol base* training at Barça is that they want all their players to think more quickly than their opponents. The *rondos* help your touch, your passing, they train fitness and are very good technically, but what helps you most is if you are very sharp at knowing what's going to happen and what to do next. That's a defining trait of what is valued at Barça."

Today we see a great number of clubs running a similar drill, but when I see these *rondos*, particularly in the English Premier League, they bear no relation to the touch, speed, technical excellence or competitiveness that is commonplace at Barça.

One FA contact told me: "In England that exercise is still seen as having a bit of a joke and a laugh."

There are other vital concepts in the training of a Barça footballer. One, unusually for this team, concerns the use of the head. As Xavi explains, it is about acquiring the vision necessary to make such quick decisions on the ball.

"In Barcelona there are many concepts we discuss at training sessions," he says. " 'Keep your head up' is one.

The ball is at your feet, but you need to keep your head high. If not, you're not watching the game. Another saying is 'look before you receive the ball'. That's a really important one for shaping your stance to control first time and then knowing what move you have to make to release the ball quickly to the next guy."

Throughout his junior career, Xavi had it drilled into his head: 'Watch Pep, he has his head up'. 'Watch Pep, he always knows when to give and where to give to'.

These will be drilled in over and again to every kid in Barça's *fútbol base*. It's easy to imagine Guardiola's name being replaced by that of Xavi or Iniesta, but both of those players think that Sergio Busquets is a more complete example of this teaching philosophy. His play is less spectacular, but Busquets embodies the work ethic, the control of possession and the speed of thought which once was Guardiola's.

"Sergio doesn't get enough credit," says Xavi. "He's a brilliant player. He doesn't dribble, he rarely scores, he doesn't do stepovers, but what a player!

"Busi is the essence of what it means to be a Barça player. He's a hard worker with real class. The other team will mark one of us, man to man, and he'll still use a first-time pass to get the ball right to you and you think to yourself, 'How did he see me? That was impossible!'"

The 'third man run' is not a tactic exclusive to Barcelona, but their superior technique and speed of passing means that few teams execute it better.

It's like the 'find the lady' con with three cards, one

of which is a queen. You think you know what's happening, you think you've followed the 'lady' when, of course, you haven't and you lose your money when the con man turns over the card you selected.

Xavi feeds the ball to the feet of David Villa, who has dropped towards him and is facing the passer, back to goal.

Villa has no intention of holding the ball up or turning. He is just a wall to play the ball off. Villa plays the ball, with one touch, straight to Iniesta, who, as Xavi was, is facing Villa.

As soon as Xavi releases the ball to Villa, he starts moving. That run takes him away from his own marker and beyond the marker who has stayed tight to Villa. Xavi is now in a space into which Iniesta, also using a first-time pass, sends the ball.

Ask any Camp Nou-trained player about this move and they'll tell you that it's almost impossible to defend against when it's done effectively and at high speed.

A *fútbol base* education goes beyond the technical. The lessons are also psychological and include the value of losing plus an ongoing debate concerning the balance between winning and learning in the early years of development.

Barcelona have built a winning machine and it may seem odd that the concept of losing is so important to it. In part, it is about learning to handle defeat with some dignity – a concept which Pep Guardiola holds dear, often speaks about and which is also taught at all levels of *fútbol base*.

Albert Puig, technical secretary of the youth programme at the Camp Nou, explains how he puts this
principle into heated match situations. "I always tell
my players that it's healthy to express anger and disappointment after losing a match, but that they should
only allow that reaction to last from the moment the
match finishes until they make it to the shower," he
says. "The second the water hits their head they should
remind themselves that football is just a game and that
there will always be winners and losers."

Charly Rexach explains the danger that comes with
unchallenged supremacy on the pitch. "Sometimes it's
important to lose in *fútbol base*," he says. "There are
times when you end up always winning because you're
up against weaker teams. Then, when you meet an
opponent of equal quality, your performance can slip
because you're so unused to playing boys at the same
level. Winning every match is not healthy because
players get complacent.

"If at half-time you're winning 3-0, you already know
that you've won and you might think there's no point
in going for 7-0 or 8-0. The coach must, therefore, add
a challenge for his players. He has to tell them to play
one-touch football, or run faster and so on. He needs
to make changes like that so that the win will be well
deserved."

Fundamental to Rexach's point is the debate between
winning and losing in the early stages of the *cantera*.

Is a winning mentality innate or can it be learned?
How did ferocious competitors who are now addicted
to winning at the highest level, like Víctor Valdés, Carles Puyol, Andrés Iniesta and Xavi become part of two
eras, between 1999 and 2004 and then from May 2006

to May 2008, when a total lack of trophies was reflected in the psychology of the dressing room?

Even Pep Guardiola plays around with the basic idea of what 'winning' means. In Puig's book *La Fuerza de Un Sueño*, he argues that: "Winning is not incompatible with a good early training. On the contrary, good early training means that youngsters develop into players who win, but who win the right way. They respect their opponents, behave at all times as representatives of the club, accept that there is someone in charge, have tactical discipline and work hard at training. That is the way to win."

Alex García, who taught Messi, Piqué, Fàbregas, Bojan, Busquets and Thiago, partly explains the concept as encouraging players to learn by never settling for what they have achieved. "That group of Messi, Cesc, Victor and Piqué were all very competitive," he told me. "They were born winners who chased every trophy. They were never willing to settle. That's one distinctive thing about Barça players, they're never happy with just being good enough. They could be winning 5-0 and they'd still want to score a sixth."

Xavi adds: "Before you become a professional you need to learn and develop, but without losing your competitive edge. In Barça we all understand that. Development is a priority. The young lads learn footballing concepts and understand why we do things in a certain way whilst maintaining their competitive spirit, their desire to win. It's good to express the anger you feel when you lose. In the *fútbol base* the priority is training and development, but the objective is to win."

I learned during the writing of this book that the NextGen Series, where clubs compete at under-19 level in a Champions League-style competition, has uncovered almost identical concepts at Tottenham Hotspur. When I talked to Tim Sherwood, in his day a title winner with Blackburn Rovers, now Spurs' technical coordinator, his take on winning versus learning was a familiar one. "In development, it's about producing players, not winning games," he said.

"There is still a lot of old-school mentality around. Some still have the perception that it's all about results at youth level, but it's not about that. The basic footballing philosophy about what to do with the ball must stay. If a wee guy is robbed by some huge guy of the same age, then we want him to keep doing the right things, not change because he's temporarily at a physical disadvantage."

Fran Sánchez is the longest serving youth coach at Barcelona, despite only being 35 years old. "Competitiveness is always essential," he says. "Whenever you play a game you go out to win and that has got to be the attitude of all our boys, from the youngest to the oldest. Today, society in general is super competitive and football reflects that, but obviously it's important to us that we play the right way. It's not about winning at all costs. We need to play our kind of football, show respect for our opponents and the referee and try to outplay the other team. Playing our style of football is essential, even if it means losing the game.

"As they grow up these boys sometimes develop the belief that, 'If I've won that must mean we're better players than the others,' but that's not our philosophy. It's perfectly possible to win a match without having played the right way and vice versa – we can play the right way and lose. What we're interested in is that our opponents make it as hard as possible, so that our own boys have the chance to develop. Winning every match 10-0 does us no good at all."

However, Thiago and Rafinha's father, Mazinho, who starred for Valencia and Celta Vigo and won the World Cup at USA 94 with Brazil, concludes the debate by providing some context and a perfect balance between winning and learning. He's in tune with García's sentiments. When Mazinho's two talented sons were at school in the Galician city of Vigo, they had a five-a-side football coach who would tell the group, 'The most important thing is to participate.' Eventually the Brazilian world champion took the guy aside and quietly told him, "You are mistaken. The most important thing for any of them to do is to compete".

There is a constant queue of people from all over the world waiting to study Barcelona's training methods: managers, coaches, directors, you name it. Depending on who they are and what they ask for, they will be given varying levels of access. However, while the Barça staff are friendly and open about their work, they are sceptical about the worth of 'spot' visits aimed at assimilating ideas that have evolved over a generation or more. Unless a person sees the development process in its entirety, then coming in for a couple of days to study the work done by a particular age group will only provide a partial, and probably false representation. Furthermore, unless the club from which the person is sent is ready for a total overhaul of its scouting, development and training structure, as well as its basic football philosophy, then picking up 'bits and pieces' of the Barça credo is a waste of time.

Pere Gratacós, Messi's last coach before hitting the first team, probably expresses the overall sentiment most bluntly. "Schools need to teach and if Barça can help coaches develop, that's positive, but it's not something you can achieve with a couple of days' work and study. It's the fruit of many years of planning; you can't just come here and observe for a couple of days and reproduce the system somewhere else."

There is another interesting development. Some of the key figures in the success of Barça's *cantera* in recent years have now gone to seek fame, fortune and personal development elsewhere. Rodolfo Borrell is at Liverpool, Alex García is charge at Dinamo Tbilisi, and Albert Benaiges is in the new football hotspot of Dubai, technical coordinator at the Al Wasl club where Diego Maradona is coach at the time of writing (but may well not be at the time of reading).

Could the Barça model be exported by hiring exceptional coaches from within its system and handing them control of youth development at a club?

"No, that would have been a serious mistake," says Borrell. "Every country has its own football culture and you shouldn't try to alter their basic footballing essence. All you can do is work out how to complement what they do already with some new ideas. I try to transfer some of the things that I believe have made Barça what it is today and make sure that all the teams, at all age levels, work towards the same basic footballing direction."

Alex García is more optimistic about taking the principles of La Masia to Georgia, but his work is pressurised by the tension between winning and learning. "We're trying to help the players here develop Barça's values and work methods, but it's a challenge because the competition doesn't really give you the breathing space and the time to teach properly," he says. "It will take time and we're determined to work hard and achieve something.

"We're restructuring the club from top to bottom according to the Barça model, but the whole project is one which takes time to reach fruition. The teams use the 4-3-3 formation, but probably the key thing is that the training methods are the same as Barça's."

From Dubai, Benaiges says: "We are working on it. It's always a challenge to bring a new style of play to a place like this and the players aren't of the same calibre as Barça's. What you can import is the order and discipline we always imposed in the Barça youth academy. There are other teams who use this model, like Ajax or Santos, and they have had great success with it over the years, too.

"A key problem for other clubs is to ask themselves what kind of player it's feasible for them to recruit. The kind of kid you put into the system is pretty much as important as the excellence with which you teach them. Barça have Xavi, Iniesta and Messi, the three best players in the world. You have players of 32 like Xavi and young guys of 19 like Cuenca coming through. They have a real mix of generations in the current team and a group of new young players snapping at their heels. They have all learned the same playing style and that essentially is the secret of our success. Replicating that elsewhere would take a long time and need the correct conditions to succeed."

The last word on this subject goes to one of the hero figures in this book, Charly Rexach. "Other teams can try to copy us, of course, but we've got 30 years of a head start."

An important, parallel development to the move to a much larger, modernised Masia building has been the professionalisation of the entire *fútbol base* system. I was first alerted to this as more and more CCTV cameras appeared across the new training ground. These are not for extra security, but to film the training sessions of as many of the age groups as possible. The idea is to review the work, to apply lessons learned and to monitor coaching standards.

Until Sandro Rosell granted Pep Guardiola one of his dearest wishes, almost all the age-group *fútbol base* coaches were part-time. They had other jobs, they earned moderate wages and they limited their time at the club to coaching and match days. Now these coaches are full-time employees of the club.

For the last couple of seasons, the staff have had the time to watch these tapes, to share notes about players who may oscillate between *Alevín A* and *Juvenil B* or between *Juvenil A* and Barça B. Planning, information sharing, review – all of these things are given more time, more attention and a higher priority than ever before.

"We're really seeing the fruits of many years' work," says Alex García. "The football and training methods have changed over time.

"In the past, the coaches were only there two hours a

day, but now they work full-time and that makes such a difference to the *cantera*."

"We work together constantly to analyse what we're doing and improve it and there's great communication between the first team guys and ourselves," adds Fran Sánchez. "As long as the information is flowing in both directions, we can keep improving. We won't end up waiting for 10 years to find out that we do not have good centre-forwards. If we know now that we need a player with certain skills then we start working to produce players with the right characteristics."

The flaws in the system that gave rise to the possibility of Lionel Messi leaving Barcelona while in the *cantera* have been all but eradicated by refinements in recent years. However, errors in judgment – either in the scouting process or when deciding which young players to release – still happen.

Jordi Alba, released by the *fútbol base* at Camp Nou at the *Juvenil* stage, is now a star at Valencia, a Spanish international and Barça consider him a candidate for repatriation. It happens less now, but it remains an occupational hazard.

A greater problem, however, are the predatory English clubs circling the Camp Nou and other clubs in Spain. When Cesc Fàbregas and Gerard Piqué left Barça, it was in part down to mismanagement and a lack of opportunity. As Rodolfo Borrell puts it: "In those days it was enormously difficult to move from the *cantera* into the first team, much harder than it is now."

The other factors that led to the loss of these talents

remain very much in play. Spanish labour law prescribes that footballers cannot sign a binding professional contract until they are past their 16th birthday. Each year, every gem within the Barça system (as with all Spanish clubs) becomes free to move when and where he chooses. Recently, Barça have lost Héctor Bellerín and Jon Toral to Arsenal. They are only two examples – there have been, and will be, more.

Each of them will earn Barcelona small six-figure sums due to FIFA rules on compensation for home-developed players who leave before a full transfer fee is due.

Players like Sergi Samper, an absolute gem in the *Juvenil* set-up who will eventually play in the style of Iniesta or Xavi, has already received significant offers; Messi and his father were approached consistently when he was still a junior.

Unless Spanish labour law changes, this situation will perpetuate and it is a vicious circle for Barça. The more quality players they select and train, the harder it will be for them to break into the first team.

The case of Oriol Romeu may represent a guide for the way forward. Sold to Chelsea for around €5m, there is a buy-back clause which rises by €5m per season in the first three seasons if Barcelona want to reclaim him. The *cantera* mines raw gems for sale as well as for keeping.

"In England it's much more difficult to sign players from other teams and it's better to invest in Spain, thereby avoiding transfer fees," Albert Benaiges told me. "The families of players in the Barça *cantera* don't know if their 15-year-old is going to make it or not and the incoming clubs offer their families loads of money.

As a result, you have a stream of young players going to England. Some of them flourish there, others less so."

Fran Sánchez summarises the situation like this: "The average age in the Barça first team is relatively young and there just isn't space for all the good players that come up. The club has to prioritise and sadly has, on occasion, to let good players go if they don't fit in the first team for whatever reason. We are constantly being contacted by clubs, particularly English clubs, who are interested in our B team players."

Guillermo Amor is the sporting director of the *fútbol base* system. At the end of his first season, in the summer of 2011, he said: "England is an economically strong country and they are on the prowl for the right moment, which is to sign from this country when our players are at the *Cadete* [under-16] age. It's also true that we notice English clubs when we are trying to sign young talents at earlier ages. We will never enter into a financial tug of war with a Premier League club for a kid. We will just continue on the guidelines we have set out and give a youngster, no matter how talented, what is the appropriate money depending on his age."

The more you talk to Barça people about this cherry-picking of their stars, the more one is reminded of the issue which originally brought Pep Guardiola to the first team. Luis Milla, the incumbent *pivote* in the Barcelona midfield, wanted more money and Real Madrid wanted him. Many on the Barça board wanted to pay Milla what he needed to make him stay. Johan Cruyff, the coach, did not. "We'll just find another Luis Milla," he said. And he did. Barcelona lose promising youth players to predators and say, "That's a pity. Good luck. We'll develop someone better".

9 – The Breeding Ground

That they have earned tens of millions by selling Rubén Rochina to Blackburn, Romeu to Chelsea, Jeffrén to Sporting, Bojan to Roma, Nolito to Benfica and Víctor Sánchez to Neuchâtel is a palliative.

The New Masia

The march of progress continued on October 20, 2011. The Masia Oriol Tort was inaugurated in a vast, colourful ceremony which added joy and optimism to the nostalgia which had accompanied the closure of the old one, four months earlier.

The new Masia is built on the Ciudad Deportiva Joan Gamper: an impressive, modern, sprawling training ground to which Pep Guardiola moved his first-team squad in January 2009. During my decade in Barcelona, the club began the building work, ran out of funding, mothballed and then finally completed a facility which has already helped secure historic achievements.

Now the new Masia, a €10m residential facility, has been added. Before its closure, La Masia, next to the Camp Nou, only accommodated 12 students, with another 48 in dormitories attached to the stadium. Now all 83 of the youth players to whom Barcelona have offered residential status live together on the site of the training facility.

Each room is home to one, two or four boys and throughout the 'house' there is an emphasis on study facilities, given that all the kids there are in full-time education.

On the night of the inauguration, when a host of former pupils and staff attended, Andrés Iniesta, who had such a traumatic early spell at the old Masia, recalled his own experience and looked to the future of the new building's first residents.

"The La Masia change brings back many memories," he said. "The development from what it was when I stayed there to the modern embodiment is huge. What I'd say to the lads who are lucky enough to enjoy this life-changing experience is, 'Value going to school every day, training, the whole process, because time passes rapidly' – I can tell them that. The process of being separated from your family is so tough that it can cause you to lose a lot of time. I'd advise these boys to make the most of every minute of the experience. When my parents left me in the old Masia all those years ago there was no better place in the world to which they could have delivered me."

But who better than Pep Guardiola to conclude this chapter. At the end of his first, treble-winning season in charge he was asked how many more trophies might come his team's way, given their extraordinary beginning. With a shrewd sidestep of a question he didn't want to answer, this La Masia graduate, turned midfield general, turned historic leader said: "The one thing which can never stop at this club is the *cantera*."

PEDRO:
THE COMEBACK KID

MAYBE IT IS A CULTURAL THING, but during my 10 years in Barcelona I can't remember many things in the sports media getting me quite as annoyed as the description of Xavi, Andrés Iniesta and Deco as '*Los Tres Juguetes*'. It was a phrase coined by the Catalan football press. It means 'The Three Little Toys'. It seemed to me, a bellicose Scot, an insulting way to talk about three such sublime footballers.

When Pedro came along, they were at it again. Pedrito means 'Little Pedro'; most footballers would bridle angrily at such a complacently chosen nickname. However, the guy from the Canary Islands comes with a stoic determination to be accepted on his own merits.

As was the case with Sergio Busquets, 'assessors' in the *fútbol base* system at Barcelona were unified in the belief that Pedro should be loaned out, or even sold, just before Pep Guardiola rescued him. Pedro, then, is one of the few to have made every step of the journey with the coach, from reserve-team football to unreserved adulation.

His pace was his most evident weapon, but Guardiola's judgment has been proven by the way in which Pedro has developed, almost from nowhere, a cold-blooded assassin's eye for turning the merest opportunity into a goal.

I also remember how easily he took to his role as the guy who had to supplant Fernando Torres in the defining stages of the 2010 World Cup. His temperament and sunny demeanour made his excursions with the Spain team look like he was popping down to the shops for his newspaper and a bag of crisps. 'World Cup semi-final, final? No problem, boss'.

In the Spain dressing room after the team had paraded with the World Cup I was hanging back, keeping a low profile while my UEFA cameraman, Adam Goldfinch, filmed the fiesta. Pedro wandered up, put one arm around me and said, "Thanks for everything". There was nothing, just the fact that he's the nicest fella you could meet.

Let's do him greater justice and remember the Champions League final one year after Soccer City. Forget the final scoreline for a moment, and forget the banquet of football Barça served up once they were in front. Recall, instead, something that those memories are already obscuring: the opening stages of that match belonged almost totally to Manchester United and it seemed that Guardiola's team faced a stern test.

Pedro's movement for Barça's opening goal and his 'look one way, finish the other' undressing of Edwin van der Sar, the United goalkeeper, punctured the tension just as surely as Sir Alex Ferguson said Samuel Eto'o did with his opening strike in Rome two years before. Pedro turned the tide.

With Seydou Keita, Pedro is probably the most unassuming guy in the squad, but his helter skelter ascension from potential Barça drop-out to champion of the world in two-and-a-half years is emblematic of the entire Guardiola era.

10 – THE SOLUTIONS MAN

"Xavi, you are going to replace me, but watch out for this young guy, because he'll retire all of us."
— Pep Guardiola.

PAIN HAS COME TO a standstill. Thousands of miles away, *La Roja* have left the Da Vinci hotel in Sandton, Johannesburg, in their luxury red coach which bears the legend 'Hope is my route – Victory is my destiny' and they are heading for Soccer City in Soweto. It is July 11, 2010. They are heading for the World Cup final.

In Fuentealbilla, (population 2067 and about three hours south-east of Madrid) José Antonio Iniesta is watching at home, alone, because his wife is down at the Andrés Iniesta / FC Barcelona fanclub in the centre of the village. Iniesta senior just hates flying and so hasn't gone to Johannesburg, just like he avoids many of his son's big dates. His dislike of flying is such that he took the train from Barcelona to Vienna, and back, for the Euro 2008 final; to Paris, Rome and London for his son's Champions League finals. He has established this tradition of choosing peace and quiet to watch the big game.

When his son scores in extra-time against Holland, José Antonio turns off the television because he cannot bear the tension of the remaining five minutes. He goes upstairs. Not until the sky above Fuentealbilla is lit up by fireworks is he sure his son has just won Spain the World Cup, and the set is switched back on.

Iniesta's mother, María Francisca Luján, meantime, is also stressed, down at the old Bar Luján, where her father was the landlord for 35 years. On retirement, he converted every full-page cutting he ever saved about his talented grandson into an archive which covers every millimetre of wall space. It's a shrine.

Despite the little town's fame for being a hotbed of *Madridismo*, Bar Luján is now both a fanclub for the village's most famous son and the club he plays for. It's not a small social space, either. On the night of the final it is packed, like most bars in Spain, and María Francisca is so uptight that she goes for a little bit of fresh air out in the street – and is still out there when her son scores his historic goal.

Exactly two weeks before Barcelona won the Champions League at Wembley in May 2011, Burgos Club de Fútbol drew a thriller 1-1 against Atlético Tordesillas. What do you mean you didn't notice? It was the result to guarantee them their regional third division title and a shot at the play-offs to reach Spain's national third division, Segunda B. Okay, I admit it, the rest of the planet didn't grind to a halt.

The thing of beauty which the match produced wasn't the result, but the outrageous goal scored by their inside-left, Jorge Troiteiro. Picking the ball up deep in his own half, he sprayed a nonchalant pass to the left wing, then sprinted 50 yards to be in place when the Tordesillas left-back, Villamañán, headed the ball to just outside the penalty area.

Controlling the dropping clearance on his left instep, Troiteiro dragged a gaggle of defenders all over the place before sending three of them the wrong way for a second time, planting one of them on his backside, and slipping the ball through the legs of the goalkeeper, Héctor Barajas.

It was the goal of your dreams, the one you fall asleep praying for. Despite being scored in front of only 2,000 people, Spanish television made a fuss over it in the days that followed and it is replayed on the internet still. Do yourself a favour, look it up on YouTube.

Better yet, this beautiful goal came with two minutes left and with the team and fans desperate for the point which would win them the title. OK, not the World Cup-winning goal, or an assist in the Champions League final, but it was breathtaking. And it was scored by the guy without whom Andrés Iniesta might never have made it at FC Barcelona.

Back in 1996, two kids from Albacete, Iniesta and Troiteiro, not only stood out at junior level but were being scouted by FC Barcelona as future prospects for the La Masia youth system.

The *Torneo Nacional Alevín de Fútbol 7* – then held every summer outside Madrid, now rotated around the country – is where under-15 youngsters from the best Spanish clubs play in a seven-a-side competition. It's where Fernando Torres, Cesc Fàbregas, Gerard Piqué, David Silva, Juan Mata, Fernando Llorente, David de Gea and Sergio Canales claimed their first real fame.

Troiteiro was with Mérida CF because his parents had moved to Extremadura in the west of Spain, Iniesta with his local side, Albacete. 'Local' meant that he and his dad, José Antonio, travelled just under an hour each way three times per week so that his eight-year-old kid could train at a professional club.

The life of a footballer is packed with coincidences, quirks, lucky and unlucky breaks which determine those who make it and those who don't. *Azar* in Spanish, fate or luck in English. For example, Iniesta had shone the year previously at his first *Torneo Nacional Alevín de Fútbol 7* without winning the best player award and without Albacete troubling the medal engravers. A year later – the fateful one which would light his path all the way to Soccer City in 2010 – Albacete had just been relegated from the Primera División, eliminating them from the *Torneo Nacional Alevín*. However, a couple of clubs suffering financial problems chose not to compete and Albacete responded to an emergency call to take their place at the tournament. They finished third, Iniesta won player of the tournament by an overwhelming consensus and Barça's scouts elevated his ranking to 'must sign'.

Troiteiro also shone at the tournament and despite each lad being only 12, and the La Masia entry age then being set at 14, Barça made approaches to both sets of parents and the little gems were offered future scholarships within the Camp Nou youth system.

However, Troiteiro's dad was in a hurry. He let Barça know in no uncertain terms that his son was ready, that rules were made to be bent and that little Jorge would be taking his talents elsewhere, perhaps to a white-shirted club, if the Catalans didn't move sharply.

Oriol Tort was one of the first men to go and see Pep Guardiola as a kid 15 years earlier, when he was playing with Manresa. By 1996, he was in charge of the youth section at Barça, having been so relentlessly successful that he had acquired the nickname 'The Professor'. The new youth centre at Barça's training ground, now that the original La Masia has been decommissioned, is named after Tort, such has been his influence on the club over the generations.

He and Rodolfo Borrell, now the coach of Liverpool's reserve team, got together to consider the problem. They wanted Troiteiro but didn't particularly want to leave a 12-year-old kid alone in a school of hard knocks, where everyone else was at least two years older. Tort and Borrell came up with the solution that Iniesta would also be offered accelerated entry. They phoned Iniesta senior, who was stunned but delighted.

However, if the player's father was keen, his wife was far less so and young Andrés was deeply unsure. He was a Barça supporter and idolised Michael Laudrup, but local values meant a lot to him. When Albacete, the team he'd grown up training with and watching when they hit the big time in 1991, were thrashed 7-1 at the Camp Nou in their first-ever top division season, Iniesta was upset.

"My dad was an Athletic fan, but I supported Albacete and Barça," he recalled. "Barça was my second team. I used to go and watch Albacete play in the First Division at the weekend. The year they were promoted was a great one for me. I remember celebrating in the village, but I also recall being furious when Barcelona put seven past them."

He went around telling people he didn't like Barça anymore. The scars were deep enough that when Barça came calling a couple of years later, offering to accelerate the move to La Masia, he told his parents he wasn't keen. Albacete seemed like a big draw to him – they'd had a four-year run in the top division, regularly turning up draws with Barça and even an away win at the Camp Nou. Moreover, father and son shared some special times in their five hours driving to and from training every week.

Iniesta's former coach, Francisco Javier Mármol, better known as Catali, explains: "I trained him when he was nine or 10. Even then you could see that he was a kid with an exceptional future. He was already playing with his 'head up' and stood out from the rest. He was a great kid from a good family, never in trouble, never sent off – always bringing a good atmosphere to the team.

"He liked to stay low-profile, but in my opinion his main virtue is that he always knows what he's going to do with the ball before he even gets it and he always gets it right. It doesn't matter which coaches he has had, Andrés Iniesta was predestined to triumph."

José Antonio Iniesta has a profile which is typical of so many superstar footballers' fathers – a professional at a good level for a while; semi-pro for a long time; talented, but missing either the special spark or the lucky break to make it big. There are some around Fuentealbilla who still tell Andrés junior that his dad was a better footballer than him, but given how their respective careers have unfolded, let's just let that one pass, shall we?

In the knowledge that his father was firmly in favour of accepting the opportunity, Iniesta eventually volunteered to meet Tort and another La Masia legend, Albert Benaiges.

His 'best player' award brought the prize of a free trip to the Port Aventura fun park near Tarragona in southern Catalonia. The Iniesta family used it to check out the La Masia set-up, to wander round the trophies in the Camp Nou museum. Iniesta was beginning to sway.

Tort, Benaiges and some of their colleagues already knew, as they were constructing a solution to the Troiteiro situation, that La Masia was too slow-moving, too conservative and needed to start opening its doors to players much younger than 14. This was an era when

Ajax, under Louis van Gaal but using a youth set-up sculpted by Johan Cruyff, were the dominant European side. Their youngsters were famously trained from as young as seven and eight and the Amsterdam club certainly didn't wait so long to recruit talented boarders. Tort, Benaiges, Borrell and colleagues were determined to get Iniesta, now that they had set aside the age rule for Troiteiro.

"I never stopped watching Andrés, I adored his playing style even at that age – it was the Identikit of what we were looking for in the Barça *cantera*," said Benaiges. "He's kept many of the qualities he had when he was 12 – he's pure technique. His passes and his decisions are constantly right. His change of pace to get away from someone with skill and speed is unbeatable."

Handily for them, despite all Iniesta's doubts and the fact that, aged 12, he probably wasn't mature enough to cope with moving nearly 500km away, the youngster admired Michael Laudrup and Pep Guardiola so much that his mind was flooded with possibilities.

This was a dream opportunity for a boy who adored the Dream Team, so, when the meeting with the La Masia eminences grises was "immensely persuasive", he took a firm decision to move to the Camp Nou. Iniesta explained the horror of the five-hour journey northwards, which everyone in the family knew was an irrevocable step into an unknowable life for all of them.

"We stopped for lunch but no-one could eat. My mum was crying, I was crying, my dad had no appetite and my grandfather kept trying to cheer me up, but even he couldn't eat.

"I couldn't even look at the food. My first sight of

La Masia was José, the youth team goalkeeper, who was 6ft 2in tall and who showed me round. At dinner, I couldn't stop crying. The next day my parents took me to school and said, 'We'll pick you up at the end of the day,' but when I came out, they had gone. It was for the best.

"There was no sense in prolonging the agony. I was still crying, but I reckon that if they had stayed I would have been in an even worse state."

Because of all his doubts, Iniesta arrived a few weeks after Troiteiro, who was already installed and, fortunately for Iniesta, had already encountered a friendly 'protector' in the shape of Víctor Valdés, two years older than the new recruits. The keeper knew the ropes, would not be pushed around by anyone, and yet was generous enough to see that two new saplings were going to be out of their depth unless they had a minder.

"Victor was the first guy I met coming through the front door and he immediately helped me take all my stuff up to the dormitory where I was staying," recalls Troiteiro. Iniesta still calls Valdés one of his best friends in football.

In their dorm, Troiteiro had the top bunk, Iniesta the bottom and despite having a noisy, friendly companion, he suffered. "Most days he'd cry a bit because he was struggling without his family," says Troiteiro. "Sometimes I'd tell him a joke or fool around a little just to cheer him up, but the greatest thing was that we could see the Camp Nou from our window and we used to dream that 'one day, one day ...'"

The history of La Masia is littered with stories of kids, often far older than Iniesta, who had not been able to cope. Those stories are replicated in academies in every major footballing nation. Loss of society with friends, parents or siblings, immaturity, indiscipline – these are all recurring themes. However, Iniesta and Troiteiro were also, by far, the babies of the system.

For all his tears, and the fact that Iniesta spent regular weekends with the Benaiges family when his parents reluctantly decided his adaptation would improve if they didn't come to visit him every weekend, what brought him through was the mental and spiritual toughness which have helped him overcome other crises in his sporting life.

He describes his early months at Barça as "hell". One favourable factor was that even in the five- or seven-a-side tournaments regularly held on the concrete pitch outside his school in Fuentealbilla he was so good, so technically advanced that he had always played against bigger, older, tougher lads. Coping with that sporting test couldn't prevent homesickness, but it did make him surer of his ability – a confidence he'd need at La Masia. Another was that his life, for all that he is an ordinary country boy imbued with eternal values of the land, has always been pressurised.

His devotion to the top-class training at Albacete meant that from the age of eight he had to beg time off at the end of the school morning, be rushed 50km to complete his 70-minute work-out with the club and then be driven back by his dad, mum, or grandfather only just in time for school starting again. Spanish schools tend to run from 9am-1pm, with two hours for lunch and then from 3pm to 5pm, or even 5.30pm. Without his school turning a blind eye to him leaving the morning session half-an-hour early twice a week to reach the Albacete training at 1.15pm, Iniesta wouldn't have played for the club, wouldn't have been spotted by Barça in 1996 − and would Chelsea in 2009 and Holland in 2011 have had different experiences against Barça and Spain because Andresito wasn't there?

He admits: "Without that *Alevín* tournament perhaps I wouldn't even be where I am now.

"Achieving your dreams is hard work. I really struggled when I started out, so when I see the youngsters who watch our training sessions in the afternoon, I think back to when I was at that stage. I'll never forget that period."

Life followed the same path for Troiteiro and Iniesta, even up to the point at which they both first became 'world' champions.

Nearly three years into their development in Barça's youth system, along came their big chance. The Nike Cup World Finals were held in Barcelona following a massive qualifying process − nearly 6000 teams had been whittled down to 16 after pre-tournaments in Africa, North America, Central America, Europe, Asia and South America.

Iniesta, Troiteiro and Barça became world champions. Less than two years later, Iniesta was UEFA Under-16 European champion, admired by the Barça first-team coach and not far from his senior debut. Troiteiro, meanwhile, as impatient as his father had been, had lost faith, chosen not to wait and debunked to the Atlético Madrid academy in search of earlier opportunities.

It was a bad choice by Troiteiro. He went down the divisions and, although he remains divinely talented and a joy to watch, his football is played in front of 2,000 people and glory means vaulting from the fourth to the third division with Burgos. *Azar*? Fate? Immaturity? Certainly, one of those moments which defines whether you are to be Burgos' king or an all-time Spanish legend.

Strangely, it was partly the loss of his family which drove Iniesta through the bad times and towards a state where he was comfortable in his independence, had friends and knew his football abilities were growing exponentially. He promised that if he had to cut himself off from his family, then his driving aim would be to succeed as soon as possible, to earn the wealth that comes with top level football and to ensure that they could all afford to stop working and to live near him in Barcelona. That was his personal credo – and it worked.

Back to the 1999 Nike Cup, because although both lads won it, there was extra significance for Iniesta. The tournament was played across a handful of days using the Camp Nou and the Barça Mini Estadi across the road, where the B team plays home games. Having already hammered Rosario on the first day, Iniesta, Troiteiro and company faced those same tough Argentinians in the Camp Nou final, in front of an impressive 20,000 crowd. With the match in extra-time and balanced at 1-1, guess who crashed home the golden goal winner? Andrés Iniesta, with that same trusty right foot which would later bury the ball in Petr Čech's top left-hand corner to take Barcelona to the Champions League final in Rome, and scythe an era-defining goal past Maarten Stekelenburg in Johannesburg in the World Cup final.

Even then there was a clue available for Troiteiro that perhaps there was much for him to learn before risking a move from La Masia. Ángel Pedraza, the Barça Under-16 coach, said about Iniesta: "He stands out for his football intelligence – Andrés is the team leader and reference point of this team. Technically, he's already great, but he knows how and when to control the tempo of a match."

About Troiteiro, Pedraza added: "The biggest impact he has is because of his vivacious nature. Perhaps his play is a bit more spectacular than it is effective. He can, and should, continue improving greatly."

It was 1999, the Camp Nou had just hosted that epic Champions League final between Manchester United and Bayern Munich, Barça were at a low ebb and were about to enter a horrible trophy drought. They were also inching towards the end of Pep Guardiola's glorious era as a Barça player but, fortunately for Iniesta, his hero was persuaded by his younger brother Pere, a key Nike figure, to attend the match and hand out prizes.

Iniesta had already caught Guardiola's attention and when he gave the golden goal boy his medal and trophy, he said: "One day I'll be up in those stands watching you do what I do for Barça." There was no question what meant more to the young lad from Fuentealbilla – the silverware or the silver words. Iniesta floated out of the stadium that night. However, that wasn't all that Guardiola had to say on the matter. He told Xavi, by then a team-mate: "You are going to replace me, but watch out for this young guy, because he'll retire all of us."

Thankfully, in the case of Xavi, he was wrong. From almost the moment Iniesta and Xavi were paired they became Barça and Spain's heart and soul. They have the work ethic of a navvy plus the geometric, imaginative vision of Da Vinci or Galileo.

Some fans and commentators argued then that Barça could not accommodate Xavi and Iniesta in the same team. Too similar, too small, too Spanish. Headline writers for years used the word *juguetes* – meaning toys or playthings – when Iniesta, Deco and Xavi played together in a midfield three. I never saw the humour – it always seemed like a complacent insult to me.

Once again the *azar* which has helped Iniesta, and which most great sportsmen need, eventually arrived in the form of Guardiola, one of Iniesta's two great heroes, returning as his club coach. Because of their age, physical dissimilarities and noticeably different personalities, it's easy to overlook the fact that there are many links between Guardiola and Iniesta. Both 'country' kids, from small, traditional communities where civility, dignity, honour and tradition matter hugely. Guardiola's father was a bricklayer and his son learned the value of hard work. Iniesta's dad was a scaffolder and of an evening he also had to work in Bar Luján, with his father-in-law as his boss.

Of his own era, Iniesta has been the player most repetitively troubled by injuries, something he admits has occasionally gnawed away at his optimism and self-belief. Thus it was with Guardiola, who suffered a year-long, apparently untreatable calf problem which depressed him greatly. Each of them has drawn maximum benefit from their strength of character. Each of them has also known what it signifies to be the icon of La Masia. Núñez, Gaspart and Cruyff chose Guardiola to be the *canterano* who helped plant the flag in the new plot of land at St Joan Despi back in 1989, when it was first planned to become Barça's training ground. When the Pope received FC Barcelona as part of their centenary celebrations exactly 10 years later, Iniesta was chosen by staff and colleagues to be the La Masia representative to meet John Paul II (*socio número* 108,000 at FC Barcelona since being given a *carnet*, or season ticket, in 1982).

Midway through his first season in charge (2008-09), Guardiola acknowledged his immense gratitude at inheriting Iniesta. Barça had just defeated Athletic Bilbao 2-0 to go six points clear of Real Madrid. Busquets and Messi scored the goals, but Iniesta played majestically and post-match Guardiola told us: "Andrés stands alone – beyond the fact that he's a terrific player, it's him that I always use as an example to the youth team players. He doesn't wear earrings; he doesn't tattoo his skin – he just looks like your average guy. He always, always trains at full effort and concentration. Play him for 20 minutes and he doesn't moan, play him out of position and he just gets on with it. That this club has a player like Andrés is beyond price."

The feeling is mutual. Just ahead of winning his third Champions League title, at Wembley, Iniesta said: "We are lucky to have Pep Guardiola as coach. He is a product of our youth programme, he understands football like no-one else and he knows all of us inside out. He is the key to our current and future success."

Iniesta would have been a star footballer under other coaches, but Guardiola's impact on him, Xavi, Messi and Piqué in particular has meant that the whole is now greater than the sum of the parts. He has improved each of them – technically and in their mentality. Given the tiny margins between best and second-best, that 'extra' is the winning element.

However, there was a decade between little Iniesta

winning his first major trophy with that super goal in 1999 and Guardiola finally taking over the Barça first team. The interim period began with what would become motifs in Iniesta's career – glory and injury.

Spain, headed by Fernando Torres and supplied with ingenuity by Iniesta, won the UEFA Under-16 European Championship held in England in 2001, but the midfielder was hacked out of the knockout stages after a brutal German tackle on his ankle. Iniesta was sent home for medical treatment and the esteem in which he was held was shown when Torres, still *El Niño* in those days, scored the first goal against Croatia in the semi-final at Middlesbrough's Riverside stadium.

Slaloming past the Spaniards running to congratulate him, Torres ran towards the TV camera filming the match. Raising the front of his jersey, he showed a T-shirt with a message of support for Iniesta and, on hearing that Spain wasn't taking live images of the match, Torres promised to wear Iniesta's No 8 shirt under his own in the final against France. He did, and he also scored the winner in front of 31,000 fans at Sunderland's Stadium of Light. Iniesta qualified for a medal but, for the first time but not the last, questions were being asked about his fragility.

Meanwhile, medical staff worked overtime to cope with the fact that repetitive, thuggish tackles on his knees and ankles, plus the stress placed on his ligaments and muscles by his explosive bursts of speed left him prone to injuries. Nevertheless, he celebrated the season of his full Barça debut by winning the UEFA Under-19 European Championship, beating Germany 1-0 in the 2002 final. The two future World Cup winners, Torres and Iniesta, stood head and shoulders above their team-mates and everyone else in the tournament. It was Barça's brilliant midfielder who supplied *El Niño* with the final-winning goal.

Iniesta's career with Spain and Barcelona was now starting to find some equilibrium. He was not part of a special generation in the Barça junior ranks, particularly in comparison to that of the early 1990s, which included Iván de la Peña, the García brothers and Albert Celades, or that of Fàbregas, Piqué and Messi under Rodolfo Borrell. Iniesta stood out as cream of his crop.

Even in his early teens, Iniesta had been toughened by the immensely painful experiences of his move from Albacete to Barcelona. However, Lorenzo Serra Ferrer, Barcelona's Mallorca-born manager, had listened to the glowing references coming up from the junior ranks and taken a look for himself.

What happened when he asked the first-team administrator, Carles Naval, to promote Iniesta to train with the first team in February 2001 is legendary, but also true. Naval phoned La Masia and told the administrators there to pass the message to 16-year-old Iniesta that he was to present himself for training at the Camp Nou, fully 100 metres away from the La Masia building, the next morning. Trouble was that Iniesta hadn't dreamed that the opportunity might come so soon and had never even been in the first-team dressing room down in the heart of the Camp Nou. The lad was a bit lost.

He presented himself at the security barrier next to the main entrance, where hundreds of thousands of tourists have sailed through before and since, and he asked for advice. The guard, unsure whether he was being spoofed, told Iniesta to wait. Not until Luis Enrique arrived for training that morning, identified the lad and agree to chaperone him to the changing facilities did he get in. Typical Iniesta – calm, unassuming, half-thinking it was a prank being played on him. But ready.

Reflecting on the moment, Serra Ferrer said: "I wanted to reward him because he was so special. He was modest, loyal, responsible and down to earth. He had tremendous emotional maturity and was very clever. He really listened and remembered all the details."

Iniesta recalls joining the first team and meeting his idol and future manager. "I was only 16 and when he [Guardiola] talked to me. I couldn't even look him in the eyes. I just couldn't believe that he was treating me so well. I was so embarrassed. It was amazing to be part of that team."

By 2002, Iniesta's key moment arrived under the newly returned Louis van Gaal, back for what would prove an ill-fated second bite at the cherry. Joaquim Rifé and Quique Costas, in charge of the youth sections, were asked by the Dutchman about which *canteranos* he could trust for a Champions League group game against Club Brugge. Not only were Patrik Andersson, Philippe Christanval, Thiago Motta, Marc Overmars and Michael Reiziger all injured, but with four straight wins behind them, Barça had already qualified for the next round.

However, it wasn't as if there was nothing at stake. Barça were already heavily in debt and their revenue streams were far from as developed as they are now. Each win in the Champions League group stage of 2002 brought €340,000, a draw half that amount.

10 – The Solutions Man

Nevertheless, Iniesta was joined in the squad by Dani Tortolero, Oleguer, David Sánchez and Sergio García and he made his debut in a team which, despite its average age of just over 22, won 1-0 thanks to a lovely Juan Román Riquelme goal.

Van Gaal's rather odd 3-4-1-2 formation on that big night for Iniesta was: the late Robert Enke; Puyol, Tortolero, Navarro; Rochemback, Iniesta, Gerard, Gabri (David Sánchez 88); Riquelme; Geovanni (Sergio García 60), Dani.

The sports newspaper *El Mundo Deportivo* called Iniesta's debut "spectacular" and it was the ease and confidence with which he transferred his intelligent movement and crisp, reliable use of the ball from B-team football to the Champions League which stood out.

Iniesta's league debut came at Mallorca, that December, with Barça already a chaotic shambles. They lay 13th, two points off relegation and 16 behind the league leaders, Xabi Alonso's Real Sociedad. One by one, Barça's directors were deserting president Gaspart, Van Gaal knew that he would be sacked and replaced by Carlos Bianchi if the team lost, and yet he threw Iniesta a league debut. Visionary? Heartless? Brave? Unfair? Whatever, Iniesta played sublimely, was the hero of the game for the Catalan press and Barça won 4-0 on the island. The team that night was Bonano; Gabri, Christanval, F De Boer (Rochemback 45); Mendieta; Xavi, Cocu, Motta, Iniesta (Gerard 59); Overmars (Saviola 79), Kluivert.

However, the moment which Iniesta still holds most dearly is his home debut. It came on what the Spaniards know as *Día de Los Reyes* (January 6, when Spanish kids get their equivalent of Christmas presents).

At home to Recre, having won away in Bruges and in Mallorca, Iniesta finally got to play first-team football in the stadium he'd been gazing at for six years out of the window in his La Masia dormitory.

It was a 3-0 stroll but, worryingly, there were only 45,000 fans there to see it – about half as many as Barça attract under Guardiola. Iniesta played in the next three games – a 0-0 draw with Málaga, a 4-2 hammering at home to Valencia and a 2-0 defeat at Celta. Added to the following fixture, a 3-0 humiliation by his old pal Fernando Torres and Atlético Madrid – it meant Barça had taken one point from 12 and the Celta defeat had done for Van Gaal. On January 28, 2003, those of us who attended his farewell press conference saw this proud, loud, normally successful Dutchman in tears as he swore, "I'm still the right coach for this club ..."

Nevertheless, by the time Raddy Antic took over, Barça were three points off third bottom and relegation. Sven-Göran Eriksson wanted the job and his agent, Athole Still, phoned me a couple of times to ask what the Camp Nou thinking was. Some at Barça were interested in the Swede, but there was a revolution coming.

Barça under Antic were unrecognisable and it was harsh on him at the end of the season that his remarkable fourth-place finish, two points behind Real Madrid, wasn't rewarded with the job. But it was to Iniesta's ultimate benefit. Frank Rijkaard took over, and things improved massively after a horrendous first six months under the Dutchman. Iniesta had a coach who saw his skill and recommended to the club that the player's contract be extended until 2010.

10 — The Solutions Man

This is the point at which I, again, have to admit a flaw. It has been a lesson to me that proper scouting needs not only rigour and attention to detail, but also great patience.

Back in 2003 and 2004, I would usually work at games but my friend, Rob Moore, was a season ticket holder. Rob was once good enough to have trials for Spurs and Chelsea. He owned Cape Town Seven Stars, sold it to Ajax as their feeder club and then became an agent to players including Benni McCarthy and Steven Pienaar. Occasionally, just to be sociable, I'd watch the game with him. He had had his card marked by the club's then general manager, Javier Pérez Farguell, that while Xavi was a player the club might be interested in moving on for big money, Iniesta was completely untouchable.

However, when we watched Iniesta together it took me far longer to be bowled over by him for one specific reason. His skill, vision and pace were evident, but it frustrated me how often he would either skip past a challenge, work a clever one-two or conjure up some outstanding piece of skill and then fail to finish the chance he'd created.

It seems ludicrous now. Think of his wonder goals – at Old Trafford for Spain against England in 2007, at Chelsea when it looked like Guus Hiddink's team were nailed on to make it to the Rome final, and the daddy of them all – super reactions, velvet first touch, body shape changed in a split second and "*GOL gol gol gol gol gol gol gol gol*" as the Spanish television and radio commentators all called it in Johannesburg that night, when Iniesta made Spain world champions. When I asked Piqué for a pithy description of each of his team-mates before the 2011 Champions League final, he said of Iniesta: "I think someone once tapped him with a magic wand to give him the power to score special goals at important moments."

So, I look back with chagrin that although Iniesta was a lovely footballer from the off, I heavily favoured others in the team – Ronaldinho, Xavi and Eto'o, for example – because I was impatient at his lack of goals. We live and learn, but I was heartened to discover that at the start of Guardiola's first season in charge, Iniesta went to him and asked the new coach for advice on how he could score more regularly.

Of his three superb goals – Stamford Bridge, Soccer City and Old Trafford – it is the former two people will always prioritise, but Iniesta explained that his sublime half-volley for Spain against Steve McClaren's England in Manchester brought a far bigger dividend than simply winning a friendly match.

He told me: "To beat the English is always an achievement simply because of their historic status, but to win in England, at Old Trafford, was a massive leap forward for us. It was a psychological boost which changed our mentality. We respect the English because of what they have given to football and you grow up in Spain hearing about the English achievement, the foundation of world football coming from them.

"It made us believe more and we have moved on with victories in the European Championship and the World Cup, but that night began the cycle of winners' confidence for Spain."

Despite helping establish him, the Rijkaard era was one of distinctly mixed emotions for Iniesta. The Dutchman promoted him and coined a phrase about

Iniesta being the player in the squad to "*reparte los caramelos*" or give out the sweets. It was a reference to the Spanish festival of Reyes, when the three wise men, Los Tres Reyes Magos, parade through the streets, handing out sweets to children. This was Iniesta, then: a treat, not for the working week; something to anticipate. However, Rijkaard offered this compliment only when asked why he was not starting his young midfielder, or keeping him on the pitch for 90 minutes.

Iniesta didn't appreciate the implication that he was the man for the sweet moments, but not for the long slog. He said: "We had good years and bad years under Rijkaard. Overall, it was a positive experience, but it all finished disastrously and that's what everyone remembers. Those last two years tarnished his whole time with Barça in people's minds."

Once the transition had been made from Dutchman (Rijkaard) to Catalan legend (Guardiola), Iniesta said in 2009: "We were flat out on the canvas when Pep arrived and all we needed was for him to show everyone how to do things properly again."

There was one tremendous, if brief, moment during the Rijkaard reign which taught me a lot about the flinty side of this normally gentle, introspective and easygoing guy. Barcelona's long pursuit of Thierry Henry had been curtailed in 2006 when he threw a strop on the Paris pitch over how Arsenal lost that Champions League final against Barcelona – the referee, the way the wind was blowing, the tightness of his boot laces; it was a full-on, toys-out-of-the-pram rant.

However, by 2007, Henry was *ici*. The presentation ceremony was on the Camp Nou pitch and with the stadium doors opened to the public there were at least 30,000 people there. It was a remarkably bouncy, noisy, proud ceremony and the fans seemed to think that Henry was their saviour. Noise poured down to the pitch where Frank Rijkaard, European Championship winner, European Cup winner, Champions League winner, was watching in awe. I asked him what had struck him dumb and he told me: "I've been at an amazing club, in AC Milan, I've played in front of fanatical fans who adored success, but I've never, ever seen anything like this."

Henry, then, was regarded by many as Barcelona's very own Sun King. Not by Iniesta, as it turned out. A few weeks after his presentation came the chance for Henry to make his home debut in the Gamper Tournament – held to honour the club's founder each August – this year against Roberto Mancini's Internazionale.

Henry started, Iniesta came on at half-time and when they had the chance to combine down the left, Henry played the ball inside to his new Spanish team-mate and Iniesta did the natural thing, sending the wall pass back round the full-back, César. The trouble was that Henry wanted to dictate the move, the pace and the rules. Not schooled in the La Masia movements and used to being Coq of the walk at Arsenal, he stood stock still, with his hands on his hips and then exaggeratedly held both hands out in front of him as if to say to Iniesta, 'listen, pale boy, just give the ball back to the feet of the maestro'.

Given that Barça were 4-0 up against a patchy Inter side, Iniesta having scored the fourth not long after coming on, the result was not at stake, but with the main stand crowd watching with bated breath, Iniesta instantly waved his arm angrily at Henry in a gesture that said: "Go and chase the ball and don't ever do that to this team again". Henry took a second to weigh him up, shrugged, and trotted off down the line to close the full-back. His acclimatisation to the Barça system started there and then, but he now knew that Iniesta, who he patently thought would be a soft touch, was as tough as nails.

Off the pitch, Iniesta is famous for his reticence and quiet manner but, again, in the 1-0 win over Real Madrid during Guardiola's second season, he belied his timid image. Fouled, once again, he was picking himself up when he saw Cristiano Ronaldo moaning to referee Alberto Undiano Mallenco about diving. Before Seydou Keita could get there to intervene properly, Iniesta was up and in his face, hushing Ronaldo with the universal finger-to-the-mouth gesture and then when that didn't suffice, jabbing the Portuguese in the chest.

There have been other moments, especially that wonderful goal he scored against Holland in the World Cup final, which tell a lot about this guy. He'd prepared his T-shirt as a message to the billions of television viewers about Dani Jarque, a Catalan central defender, a year older than Iniesta, but a companion in many Spanish youth squads, including that which won the 2002 Under-19 European Championships. They had become close friends even though football had taken them to 'enemy' clubs. Jarque collapsed and died during Espanyol's 2009 pre-season preparations in Italy and Iniesta was hit hard. He took time prior to the greatest day of his life to think of Jarque. His hand written message read '*Dani Jarque siempre con nosotros*', always with us.

I like the thought that there is a correlation between a superstar footballer being so thoughtful about someone else and the ball happening to drop to Iniesta in Soccer City that night. He has been through a lot and admits that wealth, fame and immense talent have not inured him to the impact of cruel fate. He was a team-mate of Robert Enke at Barcelona. The German goalkeeper's depression caused him to commit suicide five years after leaving the Camp Nou – just a couple of months after Jarque's fatal heart attack. Iniesta's first senior medal with Spain came at Euro 2008, when Madrid midfielder Rubén de la Red scored one of the group game goals, during the 2-1 comeback win against Greece in which Iniesta played. By the end of October that year, just under four months after Spain's victorious night against Germany in Vienna, De la Red also suffered heart problems and collapsed. After two years of tests, insurance discussions and thoughts of a comeback, he was invalided into retirement, aged only 25.

Iniesta said: "Jarque's death completely changed my vision of life. I lost personal stability and everything around me was turned on its head. Terribly bad ideas went through my mind.

"Sometimes I struggle to understand what goes on in the world. Natural disasters like the floods in Australia or the earthquake in Japan make me extremely upset. I get very down thinking about the dreadful experiences that people have – what happened in Egypt, for example, or this whole business with Gaddafi. All these things make me sad. I hate injustice, the abuse of children and mistreatment of women."

It's not the normal discourse of a world-class

footballer. Many may echo his thoughts but few take the time and trouble to explain it to their fans. Iniesta is one of those rarities in life, not just football. What you see is what you get – honest, personable, kind, not much of a fan of the limelight but mentally tough and with an old-fashioned attitude: 'I'll do what I think is right irrespective of what people think of me'.

One small example came in the first full week of Guardiola's debut season as Barça's first-team coach, in September 2008. Despite a good pre-season, the shock 1-0 defeat away to promoted Numancia, followed by the 1-1 home draw with Racing Santander, had led to panic and frustration from the Catalan press. With an away game in Gijón looming and Barça standing a good chance of being bottom of La Liga if they lost, Iniesta went to see the boss.

He knocked on the door of the man whose eye he'd been embarrassed to catch as a 16-year-old debutant with the Barça first-team squad back in 2001. He went in with the simple intention of letting Guardiola know that he, specifically, and the entire squad, from what he could gather, were 100 per cent behind the coach no matter what, and that they all fully understood what was being asked of them in training and matches. It was an impressive, but risky, gesture. Some managers would have felt embarrassed, or angered, or insulted and most players who came up with such an idea would be lambasted by their team-mates for seeking favour.

Guardiola took it as an honour. Iniesta didn't make a fuss about his moment of support when Barcelona then scored six at Gijón, romped to the title, added the Spanish Cup and triumphed in Rome in the Champions League final.

His toughness has come to his rescue on a number of occasions, but two – that 2009 Champions League final in Rome and how he won Spain the World Cup – stand out and will define his legacy.

Iniesta was injured in a 3-3 draw with Villarreal, a few days after scoring the winner against Chelsea in the 2009 semi-final. From diagnosis of a two-centimetre tear in his right thigh muscle, there were 15 days until kick-off in Rome.

He told the doctors in the Hospital de Barcelona, up on Avenida Diagonal, just a few hundred metres from the Camp Nou, that "there was no way any injury was going to make me miss this match". He told his father "not even a hole in my leg would stop me playing".

What he, his family and all the medics at Barcelona knew full well was that this muscle tear was a couple of millimetres below the one which had cost him two months' recuperation the previous November. The truth was that under no circumstances should he have played and in no circumstances, having convinced the normally conservative Pep Guardiola to risk him, should it have been so easy for Iniesta to sprint away from midfield markers, Michael Carrick and Anderson particularly, in setting up the crucial opening goal for Samuel Eto'o, or to complete 91 minutes.

At half-time, the Barça medics warned Iniesta that, at all costs, he mustn't shoot because his thigh injury had already deteriorated so badly that the stretch and strain on that muscle if he attempted to pull the trigger might cause it to rupture.

What drove him was the memory of that 2006 final in Paris against Arsenal, which he admits was "the worst day of my football career – it took until Rome to get the thorn out of my side about not starting that match".

Despite playing against Sevilla in the last Liga match before the 2006 Champions League final, Iniesta was dropped for Paris. A lot of people have the impression that Iniesta and Xavi ran the midfield – they didn't. Instead of Barça's La Masia graduates, it was Cesc Fàbregas that night who stood out – starting, playing terrifically in a 10-man side after the 18th minute and then leaving the pitch in the 74th minute with Arsenal winning 1-0.

Barça lined up: Valdés; Oleguer (Belletti 71), Puyol, Márquez, Van Bronckhorst; Van Bommel (Larsson 61), Edmilson (Iniesta 46), Deco; Giuly, Ronaldinho, Eto'o.

Iniesta's entry changed Barcelona's mobility, how much they stretched Arsenal and dragged Arsène Wenger's increasingly tired players around the centre of the pitch, but even with a winner's medal in his hand, he judged the night as having been incomplete. Hence the risk in Rome.

Guardiola subsequently described Iniesta's fitness as having been "about 60 per cent" so imagine the magnitude of his performance when Wayne Rooney disconsolately told his United team-mates in the loser's dressing room, "We've just lost to the best player in the world". He was talking about Iniesta, not Messi.

I asked Iniesta about Rooney's sentiments just before the World Cup and he told me: "If I said that I wasn't pleased then I'd be lying. It's nice to hear, but the best thing is that the description comes from a top, top player and an important footballer. From a guy like Wayne Rooney, it says a lot. I could just as easily have said the same thing about him and his talents. Wayne has always impressed me, he works so unbelievably hard for the team and, above that, he has so much quality." Typical Iniesta. Take a compliment, give one back.

His extraordinary feat in Rome meant that he didn't play a full match again until early October 2009. He missed the UEFA Supercup final, the Supercopa, the World Club Championship match against Estudiantes and then broke down again just after winning 2-0 at the Bernabéu in April. That cost him both Champions League semi-final ties against Inter, when José Mourinho's mean machine just wouldn't be broken down with the tie excruciatingly balanced in the second leg. With Iniesta? It might just have been different.

The risk Iniesta took in order to win in Rome came with an expensive bill. His own assessment is this: "We won; it was a great sacrifice because the price to pay was nearly half of the next season out injured, but I'd do it again if I had to." And, of course, the Dutch must wish that the bill from Rome had ultimately been unpayable.

In the last six weeks of season 2009-10, Iniesta played just 31 minutes of football thanks to incessant injury problems. Vicente del Bosque had it planned that his squad should have a 10-day break between the end of La Liga and Spain's first friendly – back in their lucky city of Innsbruck, around which they'd been based during victory in Euro 2008. There was enormous concern that one of La Roja's talisman players, someone for whom the system was partially designed, might not be ready for the long, gruelling tournament on the hard pitches of South Africa.

Iniesta coped with an hour in each of the first two

warm-up matches – against Saudi Arabia and South Korea – each of which was a rather rocky single-goal win, but the little wizard of Fuentealbilla looked ready. What most didn't know was Iniesta's state of mind.

After winning the tournament, he revealed the doubts that had plagued him at its onset. "I had begun to lose confidence in my game. Every injury was a real blow to me."

Emil Ricart, a Barça physio, showed Iniesta a DVD of sporting champions who had experienced enormous difficulty in overcoming a variety of hurdles to win their victories. Every night before going to bed, Iniesta watched the DVD. His massive effort to be physically and mentally prepared for South Africa worked.

Iniesta was outstanding and a goalscorer against Chile when the final group game could have sent Spain out. Then he was man of the match in the excruciatingly tense quarter-final with Paraguay. And, finally, there he was, hovering on the edge of the penalty box in the 116th minute of the final.

Iniesta ran 66 kilometres on those hard, lumpy pitches during the tournament, but gave Spain an edge, kept his nerve and reaped a reward for all the difficult, worrying, threatening times in his life. In glory, it was so typical of Iniesta to recall Dani Jarque rather than celebrate his own defining moment.

During that 2010 World Cup, I was a FIFA television producer assigned to Spain. It was a fascinating, draining, exhilarating experience which ended with Adam Goldfinch, our exceptional cameraman, and I filming shots, from just to our right, of the Spain bench.

Our position was a couple of metres from the patch of grass where the Spain subs would warm up. Just before the hour mark, Fernando Torres and Jesús Navas were sent out. Torres had been a model of patience and good nature during a World Cup where no Spanish player stopped more to chat and sign autographs with the local kids – particularly the black kids back in the training ground town of Potchefstroom – than the then Liverpool striker.

Though he started from the second Group H match until the quarter-final, he was dropped for the semi against Germany and knew he wouldn't start the final. Short of confidence, touch and pace after a long race to recover from injury in time for the World Cup, he'd nonetheless put all he had into helping the team. However, as the minutes dragged on, Navas became the first change, for Pedro. Though Torres had started doing the sprints and stretches, his morale visibly dropped. Shoulders which had been broad and straight slumped.

Then, out came Cesc Fàbregas. From the first minute, warming-up in front of us on the touchline, he was like a bull, charging up and down, shouting support to his team-mates and arguing with the linesman over a call he made on a corner kick. Fàbregas was a buzz-bomb.

Eventually, with two minutes of normal time left, Fàbregas was also chosen ahead of Torres, as Xabi Alonso came off. Torres took this hard. By now, he was largely standing watching the game, understandably mixed in feeling tension for his team and painful dissatisfaction that he might not even play a part. *El Niño*, Iniesta's great supporter from nine years previously in England, was suffering.

Finally, Del Bosque chose Torres for that tumultuous second period of extra-time. What happened next is well-recorded, but this is how I read it. A couple of minutes into that second half, Iniesta and Xavi are still sharp enough, still confident in their brilliant technique, to use volley-passes to create a one-two. Xavi's is the wall pass and Iniesta is away, past the defence and sprinting on to the ball with which, in eight minutes' time, he will score past Maarten Stekelenburg. Johnny Heitinga hauls back Iniesta by the collar and the Dutchman's second yellow tilts the game.

When that historic goal finally comes, Torres aims a hopeful crossfield punt to the back of the box which falls well short of his intended target, Iniesta. However, it is Rafa van der Vaart, not the most defensive-minded of players, who has taken the responsibility of getting back to cover for the missing Heitinga. He fluffs his left-footed clearance and falls over.

A split second before this happens, Fàbregas is covered by two defenders, Joris Mathijsen and Marc van Bommel – they are so tight he's almost hidden. But he's thinking before them, he anticipates what's about to happen and he erupts into a short sprint which loses his two orange-shirted markers and he's arriving at the loose ball almost before Van der Vaart has skewed it. If Fàbregas had warmed up the way that Torres did, that chance would have never materialised. His mind was alert, his head was up, his first touch killed the ball into his path and his second touch, played well before Van der Vaart could step up and leave Iniesta offside, was velvet perfection. Same goes for the other La Masia alumnus involved in the goal.

Iniesta sets the ball up for a volley with his first touch and buries it with his second. He recalls: "Cesc passed me the ball and Isaac Newton appeared out of nowhere. The minute I had the ball under control I knew that I was going to score. I just had to wait till it came down and I could hit it. As long as the law of gravity still applied and it came down, I knew I could score."

Not only is it a typical Spain goal – all technique, sharpness and efficient finishing – it's crafted in La Masia. Iniesta – the guy who waited for his chance and suffered. Assist by Fàbregas – another, like Troiteiro, who couldn't or didn't wait for his opportunity, finding fame and excellence at Arsenal before, eventually, feeling a burning need to return to base.

Fàbregas 'wins' the World Cup for Spain with his reactions and technique and poor old Torres, creator of the havoc because of his hopeful punt, ends up injured again, thus missing the crucial Liverpool pre-season, which conditions his poor last six months at Anfield.

I still have the highest regard for Torres as a player and as an individual, but the fact that Del Bosque looked like he wasn't going to use him weighed heavily on the striker. Somehow Cesc, who Del Bosque quite happily told me before the Chile game "is really pissed off with me", was ready for his chance.

Cesc and Iniesta share something, I think. The La Masia training, for sure, but also a determination that no matter the obstacle thrown in their way somehow they will find a solution and be ready to score, win, pass, make a tackle. Whatever is needed in the situation. I was going to call this chapter Andrés Iniesta – the Leo Messi of the midfield, because I reckon that it's chilling for other teams that the nearest thing the world has to Messi's close dribbling skills (if not his scoring) is probably Iniesta – and he's in the same club side.

However, reviewing all I know about Iniesta, another

thought came to mind. He's the solutions man. There was a moment in that World Cup final which encapsulated Iniesta. In the middle of the first part of extra-time, Arjen Robben is on the attack thanks to a nice pass from Wesley Sneijder. Iniesta runs back, gets a foot in, outmuscles the bigger and stronger Dutchman and has the ball on the touchline.

He uses a Zinédine Zidane pirouette to get rid of the full-back, Gregory van der Wiel, which leaves him face-to-face with Robben. Without a thought, Iniesta nutmegs him – but not for show, simply because he can see the pass to Carles Puyol through Robben's legs. A split-second later, he's charging back up the wing as Puyol (La Masia) finds Xavi (La Masia) and Spain turn defence into attack.

The Camp Nou in 1999, Paris, Old Trafford, Stamford Bridge, Rome, Soccer City, even Wembley – I give you Andresito Iniesta, the Solutions Man.

MAKING-OF MATCH:
CHELSEA 1 BARCELONA 1
CHAMPIONS LEAGUE SEMI-FINAL, SECOND LEG, MAY 6 2009

Chelsea, under Guus Hiddink, had drawn 0-0 in the first leg at the Camp Nou and, in my view, played very close to the perfect match, at least defensively. Quick and clever all over the pitch, they pressed aggressively and were one of the few sides to put a clamp on Barça's magical midfield.

Guardiola wasn't particularly happy. "We'll go to London to score, we will try to win, not draw. They committed so many fouls, [Michael] Ballack pulled Iniesta down clear on goal and wasn't sent off, yet Puyol's first foul is a yellow and he's suspended. It's clear that if we are to win this competition then the little details clearly aren't on our side." Others would come to argue that point.

It was the first time under Guardiola that Barça had failed to score at home in any competition. Worse, Rafa Márquez injured himself and was out for the rest of the season, while Carles Puyol's booking eliminated him from the return leg in London.

At Stamford Bridge, it goes totally bonkers.

Michael Essien's thunderous goal gives Chelsea the lead and they play far better than Guardiola's team for a large chunk of the game. Then, some of the weirdest things I've ever seen on a football pitch begin to occur.

The first thing to say is that, given the athleticism, speed and pressure of modern Champions League football, the referee, Tom Henning Øvrebø, looks overweight. He appears as if he is struggling with the pace of the game all night and several of his decisions are called into question.

The howl of Chelsea anguish which still hangs over this game – and which was maladroitly used by José Mourinho before the 2011 Champions League semi-final – has been inflated, but it has foundation. There might be some room for discussion about the two Chelsea handball claims against Piqué and Touré, but in my view both would be penalties nine times out of 10.

Abidal's straight red seems open to debate, but Øvrebø consults his stand-side assistant and between them they judge that it wasn't an accidental collision of feet with Anelka and also that it was a clear goalscoring opportunity. Didier Drogba's loudest penalty claim results from a superb penalty-box tackle from Touré, who takes the ball, and Anelka later goes down so easily under attention from the same defender that, had a penalty like that been given against Chelsea, they would have been incandescent.

Football is predicated on human error and polemic debate. The fact remains that Chelsea are 1-0 up and playing 10 men from the 66th minute. Hiddink is an immense man manager, but his decision to replace Drogba with Juliano Belletti six minutes after Abidal's red is close to inexplicable.

Barça were without Puyol and Márquez, Abidal was off and instead of plundering a second goal or at least tying up Barça's back three and pushing Guardiola's side back by having Drogba and Anelka pulling and tugging them with intelligent running and holding the ball up, Hiddink put up the Alamo signs.

There are three more key points to address:

One, Chelsea miss sitters.

Two, for all Ballack's protests about a penalty not given, he ducks – yes, that's right, he ducks – when Iniesta shoots for the equaliser.

Three, look at Messi when the Barça goal finally arrives. He picks up Essien's air-shot at clearing the ball and … he thinks. Despite being the best dribbler of the ball in the world he controls the loose ball, looks to see who is well-placed and gives Iniesta every chance of a good strike at the ball with an inch-perfect pass. I think it's the epitome of the Barça ethos.

What with Guardiola's Forrest Gump run down the touchline, Sylvinho taking over the tactical reactions and reminding the manager to make subs in order to use up time, the remaining penalty shout, nearly seven minutes of added time and Drogba's roaring at the television cameras, it is one of the most bizarre and remarkable football nights I've attended.

Chelsea (4-4-2) Cech; Bosingwa, Alex, Terry, Cole; Essien, Ballack, Lampard, Malouda; Drogba (Belletti 72), Anelka.
Barcelona (4-3-3) Valdés; Alves, Piqué, Touré, Abidal; Xavi, Busquets (Bojan 85), Keita; Messi, Eto'o (Sylvinho 96), Iniesta (Gudjohnsen 95).
Goals Essien 9; Iniesta 92.
Booked Alves; Essien, Alex, Eto'o
Sent off Abidal 65
Referee Tom Henning Øvrebø
Attendance 42,000, Stamford Bridge

11 – THE MAKING OF THE GREATEST RIVALRY IN THE WORLD

"Mourinho is a bit poisoned by the fact that he was rejected. We are the dream club, at this stage. With these players, Barcelona is the best thing that can happen to you as a coach."
— Marc Ingla

TXIKI BEGIRISTAIN AND Marc Ingla left Sevilla in southern Spain on a 460km journey to Lisbon, in early 2008, to consider one of the most momentous decisions in the history of FC Barcelona: Did they dare appoint José Mourinho as Frank Rijkaard's successor?

It seems unthinkable now. At Real Madrid, Mourinho has become an object of hatred for some in Catalonia. It turns out that the strength of feeling he generated as Chelsea coach accorded him only 'pantomime villain' status compared to the way he has been vilified in Barcelona almost from the day he took over at the Bernabéu in 2010.

In the media, he used every opportunity to suggest that other teams threw in the towel before reaching the Camp Nou; he hinted at Barça getting favourable refereeing treatment; he refused to utter the name of the club, using the word 'them' or 'they' or 'others' instead.

Eventually, his provocations reached a pitch where Pep Guardiola reacted with his famous rant at his one-time 'friend' the night before the 2011 Champions League semi-final first leg at the Bernabéu.

Then, there were Mourinho's inexcusable comments after losing that game 2-0, when he claimed Guardiola should be "ashamed" of having won the 2009 tournament because of the strange refereeing performance at Stamford Bridge and wondered whether having UNICEF on the Barça shirt helped influence referees.

By August that year, Mourinho was sneaking around the back of a ruck of players and staff at the Camp Nou to poke Tito Vilanova, Guardiola's assistant, in the eye during the Supercopa match.

For as much talent as he has exhibited and the fact

that the majority of his players hold him to be a bright and witty leader, was this really one of the options that Barça were considering as their next coach back in 2007-08?

The simple answer is yes.

Immediately prior to that furtive flight to Lisbon in spring 2007, Xavi's late goal had salvaged a point from Barça's match in the Nervión against a Sevilla side which deserved victory. Lagging eight points behind Bernd Schuster's Madrid, there were incontrovertible signs of decadence on and off the pitch and the board had been working on how best to replace the Dutchman since the previous October.

Mourinho was on the agenda.

The agony for Barça *socios* of having to suffer the extraordinary decline of the 2006 European champions was immense. Then, there was the evident *morbo*, an extra air of anticipation, over whether a man who had been at the heart of Barcelona's recent and bitter rivalry with Chelsea could be forgiven.

Had Ingla, the vice president for football, and Begiristain, director of football, been spotted meeting the Special One when Rijkaard had both the Copa del Rey and Champions League still to play for, all hell would have been let loose.

There is also such a symbiotic relationship between FC Barcelona and sectors of the Catalan media that had Begiristain and Ingla attempted to leave from Barcelona for Portugal there was a very strong chance that they would either have been observed in transit or someone at the club would have leaked news of their trip to the media.

Leaving directly from Sevilla, when the travelling

Catalan media had tomorrow's pages to fill, seemed a good bet. Ingla and Begiristain were proven correct.

Mourinho's name had been floated in the Catalan media as a bold candidate. This was partly down to cold logic – his availability and trophy-laden CV – and partly because a sector of the Camp Nou board were so infuriated by the laissez-faire manner in which Rijkaard had allowed his team to plummet from their pedestal that they wanted his polar opposite.

Why were they considering a man whose very name enraged large swathes of their support?

Well, talent for one.

Secondly, at Chelsea he had regularly played the kind of 4-3-3 football which Barça were determined would survive beyond the Rijkaard era.

Thirdly, he had spent several years at Barça, first under Bobby Robson and secondly under Louis van Gaal, who had entrusted him with important work in preparation for Barça matches.

The beauty parade for the Barça job had long began, albeit nobody had publicly admitted that Rijkaard's fate was sealed and Joan Laporta continued to announce that, "Frank has enough credit to stay here for as long as he chooses to".

Begiristain considered that Laurent Blanc, Ernesto Valverde and, most of all, Guardiola had sufficient credentials and the right coaching style for the club. Initially, Mourinho was not on the list. So, once more, what were Ingla and Begiristain doing in the Portuguese capital, interviewing a man who was unemployed and who some in Barcelona viewed as unemployable?

The first part of the answer lies with Mourinho's powerful, indefatigable and increasingly controversial agent, Jorge Mendes. The Portuguese had dealt often with Barça over the years; Deco and Rafa Márquez were both his clients, as was Cristiano Ronaldo when Barça acted so slowly that Manchester United beat them to the signature of the Sporting Lisbon prodigy in 2003. Mendes had been a regular visitor to the Camp Nou offices, he knew Begiristain well and kept a shrewdly warm relationship with vice presidents Ingla and Soriano plus, of course, Joan Laporta himself.

However, when Marc Ingla drew up his nine criteria[1] for the next Barça coach, Mourinho didn't meet enough of them to be considered in the months after his Chelsea sacking.

Nevertheless, in the autumn of 2007, as it became clear to everyone that Rijkaard was a lame duck, the circumstances unfolded which led to Barça's board agreeing that Mourinho, a free agent, had to be considered.

Begiristain's mobile phone began to ring, and ring and ring. Jorge Mendes is renowned for his loquacious skills when it comes to putting together clubs, players and even third-party agents. This time, he showed all the subtlety of a Rottweiler.

However, the message was not only well-pitched it was consistent and persuasive. Mendes reported that Mourinho was desperate for the Barça job, that he would 'change' and guarantee good football, that he knew the 'house rules' at Barcelona and that he used a 4-3-3 structure when possible.

Txiki Begiristain was an excellent winger in his time, Basque-born, tough and quick, with an eye for goal. He is one of the more robust, football-bright characters I've met in Barcelona with a profile and appetite

---

1   Ingla's document is reproduced in full in Appendix D.

which will one day adapt perfectly to a leading club in the Premier League – if they are ready to embrace a top-to-bottom conversion in the scouting, coaching and education of their young players.

What governed part of his thinking, amid the blizzard of calls from Portugal, was that Mourinho had been a shrewd, tough and sometimes victorious opponent during the Barcelona-Chelsea series of Champions League epics. As a tough-minded Basque, even if Begiristain hadn't thrilled to Chelsea's style under Mourinho, he'd appreciated its efficacy.

Moreover, Begiristain had left Barça as a player just a year or so before Mourinho arrived with Bobby Robson and therefore didn't know, personally, whether the Special One was really special. He began to think that he had better at least try to find out.

Eventually, Begiristain went to his boss, Ingla, and told him that Mendes was practically on his knees, begging that his client interview for the job – and that he had said some interesting things. The director of football asked if the board wished to consider adding Mourinho to the beauty parade, even though Begiristain himself had come to the conclusion that Guardiola was a near perfect fit for the job.

Ingla and Soriano take up the story. "The first board discussion about Mourinho was in December 2007," begins Soriano. "Retaining Rijkaard had proved a mistake so, by the December, Mourinho was pushing very hard. He had been successful, he knew Barcelona and he understood the essence of the product. He wasn't on our initial list of candidates, but he was insistent."

Ingla confirms that having lost to Madrid in the December Clásico, the board's mood changed. "Come

January 2008, honestly, Frank was in trouble," says the vice president. "We had amazing pressure from Mourinho's agent to see him, talk to him: 'he knows the club … watch him, he's prepared … he understands the playing style … he wants to meet you.' He was pitching, pitching, and pitching himself, relentlessly.

"It was important to either accept or reject a meeting based on proper criteria. Txiki assessed that Mourinho could probably play our 4-3-3 formation. At Chelsea he often used it, although in a rather physical style, but with the Barça players we had, he could probably meet our requirements. If we looked beyond his attitude, and his character, Txiki reckoned, this guy was worth seeing.

"We chose Lisbon, because if we brought Mourinho to Barcelona [for the interview] it would have been one hell of a mess. So, we arranged to go confidentially, to a safe place and have a private discussion. Of the highest importance was to run a technical checkup on his views and how he would run the club in a football sense. However, we were also dealing with the Mourinho brand, so I knew that from an institutional point of view, I also had to meet him.

"Eventually this cost me dearly, because when I was campaigning for the Barça presidency in 2010, having met Mourinho was used against me by Laporta, which was mean and miserable, because I was there to do my job. I had to see the alternatives.

"I had to be able to say with authority: [Jupp] Heynckes doesn't understand Barça, [Guus] Hiddink is a great coach but maybe he's not at the ideal age; we had to see [Laurent] Blanc and Mourinho and Pep and so on. I went to see Mourinho because I had to know him."

What happened was both fascinating and a definitive moment in the development of modern Barcelona – as well as Inter Milan and Real Madrid.

Mourinho had prepared what Ingla and Begiristain remember to be a brilliant PowerPoint demonstration. His self-belief was clearly intact; he had deduced from a distance what was going wrong and had clear views on the best way out of the mess they were in. In normal circumstances the material, and the man, on show would have been so dazzling, so convincing that the argument would have become whether to give him the job there and then.

However, in the meetings – Ingla and Begiristain each met with Mourinho individually, and then they talked as a trio – a trend started to appear and it jolted both Spaniards.

Ingla confirms: "There was one moment when I said to him, 'José, the problem we have with you is that you push the media too much. There is too much aggression. The coach is the image of the club. Three times a week, talking to the media for an hour, talking for the club, you cannot start fires everywhere, because this is against our style.'

"He said, 'I know, but that is my style and I will not change.'

"He told me, 'Look at Van Gaal. In his first era he was mean at Barça and he was a success. The second time he became like a "mother", he changed his style and he failed.'

"The summary of my visit to José Mourinho is that he can be pleasant, he can be a charming guy, very *simpatico*. I had fun with him and then Txiki came a bit later for us to listen to the football ideas. Mourinho was renowned to be No 1 and he was first class at pitching himself – but he wouldn't listen."

That was the key. To Ingla and Begiristain, it appeared Mourinho believed that because Barça had gone awry, the directors didn't know the correct way forward – only he did. The Portuguese didn't hear the warning signs when told of the board's insistence that he renounce his love of polemic. To him, it was apparently unclear which party was sitting in the power seat.

Mourinho felt that his record at Porto and Chelsea, his firm control of the transfer market thanks to the increasing influence of Jorge Mendes, his past at the Camp Nou and his ability to crack the whip (something Rijkaard didn't possess) made it a buyer's market.

It was, by his standards, a towering misjudgment.

Ingla and Begiristain had an ace up their sleeve. The job was theirs to give and they felt no desperation about filling the post – largely because they already suspected that Guardiola was the man to rescue Barcelona. It was, definitively, a seller's market

Ingla left Lisbon with his principal fears confirmed – Mourinho's attitudes were inappropriate. Begiristain, too, left Portugal racked with concerns.

The director of football was now convinced that Barça would win trophies if Mourinho was appointed three-and-a-half months down the line, in June 2008. Like Ingla, however, he had found the Special One wanting.

Begiristain couldn't imagine Mourinho understanding that the club didn't want or need outbursts in the media two or three times a week. What's more, the Basque felt that the Barça he was trying to build valued respect for the opponent, honour in defeat, dignity and other fragile concepts more highly than Mourinho did at that time, or perhaps ever would. Begiristain, on the flight back to El Prat airport, knew that they were about to play a percentage game.

He was 100% sure, and remains so to this day, that Barça would have trained well, played decent, if pragmatic, football and won trophies under Mourinho. However, he was equally sure that these would become pyrrhic victories compared with what Mourinho would cost the *socios*, the board, Barcelona's international brand and a host of other intangible concepts that the club saw as intrinsic.

Més Que Un Club? Begiristain feared that Mourinho felt that he was more than the club.

Soriano describes the mood of the expeditionary force when Ingla and Begiristain returned from Portugal. "Txiki and Marc thought that Mourinho was very well prepared," he recalls. "They spent three hours with him and both came away thinking Mourinho was not our guy. Marc said that Mourinho spoke 90 per cent of the time and didn't listen. He said: 'I just don't like him.'

"Txiki was a bit more rational. He said: 'Mourinho would do well, but the number of fires he would cause internally, and with the media, are not worth it.'

"Because of the downturn in results, and the way the players appeared to be, across the wider board of directors some people were saying: 'We've got to be bold. We've got to take Mourinho. It's a guarantee of success on the pitch.'

"Others were already saying: 'We have to go to the other extreme and be faithful to our real essence and take Guardiola. Anything in between, like Laudrup or

Blanc, and we'd be nowhere.' The debate was detailed and it was intense."

Ingla is still wounded by the way his totally justifiable fact-finding mission has subsequently been twisted, but the process didn't end in February on his return from Lisbon.

As there were still firm voices in favour of Mourinho, Ingla and Begiristain became vital components in the decision-making process. They had met him, they'd received his pitch – their voices would tip the balance either way.

Ingla bumped into Joan Laporta and one of Guardiola's main supporters, Evarist Murtra, not long after returning. He recalls the meeting: "I was in the office of Laporta and Murtra and they asked me how it had gone in Lisbon. I said, 'It was okay, worth doing – but he's not our man.' Today I'm even surer of that. I clearly recommended them that we say 'no' to Mourinho."

There was one final surprise for Ingla before he and the rest of the board made the inspired decision to choose Guardiola. That was that Pep Guardiola directly asked the vice president whether he wouldn't be better appointing Mourinho, instead.

Ingla had seen during his assessment of Mourinho what could be revealed by going beyond the surface of a candidate's ability or track record. Even though Begiristain, Alexanco and Johan Cruyff were all persuasive voices, Ingla wanted to be certain he was backing the right man before pushing the board to a final decision. In explaining what happened next, he shows just a hint of defensiveness that Guardiola was made to jump through the same hoops.

"Look, I had never hired a coach before," he recalls.

"Rijkaard came to us with recommendations after it was impossible to get Hiddink and Koeman in 2003 and the decision went via the entire board. By 2007, I was vice president for football and I felt so much respect for the decision and the process, we also had to have the same kind of formal interview we'd had with Mourinho.

"I used the same nine criteria we'd originally written down to drive the meeting and they were formed with the basic question: What should the next FCB coach be like?

"I went through the script with Mourinho and I did the same with Pep at his place. I said, 'Sorry Pep, I hope you understand – I've never selected a coach before.'

"At the end of our chat Pep said: 'Why don't you hire Mourinho? It would be easier for you.'

"I told Pep: 'No, there are some criteria which this guy doesn't fit and one criterion is attitude. He's totally unsuitable for us.'"

Ingla, Soriano and Begiristain were the three key players in this part of the story (Laporta listened to good counsel and abandoned his ideas that either Cruyff take over or that Rijkaard be given a new contract to last until the end of Laporta's presidential reign in 2010). None of them regret the decision to reject him; all of them look at the way he acted between summer 2010 and August 2011 and shudder with relief that he wasn't doing that as Barça coach.

However, neither Ingla, Soriano nor Begiristain is in any doubt that had they appointed him standards would have improved, athletic, winning football would have been produced and few people would have been hammering on the door of the Camp Nou to say, 'Why haven't you appointed an inexperienced 37-year-old Catalan instead of this Portuguese winning machine?'

What's more, I believe each man initially felt that the door was only temporarily closed to Mourinho. Each of these three decision makers believed he would continue winning somewhere else (which he did), would continue to mature and perhaps mellow his public persona (draw your own conclusions) and would come around again in five, 10 or 15 years on football's merry-go-round, just at the right time to get the Camp Nou job he craved. That makes the way in which Mourinho deliberately positioned himself as Barcelona's most implacable enemy a real puzzle. He can now never expect to work there again.

"He is a bit poisoned by the fact that he was rejected," says Ingla. "We are the dream club, at this stage. With these players, Barcelona is the best thing that can happen to you as a coach. There is bitterness, but also the failure of not performing in Madrid."

Begiristain feels even more strongly that you have to read anger at not getting the Barcelona job in Mourinho's behaviour in his first season at Madrid. These players looked like guarantees of obtaining two of his career goals: to win three European Cups with three different sides and to win three great European leagues, England, Italy and Spain.

Those who rejected him were prepared for there to be a payback at some stage should Barça meet a Mourinho team, and they were proven correct by Inter in 2010, but they were truly surprised by what they saw as 'cry-baby' behaviour from Mourinho at Madrid in the first eight months of 2011. It also added a new element to a rivalry for the ages, the recent history of which has greatly influenced the development of this Barcelona team.

The pivotal year in this story is 2000. Institutionally, FC Barcelona were inept and they were going that way at a footballing level, too.

A demoralised Pep Guardiola was just about to leave the Camp Nou. Xavi, Carles Puyol, Andrés Iniesta, Leo Messi, Gerard Piqué and Cesc Fàbregas were all at the club – but Luis Figo was a different story. That year we were first dazzled by a philosophy which has remained central to Real Madrid ever since.

The construction magnate and multi-millionaire Florentino Pérez won the July 16 elections by a landslide, despite the fact that the old regime, run by Lorenzo Sanz, had delivered a second Champions League in three years.

Both clubs were transfixed by elections that summer. Joan Gaspart was, disastrously, voted in at the Camp Nou and suffered a monumental defeat almost immediately; Madrid paid Figo's buyout clause and Barça were left helpless when the player agreed to a hugely controversial transfer.

Pérez's reign is often called the era of the 'Galácticos', a nickname that was derived from media fawning about the 'galaxy' of stars which began to twinkle at the Bernabéu.

What the original policy was described as by people like Pérez, his loyal and talented lieutenant José Ángel Sánchez and Jorge Valdano was 'Zidanes and Pavones'. The smash-and-grab raid for Figo captured everyone's imagination, but there another strategy in development, which had an economic aspect.

Pérez and Sánchez explained that they were going

to buy the player Real Madrid judged to be the best in the world each summer. Having started with Figo, their target for the following year was Zinédine Zidane. However, this initiative would be backed up by a renewed focus on their *cantera*, or youth system. Players developed by Madrid, who loved and understood the club, like Raúl, Guti and Iker Casillas, would stand alongside the superstars. At that moment, the outstanding *canterano* was Francisco 'Paco' Pavón and so Pérez's vision was baptised 'Zidanes and Pavones'.

Looking back across the 11 years since Figo's transfer, it has been a risible failure. The last player to have been developed in the Madrid youth system and embed himself in the first team is Casillas. He appeared in a Madrid squad for the first time in 1997-98 and was a full debutant by September 1999. Since then, any Real Madrid *canterano* of any merit has been shipped out to succeed somewhere else. The excellent Álvaro Arbeloa was bought back from Liverpool (as Piqué and Fàbregas were by Barcelona), José María Callejón returned from Espanyol three years after being cut loose.

Barça started 2000 almost fatally wounded – Gaspart was utterly paranoid about losing any more stars to Madrid in the manner of Figo's horrific departure. By the time Joan Laporta's board took over, the key stars at the Camp Nou were earning enormous wages, up to €6m per season and they were getting an additional match fee of up to €30,000. That was the knee-jerk reaction to being so brutally asset-stripped.

Yet during the next decade Barça, and Spain, flourished thanks to a *canterano* policy which brought through Carles Puyol, Andrés Iniesta, Lionel Messi, Cesc Fàbregas, Gerard Piqué, Pedro, Bojan, Fernando

Navarro, Sergio Busquets, Pepe Reina, Víctor Valdés, Mikel Arteta, Thiago and others. Not all were retained by Barça's football management, but the majority were.

In the same period, Madrid have developed, but failed to use properly, talents like Juan Mata, Álvaro Negredo, Borja Valero, Diego López, Dani Parejo, Javi Portillo, Roberto Soldado, Javi García and José Manuel Jurado. It is a weak record for a mighty and proud football institution like Madrid, but set against Pérez's original electoral promise of matching the best signings in the world with *canterano* excellence, it's a betrayal.

Madrid continue to make significant decisions which undercut the likelihood of their youth system bearing fruit.

Firstly, there is a drive for instant gratification, not sustained development. Pérez and Ramón Calderón, the two significant presidents of the last decade, have used the chequebook not to augment natural growth, but to cover up for the lack of it, simultaneously smothering any green shoots.

Moreover, there has been a stream of coaches (Mourinho is the 11th since those presidential elections of 2000) who have either shown no interest in promoting youth talent, because they know that they are there for a short burst of 'death or glory' football, or have been removed so abruptly that they haven't had the chance to show patience or wisdom in who to promote.

For all that, and regardless of the fact that the original Pérez era ended in farce, it is worth remembering how entranced the world first was with this project.

There was an element of the self-fulfilling-prophecy to Madrid playing well and winning trophies if they could recruit the best available player in the world every summer, and so it proved. They gave the emerging world markets what they wanted – glamour, skill, spectacle – Hollywood-style stars at Real Madrid.

In one interview, Sánchez explained to me that Madrid were using market research to assess how a big new signing would 'play' in Japan, Korea, China and Malaysia. Their research into the emerging football territories told Madrid that the standard Asian fan was hugely attracted by the power, tradition and dominance of European football and that while two clubs in particular – Manchester United and Bayern Munich – were far ahead in marketing directly to these territories, Madrid thought that they had a way to catch up.

Their research also told them that the vast majority of these new fans used their allegiances completely differently from those in Europe.

For several years I wrote and reported for the SportsCN network in Shanghai and went out there to meet the organisation. I'd been dealing with journalists and editors who were hungry for information, who got up in the middle of the night to watch Champions League football and were as much in love with the sport as I was. Therefore, it was a surprise to discover that many parents were deeply unhappy if their children played or followed football.

Chinese domestic football had been wracked with one corruption scandal after another to the extent that many families wanted their kids to have nothing to do with the sport. However, the big names of European football seemed to help turn that tide of suspicion and cynicism. I've seen absolute devotion to a club like Madrid, Manchester United or Barcelona in China, equal to anything in Europe. These fans might wear club colours, or support a particular side but, according to Madrid's research, their allegiance is to the star players at that club.

As a result, Madrid believed they could 'buy' loyalty, so long as they kept refreshing their list of stars. So from Figo through Zidane, Ronaldo, David Beckham, Michael Owen and, well, Jonathan Woodgate, to Kaká and Cristiano Ronaldo, the idea was pursued, not only by Pérez but also by Ramón Calderón.

Because there were barren, embarrassing years of failure, it is possible to forget that between 2000 and 2003 Real Madrid were capable of playing inventive, entertaining and winning football before the whole thing got bloated, lazy and had ground to a halt by the time Pérez resigned in 2006.

Errors were made that allowed Barcelona back into what was a one-horse race.

Pérez forced both Vicente del Bosque and Fernando Hierro out of the club, in part at least over their support for Fernando Morientes. Del Bosque had brought the club eight trophies in four years, including two Champions Leagues, two Spanish Leagues and the World Club Championship, but during the final year of his time in charge, his relationship with Pérez became acrimonious. Hierro, his captain, had spoken up about the way in which Morientes was being pushed out of the club and the will of Pérez that he be given as little game time as possible in order to encourage him to leave. When the title was won Hierro, and his fellow players, showed their discontent with Pérez and his board by refusing to do an extra lap of honour at the Bernabéu as the fans clamoured.

On leaving the club Hierro, a brilliant footballer who embodied the Madrid philosophy which I think has been undermined in recent years, said: "We didn't lose our heads in a heated moment. The only thing I did, as captain, was defend my team-mates. My conscience is clear. The club told us certain things and the players chose to show that we were not in agreement."

Del Bosque was told that he wasn't getting a new contract about a day after winning the title. Pérez claimed that del Bosque seemed "exhausted" and "not the way forward".

Jorge Valdano, elegant and articulate but also slavishly devoted to Pérez's ideas, added flesh on the bone back in 2003. "Del Bosque has come to the end of a cycle and it's better that he goes at his highest point. We want to avoid a gradual decline. Repetitive work with the same guy can promote inertia in squads which aren't significantly renewed every single year. If your squad isn't going to change significantly then it's important to change the messages that they hear over and over."

There was a culture where the 'Galáctico' players could do no wrong by the president, so long as their image was earning the club money. If an important player wanted a day off training, he could cut out Del Bosque, and ask for presidential or club sanction for leave, 'because my sponsors want me to work with them that day'. Those same sponsors were earning money for Madrid on a shared image rights percentage and that meant Peréz's money-making machine was on target.

Fitness declined and it's impossible not to feel immense sympathy for the way in which Del Bosque was treated. At the time, Pérez said: "Every coach has his personal style. Del Bosque is a little classical, a little traditional. We want someone who is technically superior, from strategy to physical preparation, because our team will be stronger that way. Del Bosque isn't the ideal trainer for the future of Real Madrid."

In fact, they had the ideal man, they just didn't realise it. Del Bosque is still a vital, shrewd and 'modern' football coach, eight years later. He has a winning record with Spain and became in 2010 the first man to coach a team to World Cup victory having lost the first game. After he left Madrid, it was another four years before a major trophy – the Spanish league title under the guidance of Fabio Capello in 2007 – was lifted. Of course, the Italian was kicked out as a reward for that, too, by Pérez's successor, Calderón.

Since 2003, the moment when Joan Laporta's board and Frank Rijkaard's football ideas gave birth to the modern Barcelona, two coaches have led the team: Rijkaard and Pep Guardiola. In that time, Madrid have had 11. Barcelona have had two directors of football – Txiki Begiristain and Andoni Zubizarreta – against five at the Bernabéu.

The journalist Sid Lowe and I met Carlos Queiroz at Madrid's old training ground, the day after he was presented as Del Bosque's replacement. He had just discovered that, while they'd been negotiating to lure him from Manchester United, where he assisted Sir Alex Ferguson, Madrid had taken the irrevocable decision to sell Claude Makélélé, the defensive lynchpin in midfield, behind the superstars: Luis Figo, Zinédine Zidane, Raúl, Ronaldo and David Beckham.

"They've done this without listening to me!" raged

Queiroz that day. "Asking me to win the league or the Champions League without a top-class defensive midfielder is like sending a climber up Everest without oxygen!"

Not until Fabio Capello took over for the second time was the ship steadied. That season was one of the most dramatic in recent Spanish history, with Madrid constructing a title win from a series of pulsating comeback victories. After his team played a money-earning friendly in Israel at the end of the season, Capello, who was on his way for a summer holiday in Tibet in the full knowledge that he would be sacked, summed up the position of even a successful coach at the Bernabéu: "Winning this league has been like trying to fight your way out of a swamp."

There is also no question that when Manuel Pellegrini talks of having set records and given Madrid good football during his single season in charge, he does so with justification. No Madrid side has thus far bettered the 96 La Liga points won that season. Barcelona were in the middle of their extraordinary renaissance under Guardiola and only won the title by a three-point margin. The Barça coach remains disbelieving at the way his adversary was treated.

However, the apogee of Madrid's failings came when they hosted the 2010 Champions League final – won by their next coach, José Mourinho, and Internazionale. At the semi-final stage, Arsène Wenger, the Arsenal manager, made the sly comment that, "maybe it's worth waiting outside the Bernabéu and seeing which players they let go this summer". It was an artful nudge at Madrid's habit of selling 24-karat players for the price of 24 carrots. Setting aside the potential embarrassment of Barcelona winning the Champions League at the Bernabéu, the other three teams in the tournament were driven by players rejected by Madrid.

Wesley Sneijder scored one goal and assisted on the other for Mourinho's Inter against Barcelona in the first leg of their semi-final. The Dutchman had been a key figure in Madrid's title win of 2008 but was sold, at a €12m loss, to Inter, where he immediately became a dominant force in European football. Inter really beat Barça up in that first leg at the San Siro and did it with four players sold by Florentino Pérez: Samuel Eto'o, Walter Samuel, Sneijder and Esteban Cambiasso.

Arjen Robben added to his tie-winning goals against both Fiorentina and Manchester United by thumping in another screamer to set Bayern Munich on the road to victory over OlymPiqué Lyon (conquerors of Madrid) in the other semi-final. Robben had been inexplicably off-loaded to Bayern before he could form what would have been a terrifying wing combination with Cristiano Ronaldo under Pellegrini.

The more I investigated, the worse it looked. Since being rejected by Madrid, Eto'o has won 15 club trophies, Cambiasso 15, Samuel 14, Sneijder six. Robben won three trophies in his first two seasons since leaving Real Madrid while he and Sneijder were pivotal in Holland's drive to the 2010 World Cup final.

The point is, there came a stage at which Madrid were neither capable of producing 'Pavones' nor much good at keeping 'Zidanes' when they found them. From the great revolutionary step forward in 2000, Madrid have seen their short-term football gains comprehensively overhauled.

By the mid-point of the 2011-12 season, it was clear

that José Mourinho had improved Madrid and that his era was still developing. The quality of signings such as Mesut Özil and Ángel di María is beyond question, so too the way in which the coach restored the ghost-like presence of Kaká. Ronaldo's game was maturing under Mourinho. Madrid were becoming powerful, dangerous and enjoyable to watch.

When Mourinho took over he said that, while a season without a trophy at Real Madrid given their recent humiliation at the hands of Barça was unthinkable, his teams were always better in his second year.

He also said: "My relationship with Pep Guardiola has been good, is good and will be good. If we have a problem concerning football matters that won't, ever, become a problem between José Mourinho and Pep Guardiola. It would be a problem between the coach of Real Madrid and the coach of Barcelona. It's totally different. I respect him as much as I think he respects me. There isn't any personal problem between us, quite the opposite. Of course, I can't wish him luck right at the moment, because we are both playing for the same prizes, but apart from that there's no problem."

Mourinho's actions and words subsequently betrayed all these sentiments and, by the end of his first season, there certainly was a problem between the two men.

Another of his statements as the newly-appointed coach of Madrid also reveals how far off course he strayed in that first season.

Mourinho explained: "What I tell people who work for me is that it's important to 'see' things well, but it's even more important that the information garnered gets to the right person, at the right time in the right way. The quality of the information we receive is more important than the quality of the information the guys originally spot.

"Experience has taught me that if you aren't the first-team coach you will have the time to observe and analyse, but when you are in sole charge what's important is to still be able to analyse situations and take decisions under pressure. It's what scientists call 'emotional intelligence'. It's one thing when an assistant is in the stand or when an analyst is in front of his computer watching a game once, twice, perhaps 10 times. It's quite another during the high tension of a match when you can't press pause and say 'hold on, I'd just like to see that again'. The world of the match is totally distinct – completely isolated from all the other work we do."

It's a fascinating insight into the detailed nature of Mourinho's work ethic and his attempt to make football management a scientific business, but some of his actions and decisions betrayed his own concept of 'emotional intelligence'. If his analysis and that of his assistants were as good as he believed, then on what basis did he think that he could go toe-to-toe with Barcelona at the Camp Nou in November 2010? The 5-0 hammering conditioned the whole of the rest of the season and comprised one of the most brutal and complete demolitions ever seen in a Clásico.

Perhaps the only thing which detracts from the blue riband nature of that November 2010 Clásico thrashing is the fact that it was so very one-sided. Guardiola's team ran rings around Madrid and, prior to Wembley 2011, I had never heard so many voices in the world of professional football unified in wondering if this was the greatest performance they had ever witnessed.

Freezing rain didn't dampen the humiliation and

Sergio Ramos set the tone for the following spring with a vicious foul on Messi which brought him a red card. He then pushed Carles Puyol in the face, he was dragged away from a nasty confrontation with Gerard Piqué and swapped insults with Xavi. All unwritten non-aggression pacts between the Spain players in the Barça and Real Madrid players, a legacy of the World Cup win, were ripped apart that night.

Then, during the riveting series of Clásicos in spring 2011, Mourinho reversed his bet and got that equally wrong. To play as defensively as he did in the second La Liga Clásico, a game which ended tied at 1-1, and then to do so again in the first leg of the Champions League semi-final, having beaten Barcelona in the final of the Copa del Rey in between, not only betrayed Madrid's legacy, but proved to be a strategic mistake.

And where was Mourinho's emotional intelligence when he was sent off that night, when he ranted about dark conspiracies post-match, or when he poked at Tito Vilanova's eye in the Supercopa that August?

Even from afar Guti, an arch-*Madridista*, spoke out against the man at the helm of his club. "There are things I don't like about Mourinho," said the player who left Madrid shortly after the arrival of the new coach. "The Madrid sentiment is that of honour, to try to ensure that this historic shirt is more important than the people who are passing through the club at all times. Barça are winning on their own merits – not because of help from referees."

The moment when Mourinho prevents his irritation with Guardiola and Barcelona deflecting him from his normal standards, and the suspicion of conspiracies in favour of Barça are removed from his psyche, will be the moment when Madrid have the coach they deserve – and when Barcelona will have a significantly more dangerous opponent.

ÉRIC ABIDAL:
THE CONVERT

SOMETIMES, IN THE analysis of this team, it is essential to have the benefit of retrospect. If you had known during the first days of Éric Abidal's time at Barcelona that a glorious new era was on its way, you would have bet everything you owned that the system would chew up and spit out the Frenchman before any progress was made.

Upon arrival, he complained about the atmosphere, player relationships and generally felt that life in Barcelona was not *la vie en rose*. Much as he had wanted a transfer out of Lyon, it appeared that life there had been more to his liking.

When Pep Guardiola met his new first-team squad and spoke to them extremely brusquely about the challenges ahead, while making them jump through hoops in that first, fevered summer, it was Abidal who not only found Guardiola's tone unpalatable, but who needed to have his new manager's manner explained to him by president Joan Laporta.

During all of this, Abidal's elegant, quick, leggy brand of defensive football was never in question. It was all about whether the Frenchman's attitude and the mood in the camp would mesh. Fortunately, it transpired that all Abidal was really seeking were the same elements that the new coach would try to bring out of a previously dysfunctional group.

The more daring the football, the harder the work and the more heightened the ambition, the more

Abidal flourished. As he did so, his own driven personality came out and he won respect and admiration from everyone around him.

It is also the case that without the Frenchman, Guardiola would have been less able to move to a back three so often during his time in charge. Prior to using that strategy, Abidal was often able to partner Puyol or Piqué in the middle and allow a four to become three because he is so adept, so football bright when playing at centre-half – away from his main position of left-back.

Long before the diagnosis of a liver tumour in March 2011, he had become a squad leader. In the treble season, Guardiola's first, the defence was often disrupted because of injury or suspension. Abidal always adapted and rose to whatever challenge handed to him.

Before the Champions League final at Wembley, Abidal told me that the previous November, when defeating England there with France, he had left himself a little note in the dressing room which he hoped to be able to go back and collect in May. The note wasn't there but he was, despite medical prognosis that such an idea was unfeasible.

It is possible there has not been a more emotional or emotive moment in the modern history of FC Barcelona than a recently recovered cancer patient being told by the ultimate Catalan – Carles Puyol – to take the captain's armband and raise the trophy that represents a life goal for the homegrown players at the club. It tells you everything you need about what kind of a guy Éric Abidal is.

12 – THE GREATEST

"Messi is the one who makes the difference, who takes us to another level. He'll never be repeated. He's the best player I've ever seen, the best player I'll ever coach."
— Pep Guardiola

H OW IRONIC IT IS THAT Lionel Messi's confirmation on the global stage came via winning the junior version of a tournament which is a thorn in the side for both him and his nation – the World Cup. That summer of his plenitude, turning 18 and having a queue of suitors waiting to take him out to play, was a crucial time in his relationship with FC Barcelona. His contractual status was not watertight, his stock was high and about to get higher. Stranger things have happened in football than, say, the siren song of Chelsea, Milan or Manchester United turning the head of either Leo or Jorge Messi, his father. Thankfully for Barça, that wasn't to be – partly because they had a football director who was, appropriately, on the ball. But more of that briefly.

The FIFA Under-20 World Cup, in Enschede, Holland, began inauspiciously for Messi. His coach, Francisco Ferraro, left both him and young Sergio Agüero on the bench – Argentina lost 1-0 to the United States while Spain, featuring Raúl Albiol, Fernando Llorente, David Silva and José Enrique, romped to the top of the group.

Argentina fought back with a 2-0 win over Egypt, in which Messi started and scored, followed by a 1-0 win over Germany.

He scored in the 2-1 round-of-16 victory over Colombia, got another in the quarter-final 3-1 win over Spain and topped everything that had gone before with the opener in Argentina's 2-1 semi-final win over Brazil. He started wide on the right, beat two defenders and launched a typical left-foot drive into the top corner.

Even given the extraordinary nature of all that has happened since, it's one of the sweetest moments of

Messi's life. He'd won his place in the team, put Argentina in the final, defeated their oldest enemy and Barça's director of football, Txiki Begiristain, had been in Holland to see it happen – with pen and paper in hand.

Until Messi turned 18, he couldn't sign anything more than a three-year contract. By June 24, 2005, a much more lucrative, five-year contract was ready to be signed by the club, Messi and his father, who represented him. His salary was as a 'B' team player rather than a guaranteed first-team regular and, given that fact, Barça rather stole a march by establishing a €150m buy-out clause – more usual for a footballer whose annual wage was in the region of €5m.

Barça had realised they were exposed. Even though Messi and his family were perfectly happy to be at Barcelona, the as yet unresolved nature of his nationality, his exposure to regular first-team football and his vulnerability to hawkish giants of European football buying him out of his contract – a repeat of Madrid's heist of Luis Figo from the Camp Nou – was something they had to insure themselves against.

Just before the final in Utrecht, Diego Maradona telephoned Messi in the team hotel and pleaded with him to take personal responsibility for bringing the cup 'home' to Argentina. Messi promised to do his best, then scored both goals, two penalties, in the 2-1 final victory against Nigeria. It was 26 years after Maradona had propelled Argentina to the same FIFA Under-20 title and now Messi was a world champion, the Golden Boot and Golden Ball winner of the tournament. Collecting the trophy, he wore a T-shirt with the names of his sister, a cousin and two nephews printed on it. Typical Messi.

"Diego asked me for the trophy when he phoned and now he's got it," said Messi. "So, this win was for him, my family and everyone in Argentina who loves football. My old dear [*mi vieja*] is preparing a glass case for all the trophies I'm taking home from Holland, but that's in Rosario, not Spain. These are Argentina's trophies I've won and they must stay in our country.

"I don't like it when all the fuss is centred on me. All I hope is that this now earns me more playing time with Barça – that would be the best."

Initially, the news on that front was mixed. José Ramón Alexanco, who lifted the European Cup at Wembley in 1992, took charge of La Masia that summer. "Messi will still be signed as a 'B' team player even though he starts with the first team," he said. "There has been criticism of that, but the key thing is that if Frank Rijkaard doesn't use him much he must be free to play, to develop and to enjoy his football, so it's best this way for the moment."

Begiristain, director of football, was clearer. "There is no reason for us to loan him out to get experience. I've spoken to Leo and his father and it's clear that he starts with Frank Rijkaard's squad and only if he's not getting enough game time will we talk the whole thing over again."

Relations between the Messi camp, Begiristain, and the economic vice president, Ferran Soriano, were strong. Jorge Messi, however, wanted to know if his son was going to get more first-team football. He met with Begiristain and asked whether it would be a good idea to think in terms of a loan. Coincidentally, this was the time when the concept of a loan to Rangers was still being discussed firmly by the Scottish club's assistant manager, Jan Wouters, and Rijkaard's assistant, Henk ten Cate.

It turned out that Jorge Messi had judged his son's development accurately and that there was no disparity between his and Begiristain's opinion.

However, neither of them had direct control over Rijkaard, who was at the peak of his power at the Camp Nou, having just won the club's first league title for six years. Rijkaard had the last word on who played and who didn't.

Begiristain's point of view was that Rijkaard and Ten Cate considering a loan for Iniesta and Messi was a way of dodging a thorny issue: should both or either youngster be a fixture in the first team? Were the Catalan media becoming over-infatuated with these two products of La Masia? Were either of them physically ready for the rigours of 30-something La Liga games per season?

The director of football, who had been unswervingly loyal to Rijkaard in his worst days during 2003, wanted the coaches to face up to the challenge of answering these questions.

Begiristain brought the debate to a head, telling Jorge Messi the club's view was that Leo was going nowhere 'until at least December' after which, if the kid wasn't playing regularly, the entire Primera División would be lining up to take him on loan.

The director of football also told his Dutch coaching staff to manage the issue of whether Iniesta and Messi were ready and, if not, to make them so, without recourse to loaning them out.

At this stage, Messi had been the object of avaricious eyes from the Spanish Federation. FIFA rules still meant that because he hadn't played a senior competitive match for his country he could, under certain circumstances, play for Spain. Attaining international qualification through residency tends to be a five-year process and Messi's Spanish passport had long been pushed through the system by Barça, who benefited greatly from the teenager obtaining dual nationality.

Frankly, Messi is as patriotic as Maradona ever was and burns with anger if accused of being more interested in Barça than Argentina.

However, the Spanish federation knew that Messi's passport was due in autumn 2005 and sounded him out about switching allegiances. Ginés Meléndez was the age group coach at the time and fancied the steal of the century. "I had a pal at Barcelona, Alex García, who said to me, 'Why don't you have a chat with this Argentinian kid of ours?'

"I knew about him, of course, because I often went to watch the Barça youth teams playing and he'd obviously caught my eye, but I thought it was best that if there was anything to be said, initially, it was best done by Alex in person.

"Until the Under-20 World Cup in 2005 that all stayed under wraps, but at that point some journalist asked Leo whether the Spanish federation had been in contact with him about all this and he said 'Yes'. The truth is that I left it all in the hands of Alex García and because the enquiry hit a brick wall with the player I'd never have said anything about it. Honestly, I'd love the whole thing just to be forgotten about so that in the future nobody says it was our fault he didn't play for Spain!

"Messi was just a kid, a fantastic footballer already,

Alex had a fair idea about asking him the question but we got a 'No' and that was that."

Just imagine it for a second – Messi up front for this Spain team. He'd have been more appreciated, he'd have won trophies, he'd have been playing with club-mates and friends and he'd have been far from the first Argentinian (Alfredo di Stéfano, Juan Antonio Pizzi) to jump ship to *La Roja*. However, Argentina and winning the World Cup for his country mean too much to Messi. Let's hope the majority appreciate his loyalty.

That September, he was granted dual nationality.

The Gamper tournament is held every year in August to celebrate Barça's founder, Joan Gamper, and present the squad (particularly the new signings) to the fans. This year, Fabio Capello's Juventus were guests and they eventually won a thrilling match on penalties after a 2-2 draw.

During the summer, the Internazionale president and owner, Massimo Moratti, had told Italian media: "I'd spend crazy money if I could buy Messi. He's the only guy to have inspired me this much in a long, long time".

He had become Barça's youngest scorer (since super-seded by Bojan), a World Cup winner at youth level and now he was in the sights of Moratti and Inter; Messi was, without question, the hot player when Juventus came to town.

It was the first time I experienced full-blown Messi-mania.

All football fans have that effervescent optimism as the new season approaches – sometimes it's a victory of faith and optimism over realism. However, the Barça faithful had suffered Madrid's dominance so long that the emergence of this young genius – at a time when Rijkaard, Ronaldinho and Eto'o had brought the good times back – electrified the Camp Nou. Nearly 100,000 Catalans roared in exultation of Prince Leo. They were desperate to see how he'd perform against Fabio Cannavaro, Patrick Vieira, Giorgio Chiellini, Mauro Camoranesi, Alessandro del Piero and Zlatan Ibrahimovic.

Compared with a typical match for Pep Guardiola's Barça, the statistics of the game are startling. Juventus controlled 62 per cent of possession in the first half – at the Camp Nou – and led for over an hour. However, Messi just kept on taking the fight to Juve, skipping past tackles, drawing defenders to him before releasing a pass – he was head and shoulders above everyone else on the pitch, particularly when one slalom dribble left both Cannavaro and Gianluca Pessotto sprawling on the ground.

The crowd went absolutely wild. '*Messi-Messsssi-Meeeessssssi*' chants rained down from on high. It seemed like a line had been drawn between Messi the promising youth team player and his new position as a superstar.

He supplied the goal assist for Andrés Iniesta, a wonderful, defence-splitting 25-metre pass, to cap a landmark performance. Rijkaard allowed him the hero's departure, in the 90th minute, so that he could take the applause of the crowd. It was a lung-bursting standing ovation for the 18-year-old.

Post-match, Juventus formally asked Barcelona to name a price for the player, but were instantly rebuffed. President Laporta knew a good thing when he saw it.

Backstage, Fabio Capello was left with no doubt

about Messi's potential. "In my entire life I have never seen a player of such quality and personality at such a young age, particularly wearing the 'heavy' shirt of one of the world's great clubs.

"That guy can do whatever he wants with the ball. It's impressive winning a world youth title this summer, but this was outstanding – this was playing with men, not against kids his own age."

Messi had arrived. He made his debut for Argentina that August against Hungary in Budapest, but was sent off after only 90 seconds. The red card was a terrible decision from referee Markus Merk. Vilmos Vanczák first tried to hack down the young substitute, and then hauled his shirt nearly off his back. As Messi tried to shrug his assailant off, Merk decided that the aggression had been from the Argentinian and gave him a straight red – also booking Vanczák. It was ludicrous.

That's what José Mourinho thought, too. Within a few months he'd be the author of the worst calumny I've heard about Messi (when Barça and Chelsea met at Stamford Bridge in the Champions League) but on this occasion, watching in the stands of the Ferenc Puskás stadium, he was defensive of the prodigy.

"The referee got the red card totally wrong," he said. "I saw the action really clearly and Messi only raised his arm so that he could shake off the Hungarian defender. At the very most it was a yellow."

By September, the Messi phenomenon was accelerating so rapidly that Barça needed a new seatbelt.

The extraordinarily complex nature of his status – including, but not limited to, his nationality (Argentinian? Spanish?), his registration with the league (trainee? B team? First team?) and his potential status as an 'associated' player – were preventing him making his league debut until September.

His extraordinary Gamper tournament, the offers from both Juventus and Inter Milan to buy him for sums of up to €20m and his increasing assurance in first-team football meant that a new contract to supersede the one signed only that August was urgently needed.

His wages were increased, his buy-out clause remained at €150m and the Messi family agreed to Leo being tied to what was now a nine-year deal. At the time, Barça were instituting a pyramid salary structure the essence of which remains to this day. The majority of the squad is in the base, the emerging talents are one up, the established talents are towards the apex and right at the top are the one or two superstars.

Ronaldinho, then, was at the tip and Oleguer, for example, was at the base – along with Messi.

The basic base salary was then around €900,000, but there are steep incentives for all players around goals scored, league position and, above all else, trophies.

In the press conference to announce the new contract, Begiristain pointed out that the club could easily have held on for a few months, even until after the World Cup of 2006, to renegotiate but, "We wanted to make Leo, who has a spectacular future ahead of him, feel at ease and confident in us". That was the first evidence of what has become an intelligent and proactive attitude by the club towards their genius.

Jorge Messi added: "This new, improved contract has nothing to do with all the talk about offers from other clubs. I've always been a Barça guy and wouldn't go looking for other clubs to put pressure on this one."

12 — The Greatest

My research in seeking confirmation from those involved in this contract revealed that while Barça were aware of one, sometimes two offers coming to Jorge Messi almost every year from 2005 onwards, the player's father always negotiated on a good-faith basis and never used the prospect of a better financial offer from elsewhere as a bargaining tool.

Finally, and decisively, Messi added: "This is what I've always wanted – the chance to be at Barça all my career."

As much as Messi was becoming an idol for the Camp Nou, he was still in Ronaldinho's shade. Because the Brazilian lost his way and his reign at the top of world football was shorter than it should have been, it would be easy to either ignore or undervalue how extraordinary he was.

Ronaldinho was utterly different to Messi; anyone who played against him at his peak would testify that the Brazilian was brutally strong. If you tried to take the ball from him, the first thing that happened, even before he produced a trick or a sprint, was that you bounced off one of his enormous and rock-hard thighs.

He was capable of dominating a match, and Barcelona's 3-0 win at the Santiago Bernabéu in November, 2005 is remembered as 'The Ronaldinho Match'. However, it also included one of the highlights of Messi's season.

Since September 1929, this was only the 13th time Barça had won away to Real Madrid in the league. Seventy-six years, 12 away wins. A record to indicate the scale of the task.

I had taken 10 friends from Clontarf, in Dublin, to the Madrid Clásico and was seated with one of them in the stand where Madrid players give tickets to friends and family. All around me there was horrendous racial abuse for Samuel Eto'o and Ronaldinho which, farcically, turned to applause for Ronaldinho when his two fantastic slalom goals followed Eto'o's opener. There were people crying their eyes out at such a humiliation. It was an extraordinary night.

Eighteen-year-old Messi made the first goal, brought two superb saves from Iker Casillas and was the game's most-fouled player. Quite a way to mark your first Clásico.

"Messi? It's simple – we knew that even at his age he would feel no fear at all about playing at the Bernabéu and that he'd just continue to take players on in one-on-one situations," said Txiki Begiristain after that match.

Should there be any doubt about the quality of opposition, Madrid started that night with Casillas; Salgado, Sergio Ramos, Helguera, Roberto Carlos; Beckham, Pablo García, Zidane, Raúl; Robinho and Ronaldo.

Remember the sympathetic observer to Messi's unjust red card against Hungary? By the following February, José Mourinho's tone had changed dramatically.

The Champions League last 16 paired Barcelona and Chelsea. Mourinho's team had eliminated Barça, under controversial circumstances, the previous season. Stamford Bridge was one hell of a place at which to try and carve out a result.

This time Barça won 2-1 on a cabbage-patch pitch, playing with immense confidence and ambition. Asier del Horno was booked for a knee-high, studs-up assault on Messi which should have brought him a straight red. Then, having been comprehensively warned, he was sent off for his next bookable foul on the striker.

Post match, Mourinho, reprehensibly, said: "There is lots of great theatre in Catalonia and that's what Messi showed in this game – great theatre." He would be guilty of greater demolitions of reality in his later guise as Real Madrid coach, but this was a good start.

Bang on target, however, was Spain's greatest modern football writer, Santiago Segurola – currently working for *Marca*. His verdict was poetic. That fevered night, he wrote: "In a rarely seen show of skill, intelligence and courage, Messi tore Chelsea apart to the astonishment of the English fans, who reacted as often happens when a player causes panic. Beyond the boos they dedicated to him every time he touched the ball there was dread; dread at his overwhelming demonstration of class.

"You shouldn't be able to dominate a game of this calibre aged 18. Football has few precedents and those who come to mind were geniuses. Pelé's World Cup final in 1958, Maradona in the World Youth Cup in 1979, perhaps Cruyff in the famous tie with Benfica in 1969 or George Best in Lisbon, also against Benfica, three years previously. These last two cases were from guys who were 20 or over and with a proven track record in international competition. Messi's feat comes from a guy who only began to be a guaranteed starter last November. Even that status came when his explosive performance at the Bernabéu was instrumental in Barça's resounding victory over Real Madrid."

Jorge Valdano, a man so indelibly linked with the Galáctico era of Florentino Pérez at Real Madrid that some Barça fans might think he's a *Madrileño* rather than a countryman to Messi, also buzzed with appreciation. "Messi is a player who just takes opponents out of the game, which makes him a kind of football terrorist," said Valdano. "He leaves them in his wake without a possibility of catching him again – firstly because he ties them in a knot and secondly because he possesses this unstoppable burst of acceleration over short distances."

Sadly for Messi, the triumph of Stamford Bridge was the peak of his season. In the return leg against Chelsea, he limped off with a hamstring strain, and only just made it back to full training in the days prior to the Champions League final against Arsenal in Paris. On the Sunday he trained at the Camp Nou, to the surprise and pleasure of the tourists who were on the stadium tour, with all those who had been rested in the previous game at Sevilla.

Again on Monday, before the flight to Paris and on the Saint-Denis turf on Tuesday, Messi was to be seen shooting at full force, barging Ronaldinho off the ball in a tackle and then helping tend to Eto'o when a shot hit the striker full in the head and looked, for a moment, like it would deprive Barça of the man who would haul his team back into the final just over 24 hours later.

On the Wednesday came the shocking news: Rijkaard didn't name Messi in his playing squad, deciding that the 18-year-old hadn't had enough training time, following his injury in February, to be risked. Iniesta was dropped, Xavi was also reckoned by Rijkaard to be only fit enough to sit on the bench, an unused substitute. For Rijkaard and Ten Cate, the Van Bommel-Iniesta generic debate had not yet been won and the coach lacked a total belief in his two electric but diminutive young talents.

Messi had already proven so special that the level of fitness he demonstrated should have merited a place on the bench and Iniesta still talks about learning he wouldn't start in Paris as his worst moment in football.

Van Bommel started in his place and, while he certainly didn't play as anonymously as Ronaldinho, or become as over-run as Oleguer, his lack of pace and absence of that quick pass-and-move helped 10-man Arsenal outscore and outplay Barça for much of the game before Rijkaard's replacements inspired them to the second European Cup victory in their history.

We could analyse the impact of Henrik Larsson, a game-changing substitute; the absolute thirst for a goal on the big occasion displayed by Eto'o; Juliano Belletti's pace and sense of adventure down the wing – but Xavi took Iniesta aside after the match and told him: "Thank goodness you came on, we'd have lost that without you."

Barça won and the celebrations were wild. However, when his chance came to go down on the Paris turf and celebrate with the squad and the trophy, Messi was so furious at having missed out on the game that he refused to. His unrelenting need to play revealed itself in a moment of immaturity and he regretted it almost instantly.

After the World Cup, I spoke to Messi about his refusal to celebrate with his team-mates after the Champions League final. He'd just come back from a snow holiday in Bariloche, Patagonia. It is a rite of passage for kids in Argentina and because he'd never been able to enjoy it as a youngster, having left for Spain at

12, the extra holidays Barça gave him were perfect for a break in the snow, even if he was banned from snowmobiles, skis and any other high-speed activity which might do him damage.

"All that happened is that I had a rush of blood to the head," he reflected. "Looking back, I still regret that such a poor decision robbed me of the chance to enjoy the achievement, the moment and the atmosphere because it is not every day that you win the Champions League.

"You can't go back in time and change your decision, but it was just a handful of minutes when, to be truthful, I was in a bad way and I took a decision in the heat of the moment without thinking properly. Almost as soon as the chance to celebrate with all the guys and the trophy on the pitch was gone I realised that I'd made a mistake and the regrets overwhelmed me.

"I'd been central to the team as the important stage of the tournament arrived and that injury left me on the outside looking in for many, many games. Even now, I feel completely differently about my La Liga medal and my Champions League medal.

"I feel like a champion of Spain [Messi played 17 La Liga games, scoring six goals] much more than I feel champion of Europe [six games and one goal in the Champions League]."

In between the Paris final and that interview had come another tough blow.

The Argentina coach, José Pekerman, used Messi sparingly during the early parts of the World Cup in Germany, but to good effect. He stayed on the bench for the first match, but came on with 15 minutes left against Serbia, made one and scored one.

440

Messi started the Holland game and played the whole of extra time in the dramatic win over Mexico.

But in the quarter-final against Germany, which Argentina led until 10 minutes from the end and in which Pekerman decided to 'circle the wagons' against Jürgen Klinsmann's team, Messi wasn't given a single minute. In defeat, Pekerman was fiercely criticised for not unleashing his great attacking talent.

One budding coach saw Messi's skills and his World Cup contribution differently. Pep Guardiola was writing for *El País* at the time. He was about 12 months away from becoming the coach of Barça B.

One of his articles was about the youngster with whom he would go on to form one of the most incredible coach-superstar partnerships in the history of sport.

After the win over Serbia, Guardiola wrote: "Just 15 minutes from the end of the match, Lionel Messi came on to make his debut in a World Cup. And I'll bet any amount you like that it won't be his last time on the world stage.

"For 75 minutes he had sat on the bench and watched three goals being scored. And he saw nothing else. He didn't notice how Riquelme was playing, nor Maradona dancing with his family in the stands.

"And once he was playing he had eyes only for Jevrić's goal. But that's just the way he is. He forgets everything else. All he can see are those two posts and the crossbar. The minute he came onto the pitch it was as if he was declaring to the world, 'I'm here guys! I've arrived!'

"They gave him the ball and off he went. It was like watching someone running the 100 metres, but without any need for a starting whistle, and when he runs, he's amazing. As my *El País* colleague Ramon Besa says, 'He's even faster with the ball than without it'.

"If Ronaldinho is the greatest, Messi is the most authentic. He never plays to the gallery, to the press or to the fans. For him the only focus is the goal.

"He has that special quality all the greats possess. It's like watching a piece of theatre and only seeing one actor, even though there are 10 brilliant others on stage. Or having eyes only for Sara Baras, although she is dancing with 10 amazing dancers. It's the difference between watching golf played with or without Tiger Woods. One experience can't be compared to the other.

"When Messi is playing all you can do is hope that Riquelme gives him the ball. When I watch him I always have a feeling that something amazing is about to happen. That's how I felt the first time I saw him with Barcelona. I felt the same thing yesterday watching Argentina and I'm sure that's how Charly Rexach felt the first time he saw him and said, 'What are you waiting for? Let's sign him.'

"Only Argentina's coach will know what he wants to do with this genius. It's obvious that Messi will also give him in 90 minutes what he gave in 15. Yesterday it was like that sweetie a mother keeps in her pocket and brings out to save the day when her kid is crying. And it works every time, even when there are only 15 minutes to go.

"Perhaps Luis Aragonés also has a sweetie in his pocket to offer us in Spain? A certain Andrés ..."

The next two seasons would bring some unfortunate developments for Messi, although there was one outstanding highlight, when his three goals saved 10-man Barça from defeat by Real Madrid in March 2007. His hat-trick in a 3-3 draw at the Camp Nou was the first in a Clásico for a Barça player since Romario in 1994 and made Messi the youngest, at 19 years, eight months and 16 days, to score three times in the famous fixture.

But his reaction told the story of those intermediate seasons, when injury blighted him. Post-match he said: "I really needed to score a few because I'm coming back from injury and I'm only just in shape again. Prior to the injury I was in form, but I've been missing out on that last step forward – goals were something missing from my game. I was missing chances, my luck was out and then all of a sudden I've produced a hat-trick and, what's more, against Madrid. All that was lacking was that we won the game instead of drawing."

That night the mixed zone – where media interview players – was pandemonium. While Madrid had won a valuable draw in enemy territory, a 19-year-old scoring three times in his first home Clásico was a sensation.

Most players were impressed enough to talk for longer, and more freely, than is usual. Iker Casillas, for example, despite losing two points to an added-time goal from a kid with long, floppy hair, said, "Messi played phenomenally well".

Ruud van Nistelrooy, who had scored twice and produced his best game for Madrid, said: "He's already a great. Beyond scoring a hat-trick at that age, he could easily have had more tonight."

Ronaldinho, as always without a hint of envy for the kid who was patently going to succeed him, said: "Messi is simply off the scale."

But Sylvinho's reaction was the most perspicacious. The little Brazilian had become an almost paternal figure for Messi and after his fabulous hat-trick of goals, the little full-back said: "He's got a good head on his shoulders and not just for football. He's been well brought up in the fundamental things in life and mark my words, he's going to grow a great deal more as a footballer.

"It's important now that he shakes everything else off and just concentrates on playing football. Training well and playing well should be the only responsibilities he carries at this age – the pressure which is about to surround him needs to be absorbed by those of us around him."

It was a point which kept Barça level with Sevilla at the top of La Liga, and Madrid five points behind in fourth.

However, this was also a season in which a remarkable Jornada 37 (the penultimate matchday) would see Messi score, using his hand, against Espanyol; Madrid trail in Zaragoza; Tamudo equalise for Espanyol at the Camp Nou; and finally Madrid fight back for a point in La Romareda. That drama meant that victory at home to Mallorca the following weekend gave Fabio Capello's Madrid a barnstorming La Liga championship.

Another unforgettable moment came in the Copa del Rey semi-final, first leg in April, when Getafe were beaten 5-2 at the Camp Nou. Messi scored a goal which drew comparisons with Diego Maradona's second against England in the 1986 World Cup. It was sensational – Rijkaard called it "a work of art" and Deco thought it was "the best goal I've ever seen in my life".

Getafe coach Bernd Schuster jokingly told us post-match: "We were too noble; somebody should have booted him halfway through his run towards goal."

However, Rijkaard's team embarrassed themselves in the second leg in Madrid, where the coach rested Messi. The 5-2 advantage that had tempted him to do so was wiped out in a 4-0 defeat by Getafe and the cup final was off limits to Barça. The word 'Shameful' was used across Catalan media. That wasn't unfair.

Rijkaard had lost control of parts of his squad and some players began to behave with self-indulgence and indiscipline. Barça both played and trained with lethargy.

What seemed most disturbing as far as Messi was concerned, was the repetitive nature of his injuries.

Some were pure bad luck. For example, he lost three months of season 2006-07 when he fractured a metatarsal against Gerard Piqué's Zaragoza. He missed 11 straight league matches because of the broken bone in his foot, but still racked up 2,000 league minutes that season – already a vital member of the first team.

The following season, 2007-08, his individual brilliance in a declining team earned an invitation to Zurich in December 2007 to accept his silver statuette for second place in the FIFA World Player awards. Ronaldinho had dominated the awards over the previous couple of seasons, but was fifth in the voting this time. Kaká won and Cristiano Ronaldo was behind Messi in third. The photographs taken of the top three on the podium that night suggest the Portuguese forward was seriously unimpressed with the ranking bestowed upon him by his peers.

Messi's second hamstring injury of the season ensured he was returning from Switzerland to miss a

1-0 home defeat by Real Madrid in the first Clásico of the season. He would be absent for another three matches.

Barcelona's most valuable asset had already lost six months of playing time across 2006 and 2007 due to the same injury in the muscle groups at the back of his thigh and would now sit out for a further six weeks for the same reason.

The metatarsal injury which had cost him a further three months was the kind of impact injury which can affect any footballer, but the total of nearly eight months over two calendar years was now a source of great concern for Barcelona.

Messi returned one match earlier than his prognosis, against Racing in late January, but the problem was not resolved.

He collapsed holding the hamstring of his left leg after 38 minutes against Celtic at the Camp Nou on March 4, 2008. What appeared to be a devastating new downward spiral in the series of muscle injuries digging its claws into Messi's potential would prove to be the darkest moment just before the dawn.

As he crumpled to the turf, Ronaldinho and Deco were first to arrive and console, distraught at another Messi calamity. The teenager limped off the field in unrestrained tears – his season and his team's, was up in smoke.

Barça lost to Villarreal, Betis and Deportivo without Messi. They drew with Espanyol, Getafe, Almería and Recre, taking five of a possible 18 points while he was absent. They were knocked out of the Copa del Rey by Valencia. Messi inched back for the Champions League semi-final against Manchester United, but his lack of sharpness, aligned to the team's attacking impotence and capacity for error meant that a night in Moscow and Barça's second successive final was beyond them.

In the aftermath of this latest injury, in March 2008, a war cabinet convened to discuss a change in direction in the way Messi was managed. It comprised Begiristain, the director of football and two vice presidents: Marc Ingla and Ferran Soriano. The previous October, key board members had agreed that retaining Frank Rijkaard had been a mistake and that, whatever happened, he would be removed in June 2008. Now they were free to formulate a new strategy to protect and promote their greatest asset.

Ingla takes up the story. "We were disappointed with the fragility of Messi and his repetitive muscle strains. After the Celtic match we constructed a holistic plan for his future performance: to manage the number of meals he had, what type of food he should eat, how many hours of sleep he had to get, what type of stretching he had to do every day. It was a plan to keep him healthy and to minimise injuries. We put lots of work into it and invested lots of money to help him."

Juanjo Brau was a fitness and rehabilitation coach who had been working with Messi, but not exclusively, since before the 2006 World Cup. Now Brau would be almost totally dedicated to Messi, a daily part of the player's routine. He would avoid injuries, rather than recover from them. Moreover, Brau would accompany Messi on the long, debilitating inter-continental journeys to play for Argentina.

Allied to Brau's work, a change in diet to include previously unknown quantities such as fish and vegetables left Messi leaner, stronger, less susceptible to injury and quicker to recover. However, there was more to the plan than that. Ronaldinho and Deco were to be removed from the team to clear the decks for a new coach, but it was explicit amongst those in the war cabinet that their departure was also necessary to save Messi from their negative influence.

Ronaldinho, Deco and, to a lesser extent, Thiago Motta were living the high life away from the pitch – convinced like so many gifted, rich young athletes before them that they were so talented, so full of the magic dust which makes superstars that they could bend the rules and still excel. They were wrong.

Their social calendar became notorious and, while Deco seemed physiologically incapable of gaining even a pound of extra flab, he dropped down the gears when he was playing. His contributions became ever less decisive. He also picked up more niggling injuries and took longer to shrug them off.

Ronaldinho was falling from a greater height. The difference was that he gained weight and was betrayed by the same physiology which afflicted his mother, brother and sister. From being the world's best footballer, he turned flabby.

This was disastrous for Barça, as it massively reduced their capacity to press, to break down packed defences and, worst of all, it hacked away at dressing-room harmony.

Without speaking specifically about the Ronaldinho-Deco-Messi situation, Iniesta nevertheless has touched on how such issues can be handled differently within a squad.

There is no question that the two Brazilians were and remain strong friends of their Argentinian apprentice, nor that they were vital to his adaptation to first-team life. However, according to Iniesta, there is another concept, far beyond friendship, which governs the proper running of dressing-room relationships.

"In the dressing room the key word is respect," he says. "It's much more important even than friendship. You can have one or two close friends, but you must have respect for every one of your team-mates. That's the only way the team can function, the only way we can win.

"Let me give you an example. There have been times when I didn't play as much as I do now. I wasn't starting games and although I considered myself to be in better shape than some of the guys who were making the starting line-up, out of respect I said nothing. Out of respect for the dressing room, as a good team-mate, as a decent person. Those are the kind of values I was taught and they've served me well."

Ronaldinho and Deco probably still think that they never betrayed their friendship with Messi, but did they show him sufficient respect? Did they respect his development, his potential, his status, the fact that his family's physiology is similar to that of Ronaldinho's?

The war cabinet saw that young, impressionable Leo Messi would have to be absolutely superhuman not to be led astray by these senior players, whom he not only idolised, but who had treated him like he was family.

Messi was a stocky figure by now – grown to his full height, increasingly strong and explosive with the ball – but hooked on the Argentinian diet of red meat and carbs. If he found a taste for nightlife too, Barça might lose three players instead of just two.

The Brazilians had to go and both the team and

Barça's marketing strategy would be built around Messi, whose contract would be redrawn to reflect his status as the footballing and commercial hub of the club.

It was a medium-term strategy, reliant on board approval, the right market conditions for clubs to buy Deco and Ronaldinho, opting not to renew Motta's contract and ensuring that Messi and his family were totally on board with the changes.

Ingla told me: "Ronaldinho and Deco were completely out of control. They had been our best players for a couple of years and we lost them. They were non-focused on the pitch but they remained the leaders of the dressing room. Ronaldinho and Deco had an enormous role in how badly we played in those two years from 2006 until 2008.

"The season-and-a-half when we won six trophies was a product of a lot of factors, especially hiring Pep, but one of the key explanations was getting both Ronaldinho and Deco out."

There remains a massive affection for Ronaldinho. He brought the magic back to the Camp Nou. "He added value on the pitch and off the pitch. He was the symbol of the change," Soriano recalls fondly. He calls Ronaldinho their 'rock star' signing. The Bernabéu applauded him, the Camp Nou adored him, and the world fell back in love with Barça. It wasn't easy to say goodbye.

"In late 2006 and early 2007 it was becoming clear that Ronaldinho was not going to be a lasting star, although we thought in 2004, 2005 that we could achieve this and we were talking to his brother about extending his contract to 2014," continued Soriano. "We wanted him to develop his whole career at FC Barcelona but he wasn't working. His life and the way he trained and so on ... it just didn't work for us.

"By 2006 and 2007 we knew that he wouldn't be the club's icon. We had decided – that was going to be Messi."

Ingla spoke for those present for these pivotal discussions when he said: "To unleash all the power and the image of Messi we had to push out Ronaldinho and Deco."

There was a mix of intelligence and daring in this strategy. Ingla, Laporta, Soriano, and their fellow board members, Raul Sanllehi and Txiki Begiristain, envisaged a future when Messi would be the player of reference for the coach, his fellow players and the fans.

Secondly, they saw that if Messi was helped through this stage of development he might become the best footballer in the world and still have at least 10 years of greatness ahead of him.

Thirdly, they anticipated that he would become an extraordinary marketing tool – the single greatest sales accelerator FC Barcelona had ever possessed.

Finally, they knew very well that his contract had to be enhanced and they saw value in taking the new thinking to the Messi family first, building them into the strategy and showing, very early on, how much faith Barça was willing to place in him. It was inspirational forward thinking.

Soriano continues. "My part was to design a contract that would be proactive. The logic was that this guy was going to be magic and everyone knew that we would have Italian teams, English teams, Real Madrid maybe on top of him. So, we had to react to this, so that every time he was approached by someone, we counter-attacked. We decided to do something different. I developed a good relationship with his father and we committed to improving his contract every year – a tactic designed to ensure that we were ahead of the curve.

"It was arranged so that first he would get enough money to compensate, or to signal his growth, up to the point of this new contract in 2008. Secondly, that we would develop the relationship with his father so that he would be confident that we would always be fair.

"So, the father would get crazy offers from the likes of Inter, clubs promising to double our salary, and the first thing he would do would be to call me and I would tell him not to worry, that we would manage this. And he trusted us because we were consistent every time."

Ingla is clear on who was driving the strategy. "We have to give the credit first to Txiki. He told us we must build around Messi. This credo ran the club's actions."

Begiristain's goal was to bind Jorge Messi into the process at every level. Rijkaard was on his way out and, since the previous October, he'd been working through candidates like Guardiola, Laurent Blanc, Michael Laudrup, Ernesto Valverde and José Mourinho.

The signatures of Gerard Piqué, Dani Alves and Seydou Keita were almost assured. Begiristain now put all his work into persuading Jorge Messi that there was going to be serious change and that the new era would be built around Leo Messi – albeit part of the responsibility was his. Messi's father had seen the decline in the team, influenced by the indisciplined lifestyles of Deco and Ronaldinho. There was division and resentment in the dressing room. Players who had arrived from more rigorous training environments, Eiður Guðjohnsen and Thierry Henry, were bewildered and disappointed that things were so lax.

Jorge Messi wanted his son fit, developing at the right pace and winning trophies. Thus, he was told everything about the impending departure of Rijkaard, the signings which would not be announced for a couple of months and the fact that the new coach was almost certainly going to be Pep Guardiola.

Soriano's work on the contract was fulfilled that summer. Ingla saw it through to delivery in his position as vice president in charge of football. "On the same day as the vote of no confidence [in Joan Laporta, July 2008] I signed the new contract with Messi," said Ingla. "We needed to lock him in to the club. There were some shaky scenarios which could have happened."

By which he means that if Laporta had been ousted and the club marooned in months of electoral procedure, unable to move in the transfer market and still in search of the right coach, there was a chance that levering Messi away from the Camp Nou might suddenly become a more achievable prospect in summer 2008.

Instead, the most remarkable transformation was about to take place – Josep 'Pep' Guardiola was about to arrive in Messi's life, promoted from 'B' team coach and driven by the single intention of making Barça great again.

At the start of summer 2008, the Camp Nou was a gloomy place. By its end, Messi was about to illuminate it with a talent that would leave every other footballer in his shadow.

This book has been written because of what has

happened since then. It has been an incredible journey and it is not over yet. It might be a basic point, but Messi gives all of us so much fun, so much pure enjoyment. Guardiola and his fellow players feel that way too.

It was significant that the longest single answer which Pep Guardiola gave after the Champions League final in 2011 concerned his No 10. This is a coach who consistently emphasises the group over the individual. The pass over the dribble.

Remember that in the final training session before his first game as coach of Barça B, back in 2007, he shouted: "I don't want you to be so individual, stop trying to be Leo Messi! Keep passing! Pass, pass, pass – it's about moving the ball through the team, not about one individual." Remember?

At Wembley, Guardiola was celebrating a team triumph, with three different goalscorers, with stories of individual excellence right across the pitch and a finale where the captain's armband, and trophy, were handed to Éric Abidal to celebrate his brave fight against a liver tumour. However, when the Barça coach was asked for an appreciation of Messi's performance he set his normal rules aside.

"Messi is the one who makes the difference, who takes us to another level. We have excellent players, great team work, tactics, we work hard, but it's Messi that takes us to another level.

"He'll never be repeated. He's the best player I've ever seen, the best player I'll ever coach.

"I just hope that he doesn't get bored in the future, we have to see to that. I just hope that the club has the intelligence to make sure we sign the players he'll be comfortable having around him and he stays as calm and such a centred personality, because if we do that then he never fails."

Post-Wembley, Messi explained the importance of the atmosphere and team spirit at Barcelona. "The important fact is that we enjoy a really healthy spirit at the training ground and in the dressing room. From my point of view there are a few guys around with whom I've been playing or sharing rooms in La Masia with since the youth ranks.

"Right now I've got an excellent relationship with every single guy in our squad and I think that perhaps that helps explain how easy it is for all of us to get extra from our play when it comes to matches – particularly difficult ones.

"We get on well, we have fun, we share a work ethic, but a lot of us have been trained together since we were quite young. If everyone has the same idea of treating the ball [possession] with respect, managing the ebb and flow of matches and putting the team before the individual, then life becomes much simpler."

Perhaps, given his influence on this era, the last word should go to Guardiola, but I love it when a footballer outshines us all with a lovely phrase. So thank you to Javier Mascherano.

Just after he had helped overcome Real Madrid in their torrid Champions League semi-final, I asked Mascherano about the performance of his club and international team-mate.

He told me: "Leo is the best in the world and people didn't realise for a long time that he is on the way to becoming the best ever. The strength it takes to show that kind of talent in the matches we have just been through is exceptional. Leo showed that he wears the crown and nobody is going to take it off him for a long, long time."

Messi wears the crown. That's a good line to finish on.

ACKNOWLEDGEMENTS

I ENJOYED WORKING WITH BackPage Press. They read an article of mine about Xavi in the *Sunday Herald*, came up with the concept and approached me. Writing for people who are passionate about their work, deeply in love with football and unashamed to be old-fashioned and up front about their values has been a big experience. No cynicism, nothing flash just talent and energy. Can't sing though.

Most importantly of all, the fact that my wife Louise was able to add so much to the process via her smart mind and razor-sharp editing skills, plus the fact that she has met some of these characters and has been increasingly won over by their talents, meant an enormous amount to me. The whole thing has been her idea from the start.

I know my daughters Cara (who has met Ronaldinho and played in Johan Cruyff's back garden) and Annie (the only one of us born in Catalonia and probably Leo Messi's biggest fan) love going to the Camp Nou. They have been supportive of all the endless hours I've spent writing or interviewing or proofing.

To my Dad, Mum, Pete and Andrew who have all had to put up with my football rants for some considerable years, thanks to you all. They have all done their utmost to calm me down, encourage and steer me in the correct direction. I know where my original football roots come from: Pittodrie.

Graeme Runcie had the vision, back in 1982, to follow the torch to Spain – and he was just about right. Rob Moore gets a couple of mentions throughout the chapters and he deserves them. Aurelio Capaldi and

Ian McGarry always guide me, occasionally on important matters. Sid Lowe very kindly spent time giving his attention to the book.

Silvia González helped greatly with her interviews, Luis Martín is a journalistic legend and a great friend, Cordula Reinhardt is also both of those. Kevin Bridges, John Bridges and Greg McHugh must be able to hear their voices in these pages.

APPENDIX A: TIMELINE

1973	Johan Cruyff arrives in Barcelona as the world's first $1m footballer
February 17, 1974	His performance in the 5-0 win over Real Madrid inspires a generation of Barça fans, including Joan Laporta and Sandro Rosell
1978	Cruyff leaves Barcelona
1988	Cruyff returns to the Camp Nou as manager, reshaping the youth system and playing style
1990	Pep Guardiola is one of several La Masia products promoted to the first team
1992	Cruyff's 'Dream Team' win the European Cup at Wembley, beating Sampdoria 1-0 in extra time thanks to a Ronald Koeman goal

1996   Cruyff is sacked in the dressing room as his players report for training. At this time 16-year-old Xavi is in La Masia, as is Víctor Valdés; Carles Puyol has just been signed and Andrés Iniesta is being scouted and will soon be recruited, aged 12

2000   Thirteen-year-old Lionel Messi moves with his family from Argentina to Barcelona and enters La Masia

2001   Guardiola announces his departure from Barcelona at an emotional press conference

2003   Laporta, a lawyer and the leader of the *Elefant Blau* protest movement against former president Josep Lluís Núñez, wins the presidential elections. Rosell is a vice president and a key strategist in the victory. The new regime appoints Frank Rijkaard as manager

October 16, 2004   Messi, 17, makes his La Liga debut against Espanyol

2005	Rosell resigns from Laporta's board, claiming his former colleague had veered away from the manifesto that had taken them to power
2006	Barcelona come from behind to beat Arsenal in the final of the Champions League, their first European Cup since the Dream Team
2007	Guardiola appointed coach of Barça B
2008	After a single season with the second team, Guardiola succeeds Rijkaard as manager. He announces that Ronaldinho, Deco and Samuel Eto'o have no part in his plans
May 27, 2009	Goals from the reprieved Eto'o and Messi win the Champions League final against Manchester United, completing a treble in Guardiola's first season in charge, following victory in La Liga and the Copa del Rey

December 19, 2009	Barça win the Club World Cup for the first time in their history, Messi scoring the winner against Estudiantes
2010	Barça defend their La Liga title, but are knocked out of the Champions League by José Mourinho's Internazionale
June 13, 2010	Rosell becomes the 39th president of Barcelona, replacing his former colleague, Laporta
July 11, 2010	Seven of the nine La Masia graduates in the Spain squad take part in the World Cup final, as Iniesta's goal adds the world title to victory at Euro 2008
May 28, 2011	Goals from Pedro, Messi and David Villa give Barcelona a 3-1 win over Manchester United and their second Champions League title in three years under Guardiola, having already completed a hat-trick of La Liga championships

December 18, 2011	Barcelona are world champions again, beating Santos 4-0 in Yokohama, Japan
2012	Messi is the second player in history, after Michel Platini, to win three consecutive Ballons d'Or

APPENDIX B: REFERENCES

I AM EXTREMELY GRATEFUL for the exclusive interviews the following gave for this book:

Manel Estiarte, Arnau Riera, Tito Vilanova, Josep Maria Minguella, Joan Lacueva, Charly Rexach, Alex García, Marc Ingla, José Ramón Alexanco, Albert Benaiges, Rodolfo Borrell, Ferran Soriano, Fran Sánchez, Ginés Meléndez, Txiki Begiristain all gave their time to help this book explain FC Barcelona concepts and special moments in the club's recent history. Alex McLeish, a good friend, shared Messi and Iniesta details. Paul Jewell told me of how close he came to signing Guardiola, Joachim Björklund kindly shared his always sharp football views. Martin Ferguson, Steve Archibald, Darren Fletcher and Jordi Lardín guided me.

Prior to writing this book, I'd say that the interviews and the exceptionally kind and helpful treatment I've received from the majority of players at the Camp Nou over the last 10 years has been vital, but particularly Xavi Hernández, Gerard Piqué, Carles Puyol, Josep Guardiola, Éric Abidal, Javier Mascherano, Andrés Iniesta, Dani Alves, Juliano Belletti, Gio Van Bronckhorst, Henrik Larsson, Víctor Valdés, David Villa, Leo Messi, Ronaldinho, Pedro Rodríguez, Sergio Busquets, Sylvinho, Thiago Alcántara, Oscar Garcia, Johan Cruyff, Rutger Koopmans and also the FC Barcelona staff – Chemi Teres, Francesc Orenes, Sergi Nogueras, Xavi Guarte, José Manuel Lázaro. Then

Joaquin Macanás; all at IMG Spain, the excellent Juanjo Castillo and Spain's press team: Paloma Antoranz and Susana Barquero.

Senda de Campeones by Martí Perarnau was a good guide in preparing for the La Masia interviews.

In addition I would like to acknowledge the following texts which have been represented in part in this book:

Chapter 1: The Road to Wembley
The comments on Barça's performance in the Champions League final include: Graeme Souness, speaking on Sky Sports; Ossie Ardiles, on Revista de La Liga; Ottmar Hitzfeld, in *Kicker*; Juste Fontaine in the French sports newspaper *L'Equipe*. Marcello Lippi was interviewed in *Corriere della Sera*. Roy Keane spoke on ITV. Guti chose Twitter to praise Pep Guardiola

Chapter 2: The Making of Messi
This chapter includes parts of interviews with Lionel Messi which first appeared in *El Mundo Deportivo* and *El País*, as well as the following: Dr Schwarzstein was speaking on the television programme Informe Robinson, as was Matías Messi; Leo Messi's description of injecting growth hormone is on his personal website

Chapter 3: The Exile Returns
Xavi Hernández was talking to Luis Martin of *El País*. Zlatan Ibrahimovic was speaking to the author for an interview which appeared in *Champions* magazine and, later, to *El Mundo Deportivo*. Pep Guardiola's mother, Dolores, was talking to the television station Cuatro.

Chapter 4: The Machine
Two interviews with Xavi Hernández feature here. He was talking to Canal+ about playing football as a child, and to Luis Martín of *El País* on the subject of his 10th anniversary at Barça.

Chapter 5: Johan Cruyff's Theory of Evolution
Extracts from the following interviews with Johan Cruyff are used: he was talking to *GQ* about his deal to join Feyenoord; his newspaper columns appeared in *La Vanguardia* and *El Periódico*; he spoke to Frits Barend and Henk van Dorp for *Nieuwe Revu* about the state of the club when he arrived as coach and his impact on Frank Rijkaard; Charly Rexach was talking to the author for an interview which appeared in *Four Four Two*.

Chapter 6: The Making of Pep Guardiola
This chapter includes extracts from interviews Pep Guardiola gave to Gabriel Marcotti of *The Times* and the Barcelona-based newspaper *El Mundo Deportivo*. Pep Guardiola's mother, Dolores, Francesca Guardiola, Carles Naval, Luis Milla and Guillermo Amor spoke to La 2.

Chapter 7: The Emperors of Barcelona
This chapter includes extracts from an interview Joan Laporta gave to *El País*. Laporta was also talking to the author for an interview which appeared in *Champions*.

Chapter 8: The Odd Couple
This chapter features extracts from the following interviews: Jordi Mauri spoke to TV4, Gerard Piqué was

talking to Luis Martín of *El País* about homesickness. Carles Puyol spoke about attitude-versus-talent and hunger for winning to Albert Puig in *La Fuerza de un Sueño* and to *Marca* about Real Madrid. Xavi was speaking to Canal+.

Chapter 9: La Masia: The Breeding Ground

In this chapter I used excerpts from the following interviews: Pep Guardiola spoke to Albert Puig in his book, *La Fuerza de un Sueño* where Mazinho also shared his anecdote; Xavi spoke to *L'Equipe* newspaper; Guillermo Amor was speaking to *El Mundo Deportivo*, Charly Rexach spoke to *El País*.

Chapter 10: The Solutions Man

This chapter includes extracts from interviews with Andrés Iniesta talking about his childhood to *El País*; he talks about the *Alevín* tournament on his own website; he was talking to his friend, Luis Martín of *El País*, ahead of the Champions League final at Wembley and in an interview with the same paper in 2009. Llorenzo Serra Ferrer was talking to *El País*.

Chapter 11: The Making of the Greatest Rivalry in the World

This chapter features extracts from an interview Jose Mourinho gave to *El País*, Guti spoke to Ona FM

Chapter 12: The Greatest

José Mourinho spoke to Cristina Cubero; Pep Guardiola was writing for *El País*. Santiago Segurola was writing for *El País*.

APPENDIX C: GLOSSARY

Alevín   The stage of the *fútbol base* system
                    for boys aged 10-12.

Azar   Fate; luck.

Cadete   The stage of the *fútbol base* system
                    for boys aged 14-16.

Cantera   Generic term for the youth system
                    of a Spanish club.

Canterano   A player from the *cantera*.

Carnet   Season ticket.

Colchonero   Supporters of Atlético Madrid.
                    Literally 'mattress-makers', as their
                    first striped shirts supposedly
                    resembled the material old
                    mattresses were made from.

Concentración   The practice of taking a team to a
                    hotel the night before a game to
                    focus their minds.

Culés   Affectionate term for FC
                    Barcelona fans. Derived from
                    the backsides of fans which used
                    to stick out from between the
                    wooden slats at the top of the
                    club's old Les Corts stadium.

Derbi	A derby game, between rivals .
El Niño	Nickname of Fernando Torres, 'The Kid'.
El Submarino Amarillo	Nickname for Villarreal, the Yellow Submarine.
Entorno	Collective of influencers, in this case including fans, media and some board members.
Fútbol base	Summary term for the entire youth system that provides 'basic football education'.
Gol Nord	The north goal of the camp nou.
Jornada	A matchday in La Liga season.
Juvenil	The stage of the *fútbol base* system for boys aged 16-19.
La Roja	Nickname for the Spain national team – 'The Red'.
Madrileño	Someone from Madrid.
Més Que Un Club	'More than a club,' a motto for FCB on and off the field since January 1968.

Pañolada   An in-stadium protest where fans wave white handkerchiefs to signify their displeasure.

Pasillo   The guard of honour traditionally afforded league champions by their next opponents.

Patio   Playground, where football is played at school or in the neighbourhood.

Pivote   The pivot position between defence and midfield, played by Pep Guardiola among others.

Rondo   A possession drill at the heart of Barcelona training from the earliest age groups to the first team that involves one or two players trying to intercept passes by players forming a circle around them.

Socios   Members of FC Barcelona (*socis* in Catalan), who pay an annual fee and vote in presidential elections.

APPENDIX D: HIRING CRITERIA

Mentioned in Chapter 11, reproduced below is the document Barça vice-president Marc Ingla drew up to outline the criteria Frank Rijkaard's replacement as coach would have to meet.

The New Coach of FC Barcelona

I. Respect the model of sports management and the role of the technical secretary.

- Work with the first team technical staff
- Co-ordination of the *fútbol base* locally and globally
- Signings, new contracts, player releases, sales, etc
  - » Work with the technical team on these from December to January
  - » Although the technical secretary is responsible for the final decision, the coach can make proposals and offer vetoes.
- Neither the board nor the technical secretary will act as coach or influence training sessions and preparation for matches.

2.   Style of Play

- Balance between playing the most attractive, most spectacular football possible and efficacy.
- 4-3-3 formation with alterations as necessary
- Management and control of matches – maximum concentration and attention

3.   Values to be promoted in the first team – some of these are new

- Work, work, work
- Continue to promote players from the *cantera* (this is part of the club's identity and will help maintain our style of game and contribute to the level of cohesion in dressing room.)
- The team
  » Encourage solidarity, team play, passing and speed of movement, generosity above "prima donna" which is not effective
  » superstars and each players' talents and skills are at the service of the whole team
- Maintain total concentration at all times (remain detached from the noise and distractions of daily life and focus on the competitions)
- Pay attention to the tiniest of details (eg permission to be absent from training)

4. Training and performance: "How you play is a product of how you train"

- Each and every training session is of maximum importance
- The coach must manage closely every activity which might impact directly on players' performances
  - » Strategy and the tactical approach to matches
  - » Physical preparation at an individual and team level
  - » The players' health and the involvement of the medical staff in training to ensure players are protected from injury as far as possible
  - » Nutrition and rest
- More emphasis on physical preparation (a new value for the club)
  - » Football has become more and more physical and competitive. FCB are No 1 in terms of our talent ... but we also need our players to develop in terms of strength and power.
- Emphasis on preparatory and post-match work
  - » The analysis of our opponents (video, new tactical solutions, etc)
  - » The day after a match, look at our mistakes, the things that worked and what we can learn
- Other considerations
  - » Training should be more "closed" in line with our continued professionalisation

» More training in the Mini Estadi and the Ciutat Esportiva.
» Extension of the working day: more rests, more controlled meals at the training ground, etc.

5. Active management of the dressing room

- Application of the "house rules"
- Permission to be absent from training – in case of doubt the coach should agree these with the technical secretary
- The captaincy model – in this meritocracy we promote those who have natural leadership skills and influence over the group
- Management of our superstar players

6. Other duties and agreements with the club. The media

- As one of the abiding and permanent images of the club the coach must
  » behave in a prudent manner at all times
  » adhere to the concept of a clean game and show respect to opponents, referees and other institutions
  » Avoid the overuse of the media and the creation of artificial polemic. The focus should at all times be on the football and where the team is at any given time

- The players
  - » Mixed zone – the players should be there after matches
  - » They should fulfill their duties regarding press conferences
  - » Marketing – a balance needs to be achieved between the club's commitments and those of the players
  - » Social area

7.   Experience

- Experience in elite, international football as player and coach
- Proven personal qualities of the highest order if extensive experience is lacking.

8.   Contribution to and support for the effective management of the whole club

- An emphasis on explicit and formalised methods of communication to ensure that the needs of the team are identified
  - » Weekly plan of training sessions, attendance at Mixed Zone, notes of all absences from training, notes on the health and fitness of the players and, if required, a "book on every player".
- Regular internal co-ordination meetings to develop the work of the team and ensure continual progress. These should involve

Appendix D: Hiring criteria

> » The technical team, physios and medical staff (frequency is at the coach's discretion)
> » The vice president of sport, the technical secretary and the first team coach (fortnightly)

- The management board will strictly avoid bringing influence to bear on technical decisions and will respect the work of the professionals with the sole exception of matters relating to the club's global strategy.

9. Other highly desirable qualities

- A good knowledge of the Spanish league
- A good knowledge of the club
- International experience

APPENDIX E:
BONUS CONTENT

BACKPAGE PRESS

On BackPage Press' YouTube channel, we have a series of exclusive video diaries with Graham Hunter discussing Barça in greater detail in and around the city and Camp Nou on a match day.

Visit: **www.youtube.com/backpage2010**

Or, if you have a smartphone, use a QR reader to scan the below code and be taken straight to the Barça playlist:

Follow us online:
www.facebook.com/BackPagePress
www.twitter.com/BackPagePress
www.backpagepress.co.uk

DAN LEYDON

The illustrations in this book were comissioned for the title and are the copyright of Dan Leydon, an illustrator and graphic designer from Sligo on the West Coast of Ireland. To buy or see more of his work, visit
http://hotfootynews.blogspot.com
Twitter: @danleydon.

PRODUCTION ATTIC

The video diaries were expertly shot by Production Attic **www.productionattic.com**.
Twitter: @ProductionAttic